The
Theory
Of The
Firm:
Production,
Capital,
And Finance

Economics Handbook Series
SEYMOUR E. HARRIS, EDITOR

THE BOARD OF ADVISORS

Neil W. Chamberlain
Columbia University—Labor
John M. Culbertson
University of Wisconsin—Monetary Theory
Seymour E. Harris
University of California, La Jolla—International Economics
Social Security; all other areas
Franco Modigliani
Massachusetts Institute of Technology—Economic Theory
Richard A. Musgrave
Harvard University—Public Policy
Marc Nerlove
Yale University—Econometrics and Mathematical Economics

The
Theory
Of The
Firm:

Production,
Capital,
And Finance

Douglas Vickers

Professor of Finance
University of Pennsylvania

*McGraw-Hill
Book Company*

New York,
St. Louis,
San Francisco,
Toronto,
London,
Sydney

**The Theory of the Firm: Production,
Capital, and Finance**

Library of Congress Catalog Card Number: 67423

1 2 3 4 5 6 7 8 9 0   M A M M   7 5 4 3 2 1 0 6 9 8

To Miriam

Preface

In this book I have tried to break new ground in the theory of the firm and in the application of theoretical thought forms to what I have called the optimization of the owners' economic position. For this purpose my objective has been the integration, on a more logically satisfying level than has hitherto been realized, of the microtheories of production, capital, and finance. This is necessary, I feel, before it can be said that analytical economics has provided a relevant and usable model of the firm's behavior problems and policy decisions. Against the background of this analytical trilogy I have examined the corresponding trilogy of decision problems in production, investment, and finance. The solutions to these problems are reflected in practice in the structure of the firm's financial statements, and it has therefore been my main concern to look behind these statements, discover the nature of the interdependent causal relations determining the firm's position, and argue consistently for models designed to explain the optimum structure of the firm as a whole.

My concern, therefore, has been with the development of new theoretical constructs and models, and I hope thereby to have opened new avenues for further extensions, refinements, and empirical applications. At the present stage of the development of microtheory, the pressing need is for an integration of the areas of theory I have referred to. To contribute to this end it has been possible to build on some promising starts already available in the literature, and I have indicated the intellectual indebtedness of my work at each stage of the analysis. Notably, on the level of theoretical development, I have endeavored to give a new treatment of the firm's production function, designed to clarify the significance of capital as a factor of production, and distinguish carefully between real capital factors on the one hand and money capital on the other. The former are included, in a suitably defined way, as arguments in the production function, but money capital, it is shown, is not a factor of production; its theoretical relevance resides on a rather different level.

The understanding of money capital as a constraint against which optimizing decisions as to production and investment are made facilitates new progress in defining the firm's financing problem. It provides also for the integration of the new theory of finance with the theory of capital and production. The following decision problems of the firm can then be seen as mutually relevant, and their solution values recognized as the precipitate of a set of mutually determinant forces: First, what optimum quantities of various products should the firm produce and what optimum combination of factors of production should it employ? Second, what optimum investment in assets should it make to establish and maintain the productive process, and how should this investment activity be reflected on the assets side of its balance sheet? Third, with what optimum combination of sources of money capital should the firm's investment be financed, and how, as a result, will its stance in its economic milieu be reflected in its financial statements?

The unity of the book lies in its consistent search for an optimized enterprise structure, and the several chapters present a logically ordered development of the analysis. In the first two chapters I have defined the optimization problem with reference to the economic position of the owners of the firm, and the argument develops in summary fashion the relevance of the owners' utility functions, the stochastic interpretation of value outcomes, and the meaning of the risk-adjusted valuation of the firm. Chapters 3 through 5 look closely at the financial statements of the firm, not in the detailed descriptive fashion of the finance texts, but in such a way as to expose the economic forces determining the firm's optimized decision solutions. My objective in these chapters is to erect the empirical categories with which the ensuing models must come to grips and to exhibit also the logical content of the traditional analysis from which, in many respects, I have had to dissent. In Chapters 6 and 7, then, it is possible to explore the main notions of production and capital theory and to put the constructs in order for use in the model building of the remainder of the book. I have discussed the plan of analysis at somewhat greater length in the concluding section of Chapter 1.

A word should be said at this point on the use of mathematics. Some acquaintance with differential and integral calculus is necessary for a full understanding of the work, but the mathematics has been kept on a simple level throughout. A basic college course in the calculus, such as undergraduate seniors and beginning graduate students in economics and finance nowadays possess, is sufficient preparation. In several important applications of differentials and Lagrange multipliers I have made the work as self-contained as I thought would be necessary or helpful. For this reason some mathematical arguments, while inherently simple, are deliberately presented at more length than might have been necessary for professional reading, with the intention of serving the interests of the student making his way in this area for the first time.

It is my hope that this reconsideration of the theory and problems of the firm will provide a new basis for work in the relevant parts of economic theory. But I hope also that a new framework is hereby provided in which the nascent theory of business finance can develop, and that students in both the theoretical and applied sides of the discipline can, with the kind of perspectives now opened up, assist in bringing the subject to higher stages of maturity.

It is impossible adequately to acknowledge the obligations I have incurred in writing this book. I am deeply indebted to my colleague Prof. Sidney Weintraub for his continual interest and encouragement. At various stages of the work I have benefited from the critical comments and gracious assistance of Profs. Richard Clelland, Jean Crockett, Morris Mendelson, and James Walter. Professor Michael Adler repeatedly refused to be satisfied with easy answers to probing questions and helped me in clarifying several parts of the argument. I cheerfully absolve all these friends from responsibility for the blemishes, unevenness, or other shortcomings of the finished work. My special thanks are due to Mrs. Ann Hopkins, whose unusual skill in transforming a tangled manuscript into a perfectly typed copy I remember with true gratitude. I wish to record also my thanks to Mrs. Judith Warren, who assisted me in preparing the typescript for the press, to my son Paul, whose expert training in mathematics happily caused him to raise many important questions during my construction of the analysis, and to Miss Nesta Betts, who assisted in the preparation of the index.

I am happy to acknowledge the assistance of the Ford Foundation, whose award of a Faculty Research Fellowship facilitated the completion of the work. However, the conclusions and opinions expressed in the book are those of the author, and not necessarily those of the Ford Foundation.

Douglas Vickers

Contents

The
Theory
Of The
Firm:

Production,
Capital,
And Finance

1

The
Optimization
Problem

The economic theories of production, capital, and finance are viewed in this book as an analytical trilogy, the demonstration of whose unity and logical coherence is of foremost importance for the theory of the firm. To the extent that an optimization objective requires the production of a specified level of output, with an optimum combination of inputs of factors of production, to that extent there arises also a further and twofold problem: first, the interpretation of capital as a factor of production; and second, the provision of funds to finance the production process and the necessary capital investment.

In actual fact the problems that confront the firm on all these levels have somehow been solved. Production levels and processes are decided upon, investments are made, capital is employed, and finance is obtained from various sources to bind the enterprise structure together. But clearly, the question that begs for an answer from economic theory is whether the causal forces in the decision areas are interdependent, and their solution outcomes mutually determinate, in such a way as to require and permit a general theory of the total optimization of the firm. If this should be so, it is then a reproach to economic analysis that such a theory does not exist.

Considerable time has been spent, and no little energy absorbed, in refining aspects of theory which, properly conceived, might be shaped as building blocks in the grander theoretical structure. But the firm in fact is still without guidance as to how theoretical advances in production, capital, and finance can provide it with guidelines for consistent policies adapted to total optimization. It is therefore with the gaps in the theory of enterprise structure and policy that our work will be principally concerned.

The Theoretical Problem

The following chapters comprise an essay in economic and financial theory. The task and method of the work are analytical, and the principal conclusions reside on a theoretical plane. But given the need for a more robust theory of the optimization of the firm, and given, therefore, the desirability of sounder methodological bridges from economic to financial analyses, the work is motivated also by the pragmatic objective of developing sounder policies for efficient business behavior.

In recent times the study of business behavior, or, as we shall be principally concerned with it, the analysis of financial policies and objectives, has moved away from a preoccupation with description and its earlier shallow empiricism. It has searched for principles that might be used in a genuine optimization and equilibrium analysis, and it is to the discipline of microeconomics that the new analytical consciousness has applied for its guiding theoretical principles. In many respects, significant advances have been made toward marrying theoretical thought forms with empirical findings and data, generated and discussed with the aid of newer statistical and mathematical techniques. But the conclusion cannot be avoided that the importation of theoretical thought forms into problem solving in business has realized little of the achievements that might be expected.

For this there are two main reasons: First, the received traditions in the theory of the firm simply do not exist in the form in which they can be applied directly to the kind of problems with which the business enterprise deals in actual fact; and second, business analysts have not consistently asked the most meaningful or significant questions from the point of view of the economic position of the firm or its owners. Optimized equilibria have not in general been achieved, partly because the theoretical disciplines have not been approached with the most significant questions and partly because the available and underlying theory itself has not existed in a very readily or easily applicable form.

Some Summary Propositions

The foregoing, of course, is a severe and still too generalized complaint against the relevant economics, in both its applied and analytical forms. It will be useful, therefore, to spell out immediately the conclusions to which our work will lead. This can be done in brief compass in the following summary statements.

First, economic theory has developed, unfortunately along somewhat disparate lines, a theory of production and a theory of capital. What remains to be done on the level of analysis is to integrate these theories into a coherent system, or a logically consistent organon. On the level of the theory of the firm their mutual relevance can thereby be exhibited and their empirical significance enhanced. The theory of production, it needs to be shown, is logically sustainable only in conjunction with a theory of capital use; and the theory of capital is viable, in turn, only so long as its logic is embedded in a production and factor-employment analysis.

Second, at the level of the business firm a clear understanding needs to be gained of the requirements and use of capital funds and their reflection on the assets side of the balance sheet, and of the availability of money capital for financing investment in assets and its reflection on the liabilities side of the balance sheet. It needs, moreover, to be shown that (1) it is possible to describe what can be called the *optimum structure* of assets and the *optimum structure* of liabilities, (2) it is possible and necessary to understand the mutual relevance and interdependence between these optimum structures, and (3) the relationships that thus emerge are relevant also to the optimum structure of the productive processes in the firm and in part determine these structures. This implies that the relationships here envisaged determine also the choices the enterprise makes as to product outputs on the one hand and its factor input combinations on the other.

Our third summary proposition follows from the fact that it can thus be shown, on the level of economic theory, that the availability and use of capital in the firm, depending in part on the terms on which it is available, will influence the optimum relationships of capital and other factors in a given productive process, or their relative employment in an optimum enterprise structure. Thus it will influence also the envisaged growth or expansion path of the firm.

In the empirical environment, therefore, the enterprise problem of capital investment, or what has become known as the capital budgeting problem, cannot logically be separated from the question of the total enterprise structure. It will be seen that the seemingly simple desideratum of equating the marginal cost of money capital with the marginal productivity of its investment in specific projects will not in general lead to an optimum situation unless the notion of marginal productivity is connoted with a more radical thoroughness than is generally the case. Specifically, the marginal productivity of capital investment projects will be seen to have no meaning if projects are considered in isolation. The relevant and meaningful notion is that of the marginal superiority of one total enterprise structure over alternative enterprise structures, given the constraint of the money capital or investable funds availability with which the firm is working. It will emerge, in other words, that the amount of money capital available, and the terms on which it is available, will influence the capital intensities of the factor combinations which the capital funds are used to finance; thus the enterprise structure decided upon is in part determined by capital availability. In terms imported from other contexts, the availability of capital funds for the business firm affects not only the extent of capital widening in the firm, but also to a significant extent the degree of capital deepening.

The spelling out of the background, content, meaning, and empirical relevance of the analysis implied in the foregoing paragraphs will be our principal task in this book. The total effect, it can thus be hoped, will imply a reorientation and a redirecting of work in the microeconomic theory of the firm and a reconstruction of the groundwork from which the new theories of business finance can develop.

The Optimization Theorem

In the remainder of this chapter we shall consider in more detail the nature of the optimization problem we shall be dealing with, preparatory to discussing in the following chapters the recent developments and necessary reconstructions in economic theory on the one hand and the firm's financial problem analysis on the other.

Augustin Cournot

The explicit formulation, in rigorous analytical form, of the enterprise optimization problem is at least as old as Cournot's *Researches into the Mathematical Principles of the Theory of Wealth*.[1] Consider, for example, his famous proprietor of the mineral spring. If the operator of the spring set out "to make the most of his property," Cournot argues,[2]

> he will therefore successively reduce the price of the liter to the point which will give him the greatest possible profit; i.e. if $F(p)$ denotes the law of demand, he will end, after various trials, by adopting the value of p which renders the product $pF(p)$ a maximum, or which is determined by the equation
> $$F(p) + pF'(p) = 0$$

Quite simply, Cournot is saying that in the case of costless production the total revenue from the operation will be maximized at the price (output quantity) at which the marginal revenue, here explicitly the first derivative of the total revenue function, is equal to zero.

Moreover, Cournot then goes on to consider the case in which the production of the mineral water will involve material and labor costs of production.

---

[1] Augustin Cournot, *Researches into the Mathematical Principles of the Theory of Wealth*, 1838, republished by Augustus M. Kelley, *Reprints of Economic Classics*, New York, 1960.

[2] *Ibid.*, p. 56. For an example of the many discussions of the Cournot point in the literature see Sidney Weintraub, *Intermediate Price Theory*, Chilton Company, Philadelphia, 1964, p. 199.

It will no longer be the function $pF(p)$, or the annual *gross receipts*, which the producer should strive to carry to its maximum value, but the *net receipts*, or the function $pF(p) - \varphi(D)$, in which $\varphi(D)$ denotes the cost of making a number of liters equal to D. Since D is connected with p by the relation $D = F(p)$, the complex function $pF(p) - \varphi(D)$ can be regarded as depending implicitly on the single variable p, although generally the cost of production is an explicit function, not of the price of the article produced, but of the quantity produced. Consequently the price to which the producer should bring his article will be determined by the equation

$$D + \frac{dD}{dp}\left[p - \frac{d[\varphi(D)]}{dD}\right] = 0$$

This price will fix in turn the annual net receipts or the revenue of the inventor, and the capital value of his secret, or his *productive property* . . . .[3]

Thus we are told that the optimum price (output level) is that at which the marginal cost equals the marginal revenue or where the first derivative of the complex net revenue function (revenues minus costs) equals zero. This level of price and output, moreover, is also thereby recognized as determining the capital value of the ownership, a maximand notion we shall discuss more fully in what follows.

It is not necessary for our present purposes to multiply instances of Cournot's early insight into the optimization problem, or to discuss either the lack of impact of his ideas in the subsequent history of economic thought or the rediscovery and rehabilitation of his contribution in the work of Jevons, Marshall, and others. In discussing developments in the theory of the firm, Boulding has noted that

The hundred years of development from 1838 to 1938, however, merely made more explicit and usable what was already in Cournot, where all that is essential in what has come to be known as the marginal analysis is found in embryo, expressed in the formulae of the differential calculus.[4]

We might add, for historical perspective, Schumpeter's comment with reference to the "marginal revenue curve" that "We must not, however, forget that the tool was first used by Cournot, and no author of the 1920's or 1930's can have any *objective* claim to it."[5]

---

[3] Cournot, *op. cit.*, p. 57; italics in original.
[4] Kenneth E. Boulding and W. Allen Spivey, *Linear Programming and the Theory of the Firm*, The Macmillan Company, New York, 1960, p. 2.
[5] Joseph A. Schumpeter, *History of Economic Analysis*, Oxford University Press, Fair Lawn, N.J., 1954, p. 1152.

We shall return in a subsequent chapter to the main lines of development of the theory of the firm and to the building blocks we shall need to derive from it. Without stopping to examine the considerable achievement of Marshall at this point, we might introduce our comment on the need for a more fully integrated and generalized body of analysis by noting Marshall's acknowledgment of Cournot, whose work we have just referred to. "He taught," Marshall says in the preface to the first edition of his *Principles*, "that it is necessary to face the difficulty of regarding the various elements of an economic problem — not as determining one another in a chain of causation, *A* determining *B*, *B* determining *C*, and so on — but as all mutually determining one another."[6]

Mutual Determination of Decision Variables

The notion that Marshall here expounds is the mutual determination of the optimum values of interdependent variables, which we shall explore in some depth in the following chapters. In the context of the firm's policy problems and the underlying economic theory, we shall refer to the mutual determination of the solution values of the firm's decision variables: its factor inputs, product output, asset acquisitions, financing sources, etc. The kind of integration problem we shall encounter is similar in one of its aspects to that of Smith, whose *Investment and Production* set out "to develop a unified theory of production and investment."[7] And in similar vein F. and V. Lutz attempted "to develop a method of analysis which integrates the theory of production with the theory of capital as the latter applies to the individual firm."[8] Again, Carlson, in an important work to which we shall refer further, indicates that he "tried particularly to emphasize the bearing of the capital and interest theory on the cost and revenue calculations of a single firm's production."[9] Each of these positions will be examined further and more critically in what follows.

The Problem of the Maximand

Before we can make much progress with the integration, on the theoretical or the empirical level, of the causal relations in the firm's optimization

[6] Alfred Marshall, *Principles of Economics*, 9th (variorum) ed., C. W. Guillebaud (ed.), Macmillan & Co., Ltd., London, 1961, vol. 1, p. ix.

[7] Vernon L. Smith, *Investment and Production: A Study in the Theory of the Capital-using Enterprise*, Harvard University Press, Cambridge, Mass., 1961, p. vii.

[8] Friedrich Lutz and Vera Lutz, *The Theory of Investment of the Firm*, Princeton University Press, Princeton, 1951, p. 3.

[9] Sune Carlson, *A Study on the Pure Theory of Production*, published in Stockholm, 1939, republished by Augustus M. Kelley, *Reprints of Economic Classics*, New York, 1965, pp. v–vi.

problem, we must first confront the thorny question of just what it is the firm should set out to optimize. We need to consider what form of a maximand, if any, should be introduced into the discussion. Classically, following the developments from the lead laid down by Cournot and his notions of total and marginal net receipts, the maximand has been taken to be some form of suitably defined profits, or the capital values implicit in definable streams of profits which, it was envisaged, could be generated by certain asset holdings or by certain investment commitments. More recently, however, controversy has developed regarding the general acceptability, and the empirical applicability, of the classical marginal analysis.[10] Simon's "satisficing versus maximizing"[11] and William Baumol's questioning of "the revenue maximization hypothesis" and his discussion of "sales as an ultimate objective"[12] are examples of directions taken by the newer discussions.

For our own part, however, we shall rely heavily on the insights of marginal analysis inherited from the general neoclassical tradition. But in defining our maximand we shall also adopt the overriding proviso that the thing to be maximized in the search for enterprise optima will not be profits as such, nor the rate of profits generated on investment commitments, but the capitalized values of the income streams that investment and productive activity can be expected to produce.

On the simplest level of generalization the distinction between profit maximization and capital value or wealth maximization is that the latter is required to pay close attention to four important aspects of analysis: first, the timing of the expected receipt of the components of the projected income stream; second, the quality of the income stream, or the relevant degree of risk or uncertainty attaching to the income expectations; third, the possible variations in income receivers' attitudes to the quality of income, or to risk and uncertainty, and the manner in which such attitudes or predilections may be analyzed under a definable utility function; and finally, the choice of an appropriate discount factor or factors, and the method by which income receivers' time preferences and risk preferences should influence the reduction of expected values to present or capitalized values. Probably it will never be possible, if only because of the subjectivities inherent in the problem, to give, in a single and unambiguously usable model,

---

[10] See, for example, Boulding and Spivey, *op. cit.* pp. 4f., for a perspective on the "criticisms of marginalism." See also Martin Shubik, "Objective Functions and Models of Corporate Optimization," *Quarterly Journal of Economics*, vol. 75, pp. 345–375, August, 1961.

[11] Herbert A. Simon, "Theories of Decision-making in Economics and Behavioral Science," *American Economic Review*, vol. 49, pp. 253–283, June, 1959, and "New Developments in the Theory of the Firm," *American Economic Review*, vol. 52, pp. 1–15, May, 1962.

[12] William J. Baumol, *Business Behavior, Value and Growth*, The Macmillan Company, New York, 1959, pp. 45–53.

a complete answer to a complete listing of all the conceptual and procedural questions that can be raised on the levels just indicated. The thing that can hopefully be done is to open up some new perspectives and approaches and discover some new dimensions of awareness of the logical orders and causal relations in the overall area of enquiry.

The Owners' Economic Position

In the present work the optimization problem will be referred to in specific terms, and we shall speak of the optimization of the economic position of the owners of the firm. In the general case this will involve the maximization of the value, or what we shall call the economic value, of the ownership investment in the firm. This in turn involves the maximization of the capitalized value, or present discounted value, of the income stream the business can be expected to generate. The thing we implicitly have in view, therefore, is the economic value of the asset investment at work in the firm, and we shall be concerned to ascertain that the structure of income-generating assets to which investable funds have been committed is in some sense, yet to be defined, an optimum structure. We shall require at the same time that the sources of money capital by which the investment has been financed comprise, in some similar sense, an optimum structure of financing sources.

But the need for assets to support the productive process depends, in turn, on the magnitudes and capital intensities of the factor capacities employed in the firm. The demand for assets, and thus the requirements of money capital resources, hangs on the technological potentialities of substitutions between asset capacities and other factors in the production function, and on the economic margins determining the extent to which such elasticities of substitution as exist should profitably be exploited. Thus our optimization objective will involve the optimization, in a more radical and thoroughgoing fashion than is generally confronted, of the productive and operating structure of the firm. Our analysis will lead us to the concept of what we shall call "sequential decision-making" points, at which the enterprise structure is examined for its consistency with the solution outcomes of the explanatory planning models we shall construct.

A Simple Model

We might profitably introduce the argument by looking at the simplified value maximization model set out by Solomon in his recent *Theory of Financial Management*.

The gross present worth of a course of action is equal to the capitalized value of the flow of future expected benefits, discounted (or capitalized) at a rate which reflects their certainty or uncertainty. Wealth or net present worth is the difference between gross present worth and the amount of capital investment required to achieve the benefits being discussed.[13]

At this point Solomon's model contains a couple of features that we shall incorporate in more complex form at different levels of approximation. We note therefore that he continues: "In order to define the net present worth of an asset or a course of action more exactly, it is useful to begin by thinking in terms of benefits that are not expected to undergo secular growth or decay."[14] In such a case, the net profit or income accruing to the owners of the firm can be understood as the gross annual earnings less all costs of production, including depreciation on the firm's capital assets, taxation payments, and the interest on those capital funds supplied to the business by creditors and other nonownership sources. The point of principal interest at present is that the enterprise may in this way be looked upon as having perpetual existence and as generating an income stream extending over an infinite time horizon. This will be the case if the annual residual profit of the firm is reckoned after the deduction from total earnings of a depreciation or reinvestment sum necessary to maintain the earning ability, or the projected annual gross cash flow, at its currently estimated level.

Leaving aside for the moment the stochastic interpretation of the annual cash flow of the business and the possible description of the cash flow components in terms of the decision maker's subjective probability distributions, the following notation describes the basic Solomon model.

G = average annual earnings before depreciation, interest, and taxes
M = average annual reinvestment required to maintain G at the projected level (which may differ from the conventional accounting depreciation allowance)
I = annual payments of interest, preferred dividends, and all prior charge payments to nonowner sources of capital
T = annual tax payments on the expected income implicit in G, M, and I

Then the perpetual stream of earnings available to the owners can be described as

$$E = G - (M + I + T)$$

and in the nongrowth case this will equal also the annual dividend payments to the owners. Given also that k is a capitalization rate (describable on the basis of subjective estimates of outcomes and risk aversion or predilection)

---

[13] Ezra Solomon, *The Theory of Financial Management*, Columbia University Press, New York, 1963, p. 20. This work contains a convenient and valuable summary of the principal points of discussion in this area at the time it was written.
[14] *Ibid.*

consistent with the degree of uncertainty attaching to the estimates of the underlying flow of benefits, the value of the ownership may be described as

$$V = \frac{E}{k}$$

Then the wealth or net present worth of the firm can be understood as the difference between this gross calculated value of the income stream and the amount of ownership capital committed to the firm:

$$W = V - C$$

First Extension of the Model

Let us expand this basic model slightly to give an indication of the direction of approach we shall take to the problem of economic valuation. As a first approximation the maximand in our model can be written as follows:

$$\pi_t = p_t Q_t - \sum_i b_{it} X_{it} - r_t D_t \tag{1-1}$$

where the following notation applies, with all variables being appropriately dated as indicated by the time subscript t:

π = net residual income available to the owners
p = selling price per unit of output
Q = number of units of output sold
X_i = quantity of units of factor capacity employed for each factor i incorporated in the productive process
b_i = input cost per unit of factor capacity
r = average rate of interest per annum payable on funds obtained from nonowner sources of capital
D = total amount of nonowner funds employed in the firm

It will be noted that, for purposes of simplicity, we abstract at present from the problem of corporate income tax liability. If it were desired to incorporate a tax factor T as in the Solomon case, the residual income available for the owners could be written as $\pi(1 - T)$.

More important, the b_i in Equation (1-1) is understood to include, in the cases where so-called factor capacities are provided by assets whose durability or economic lives extend over more than one time period, an appropriate depreciation allowance necessary to maintain the asset investment and its earning ability intact. It will be seen subsequently in more complex contexts that such a treatment of the depreciation problem not only enables us to conceive of an infinite income stream in an effectively perpetual enterprise, but serves also as a conceptual link between the theory of capital, in its microeconomic context, and the pragmatic optimization procedures of the firm.

Our immediate problem, on the basis of this first approximation model, is to describe the economic value of the ownership. This is defined as the present discounted value, or present capitalized value, of the anticipated income stream, and assuming an appropriate time rate of discount r, this may be written as

$$V = \sum_{t=1}^{\infty} \frac{\pi_t}{\prod_{s=1}^{t} (1 + r_s)} \qquad (1\text{-}2)$$

or, assuming continuous discounting, as

$$V = \int_0^{\infty} \pi_t \exp\left[- \int_0^t r(s)\, ds\right] dt \qquad (1\text{-}3)$$

In the event that the time rate of discount can be assumed to remain constant, the value of the ownership reduces to the simpler and more familiar form

$$V = \sum_{t=1}^{\infty} \frac{\pi_t}{(1 + r)^t} \qquad (1\text{-}4)$$

or

$$V = \int_0^{\infty} \pi_t e^{-rt}\, dt \qquad (1\text{-}5)$$

But this initial statement does little more than focus attention on the three principal points at issue in the optimization argument: first, the decision to concentrate analysis on the economic value of the ownership investment in the firm; second, the need to specify, in an expectational form, the future income stream attributable to the ownership investment; and third, the reduction of future income values to present capitalized values by applying an appropriately defined capitalization rate. The second and third of these issues will be seen to be tightly meshed, for the nature of the risks and uncertainties in the income expectation will determine the way in which it will be valued by an individual owner or investor. If, as will be proposed in Chapter 2, an individual may logically assess the quality of income expectations in terms of a utility function defined over the twofold arguments of profit on the one hand and risk on the other, then the degree of risk and its utility or disutility significance will, via the utility function, determine the capitalization or valuation rate.

The concept, moreover, of the profit expectation as defined in Equation (1-1) and evaluated in Equations (1-2) through (1-5) needs also to be defined in detail, taking account of the ways in which the firm's production, investment, and financing decisions determine the arguments and magnitudes on the right-hand side of Equation (1-1). It will be useful, therefore, before proceeding to the uncertainty and utility analysis, to summarize in the remainder of this chapter the terrain of theory through which we shall move and the nature of the conclusions we shall reach.

Plan of Analysis

The following paragraphs indicate in only a highly adumbrated form the nature of the analysis that follows; they do not disclose the structure or nuances of the argument in very significant detail. The statement that follows, however, will be useful as a guide through the ensuing discussion, and reference to it may be helpful as the argument unfolds. The reader may find it advantageous also to bear in mind the summaries of the analysis in the concluding sections of Chapters 3, 7, and 9 and in the opening sections of Chapter 10, where the final objective is reached in the setting forth of what we have called the *maximum maximorum* of the ownership valuation of the firm.

A principal task in Chapter 2 is the forging of a linkage between the owner's, or decision maker's utility function on the one hand and the equity capitalization rate on the other. Utility will be defined as a function of income and risk in the general form of

$$U = f(\pi, \sigma) \tag{1-6}$$

where π refers to the profit expectation and σ to the standard deviation of the probability distribution of the profit variable. It will be posited that the utility function in general takes a risk aversion form, and while the properties of more than one possible form of the function will be examined, the assumption will be made that utility is positive in the profit argument and negative in the risk argument. From this foundation the capitalization rate function will be derived, and it will be shown that in general the form of this function is the logical precipitate of the form of the utility function. For concreteness, an analysis will be made of the properties of the capitalization rate function of the form

$$\rho = a + w\sigma^2 \tag{1-7}$$

where the capitalization rate ρ is a linear function of the square of the standard deviation of the distribution of profit expectations, previously encountered in the utility function and here taken as a measure of the degree of risk. The parametric constants in Equation (1-7), a and w, will be seen to depend on the magnitudes of the coefficients on the arguments in the utility function. The value of the ownership, given the income expectation and the rate at which it is valued, will be determined by a relation of the general form

$$V = \frac{\pi}{\rho} \qquad (1\text{-}8)$$

where the variables are as previously defined.

In Chapter 3 the empirical financial statements of the firm are discussed, and the income statement and the balance sheet are examined. The objective there is not the description of the accounting problems and techniques involved in the construction of the statements, but rather the discovery of the economic forces which determine the structure of the firm and its income-generating process and which are therefore reflected in the firm's financial statements. The attempt is made in Chapter 3, as in the two chapters that follow it, to discover the empirical categories with which the subsequent economic analysis, and in particular the general optimization models, must come to grips.

The argument in Chapter 3 will therefore establish the firm's decision nexus as concerned with a trilogy of decision problems: the production problem, the investment problem, and the financing problem. It will be seen that lurking behind this trilogy of decision problems is the logical and analytical content of the economic theories of production, capital, and finance. The mutually determinate solutions to the problems are reflected in the structure of the firm's financial statements that we have already referred to. In brief, the production problem has to do with optimum product outputs and optimum combinations of factor inputs employed in the firm; the investment problem takes up the question of optimum capital usage and is accordingly concerned with the optimum structure of the firm's investments, reflected in the assets side of the balance sheet; and the financing problem is concerned with the optimum combinations of sources of money capital used to finance the firm's investments, and described in the liabilities side of the balance sheet.

In Chapters 4 and 5 the partial optimization analysis sets in perspective the relevant content of current and recent traditions in the financing and capital investment of the firm. But the problems there are highlighted as problems in partial optimization, because the questions asked have generally to do with issues such as the following: Given the availability of certain investment projects and the availability or cost of money capital to the firm, how can decisions be made as to the optimum projects or set of projects in which to invest; or given the level of total money capital employed in the firm, is it possible to define an optimum combination of financing sources from which to obtain that capital, raising in particular the question whether the overall cost of capital to the firm and thus the value of the firm are or are not dependent on the financing mix employed.

While various extensions of the capital budgeting analysis implicit in the foregoing will be explored, it will be seen that the partial optimization analysis in its usual form does not achieve a significant integration between the investment and financing problems. The logical difficulties bypassed by the analysis have to do mainly with the need to show a clear linkage between the production and factor employment problems on the one hand and the asset requirements and capital intensities of production processes on the other, thus determining the optimum level and structure of real capital investment. The partial optimization analysis founders in its failure to examine the linkage between the cost and availability of money capital and the optimum capital intensity of the firm's production process. In the form in which it traditionally exists, it fails to examine the extent to which the solutions to the capital employment and financing problems are interconnected, via the manner in which the money capital constraint may induce a degree of substitution between available factors of production. The possibilities of such substitution and the economic significance of their exploitation depend on the capital intensities of the various factors at work in the firm and on the technological characteristics of the firm's production function.

The foregoing, of course, is a highly compressed and summary statement of issues that will engage us at some length. But it does point up the principal methodological problem. Analytically, the interconnections between the theory of production and the theory of capital need to be securely established; and empirically, their relevance for optimum decision making in the firm needs to be shown. In Chapter 6, therefore, we have sketched the ways in which economists have historically lived with the awareness of this kind of problem. We have done so, not for the sake of an indulgence in intellectual history as such, but in order to establish the theoretical standpoint from which our subsequent model building can be approached.

The elements of the general optimization model of the firm are introduced in Chapter 7 and then employed with increasing complexity throughout the remainder of the book. At this point it will be useful to present a simplified example of the kind of constrained objective or maximand function with which we shall be working and to indicate, on the basis of it, the principal elements of the model. Consider a function of the following form:

$$\varphi = \frac{1}{\rho(D)} [p(Q)f(X,Y) - \gamma_1 X - \gamma_2 Y - r(D)D]$$
$$+ \mu[\overline{K} + D - g(Q) - \alpha X - \beta Y] \quad (1\text{-}9)$$

where the following notation applies:

ρ = equity owners' capitalization rate, here shown as functionally dependent on D, the total amount of debt capital, or nonownership capital, employed in the firm

p = unit selling price of the firm's product, here shown as a function of the quantity of output produced and sold, Q, thereby recognizing the pervasiveness of imperfect competition in the firm's output market

X,Y = input factors of production, to be described more precisely as the number of units of the respective factor capacities employed; it is noted that the production function is written in the standard form as $Q = f(X,Y)$

γ_1, γ_2 = unit factor costs of inputs X and Y respectively

r = average rate of interest on the total debt or nonownership capital employed in the firm

$\overline{K}$ = amount of equity or ownership capital invested in the firm, assumed for purposes of Equation (1-9) to be given and fixed

$g(Q)$ = a net working capital requirement function, the full specification of which will describe the firm's net investment in working capital assets, cash, accounts receivables, and inventory, as functionally dependent on the level of production and sales

α, β = money capital requirement coefficients of factors X and Y respectively, indicating, for example, that for each unit of factor Y capacity employed in the firm an investment in fixed assets of β dollars is required

It will be recognized that the first term on the right-hand side of Equation (1-9), or the expression to the left of the plus sign, is of the same form as the right-hand side of Equation (1-8). It is describing the value of the ownership of the firm as the capitalized value of the net income or profit. The expression in brackets in this term is thus defining the net income as equal to the gross revenue, or selling price times quantity of output sold, where the production function $Q = f(X,Y)$ is substituted for the output variable, minus the direct factor costs and minus also the total interest cost of debt capital being borne by the firm.

It is seen, moreover, that Equation (1-9) is describing an ownership valuation function where the value, here referred to as φ, can be maximized by choosing the optimum input values of the three decision variables, factor X, factor Y, and the use of debt or nonownership capital D. But it is clear also that the procedure envisaged is that of constrained optimization, or the maximization of the function subject to the constraint or side condition described in the second term on the right-hand side of Equation (1-9). The economic and mathematical meaning of the constrained optimization procedure will be clarified fully, but for the present it can be said that the expression in the final brackets on the right-hand side of Equation (1-9) will be referred to as the firm's money capital availability constraint. As it stands in Equation (1-9) it is made up of two parts: first, the total supply of money capital available to the firm, the given amount of equity capital, $\overline{K}$, and the amount of debt it is economically advantageous to borrow, D, subject to the interest cost function, $r(D)$; and second, the total money capital requirements of the firm.

Bringing the two parts of this constraint together, the following three-fold proposition can be advanced: (1) Whatever level of output is decided upon by the firm as the optimum level, this will call for the employment of a unique optimum combination of factor inputs; (2) such a factor input combination will necessitate definable investments in assets, in accordance with the money capital requirement coefficients of the factors, in this case α and β; and in addition, the output level will necessitate a net investment in working capital assets, here referred to as $g(Q)$; (3) finally, the total amount of money capital that the firm may use for these several purposes will be restricted to the total amount of money capital available to it, and the constraint condition may accordingly be specified in the following form:

$$g(Q) + \alpha X + \beta Y \leq \overline{K} + D \qquad (1\text{-}10)$$

It will be seen in the fuller development that the variable μ in Equation (1-9), the coefficient of the constraint condition, sometimes referred to as a Lagrange multiplier, can be interpreted as the marginal productivity of the constraint variable, or in this case as the marginal productivity of money capital. It will be seen more clearly in due course also that the input factor costs γ_1 and γ_2 and the money capital requirement coefficients α and β may be specified uniquely, depending on conditions in the factor, the asset, and the money capital markets.

The objective before us now is that of choosing an optimum structure of the firm—the level of output or in a multiproduct firm the combination of outputs, the factor combination and thus the structure of the production process, the structure of asset investments, and the structure of financing sources or the combination of debt and ownership capital. The analysis thus takes the form of an optimum structure analysis, and the consistent objective is that of making the structural decisions that will lead to the maximization of the value of the ownership. In general terms the problem will be solved, on the basis of the form presented in Equation (1-9), by maximizing the φ function at the optimum solution values of the input or structural decision variables X, Y, and D. Thus the factor employment decision and the real capital investment decision implicit in it are linked to the mon-

ey capital financing decision, pointing in the direction of the desired generalization of the microtheory of the firm. It will be seen that by taking the
partial derivatives of Equation (1-9) with respect to the three decision
variables and μ, a set of simultaneous equations is derived, sufficient to determine the required solution values of X, Y, D, and μ. Substitution into the
determinant functions implicit in the model, the production function, revenue function, interest cost function, etc., will provide the solution values
describing the total structure of the firm, its processes and operations.

In Chapter 10 the argument recognizes a crucial limitation of the analysis to that point. The preceding structural optimization, it might be noted,
has rested completely on the assumption that the amount of equity or ownership capital in the firm, $\overline{K}$, was given and fixed. We have spoken of the optimum structure, including in particular the optimum debt-equity money
capital ratio, for a given amount of equity capital at work in the firm. We
are required now, therefore, to consider not only the optimum structure for
a given amount of equity, but also the optimum structure for the optimum
equity. It is this latter that we have called the *optimum optimorum*. It will
be seen in this connection that very important signals are given in the optimization process by the solution values of μ, the marginal productivity of
money capital.

Beyond the *optimum optimorum* of the basic analysis there remain
many issues related to the structural planning and operations of the firm.
These are examined in Chapters 11 and 12, and it will suffice at this point to
indicate only three of the further areas of analysis. First, at any of the sequential-planning or structural decision-making dates, the optimum plan
may call for a disinvestment in certain of the firm's existing activities as
well as for a change in the structure of the firm to incorporate new activities. The optimization model must therefore provide for the incorporation of
partial or segmental liquidation values, and for the generation of alternative enterprise plans, from among which the future operating base may be
chosen.

Second, in certain situations a firm might rationally choose to operate
at what, on the basis of the decision signals given by the planning model, is
a suboptimum structure, if by doing so it preserves a larger degree of flexibility in its future operations than would otherwise be the case. We shall
consider, therefore, the notion of the economic cost of structural flexibility
in the operating plan decided on by the firm.

Third, the principal parts of our analysis in the following chapters will
assume that we are dealing with a single-product firm whose production
function is of the two-argument type we have already referred to. It will
be necessary to indicate, therefore, the nature of the generalization to multiproduct firms, considering the economic relations between different prod-

uct outputs on the one hand and the wider range of the uses of different factors inputs on the other.

In the final chapter of the book a comment will be made on the relations between the new directions of analysis we are hopefully opening and some recent traditions in the theory of the finances of the firm.

2

Uncertainty
And
Utility

The rate at which an individual values an income expectation can be assumed to depend upon (1) the degree of risk or uncertainty inherent in the expectation, and (2) the aversion or predilection with which, in accordance with a suitably defined utility function, the degree of uncertainty is contemplated. In the context of the ownership of a firm, these issues together establish the capitalization rate at which, as in Equation (1-8) for example, the equity investment should be valued at any given time. The problem of valuation is simply, we have seen, the problem of reducing future expected income components to their present value equivalent, or to present capitalized or present discounted values. In this chapter we shall explore briefly the main issues involved in this capitalization relationship, in such a way as to exhibit their relevance and applicability to our consistent problem of maximizing the ownership value of the firm.

To this point the model of the preceding chapter has suppressed fairly completely the question of the degree of risk or uncertainty surrounding the income expectations, or the quality of the income stream. We may therefore reinterpret the profit function in Equation (1-1) in the following manner:

$$\pi = R - C + u \qquad (2\text{-}1)$$

In this expression, R and C are understood as summarizing the total gross revenues and total costs, including depreciation and financing costs, as previously incorporated in the model. The profit-earning opportunities of the firm, described in terms of a probability distribution of outcomes, are taken to be constant from year to year, the time subscript is dropped from the equation, and the revenues and costs are now regarded as annual expected values. What is most important, however, is that the final term u in Equation (2-1) is now introduced to represent a random variation or random disturbance term, summarizing the effects on the dependent variable π of the annual determinant forces not fully subsumed in the expected values R and C. Our new profit function, Equation (2-1), is therefore a statistical function that envisages random variations of annual profits about a calculable expected value.

In order to make any judgment about the degree of risk in the projected income stream it is necessary first to specify a set of expectations about the behavior of the random term u. Let it be supposed, for purposes of concreteness, that the characteristics of the random component can be described as follows:

$$E(u) = 0$$
$$E(u_i^2) = \mathrm{Var}(u) = \sigma_u^2 = \mathrm{const}$$

This implies that the variance of the random component, or the dispersion of the distribution of the deviations of the profit observations about their expected value, is assumed to remain constant over time. It would be possible, of course, to imagine that the variance of the random term was itself a function of time, but it is not necessary, for purposes of our present objectives, to go beyond the simple assumptions already indicated. If, in fact, such a further complex assumption were made and the variance of the profit expectation were understood to depend on the time horizon of the expectation, a rather more complex form of the utility function involved in the valuation process would also have to be specified. For as will be seen, the variance we now have in view will serve as an index of risk in the utility function on the one hand and in the implied capitalization rate function on the other. The assumption of constant variance, or homoscedastic expectations, will enable us to establish the relationships included in the argument without significant loss of generality.

The Utility Function

Subject to a fuller analysis in the remaining sections of this chapter, we can now make the preliminary assumption that it is possible to describe the owner's attitude to risk and expected returns in terms of a suitably defined utility function. Let us suppose that the total utility of the outcome of the investment in the firm is positively related to expected returns and negatively related to the associated degree of risk. If, now, the standard deviation of the fluctuations of the random disturbance is taken as a measure of the degree of risk, the utility function in view may be written as

$$U = f(\pi, \sigma) \tag{2-2}$$

or, for concreteness,

$$U = \alpha\pi - \beta\sigma^2 \tag{2-3}$$

It would seem, then, anticipating the subsequent mathematical argument, that the owners of the firm will assess a less risky income expectation at a higher value, per dollar of income, than they would value a more risky expectation. We might consider, therefore, that the rate at which income streams of differing degrees of risk will be capitalized to determine their present values will be an increasing function of the measure of risk. We might write, for example,

$$\rho = a + w\mathrm{Var}(u) \tag{2-4}$$

where ρ, the rate at which the income stream is capitalized, is a linear function of the variance of the expectations. The intercept a can be taken as the required rate of return or yield on riskless or default-free securities. The yield on perpetual government securities may be taken as indicating this riskless rate. Figure 1 indicates the required yield function, or the capitalization rate function, in view.

On this basis, we are now in a position to specify (1) the expected annual income of the firm, designated as $\bar{\pi}$, (2) the degree of risk or variance associated with that expectation, and (3) the attitudes of the owners to the projected outcomes, summarized in the capitalization rate ρ at which the income is valued. Our valuation model may then be amended from the form in which it stands in Chapter 1 to

$$V = \int_0^\infty \bar{\pi} e^{-\rho t}\, dt \tag{2-5}$$

And in the case we are considering for the present illustration, this reduces to

$$V = \frac{\bar{\pi}}{\rho} \tag{2-6}$$

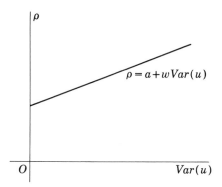

Figure 1. The equity capitalization rate function

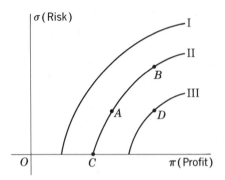

Figure 2. The investor's indifference map

The Certainty Equivalent Approach

The foregoing procedure is not, however, the only way of valuing expected income streams or a firm's income-earning ability in the presence of
risk and uncertainty. A discussion of an alternative approach, or what will
be known as the certainty equivalent method of valuation, will serve to
bring into focus some additional aspects of the underlying relationships with
which we are concerned. Let us begin by considering a hypothetical investor's indifference map as drawn in Figure 2.

Each member of the family of indifference curves in the figure is the
locus of a set of risk-profit combinations between which the investor, or in
our previous context the owner of the firm, is indifferent. Consider two investment opportunities whose expected profits and associated risks are as
indicated by the coordinates of points A and B on the indifference map. We
can say that the investor would find the two projects equally attractive,
and, as would be the case with any other project whose risk and profit coordinates fell on indifference curve II, he would be indifferent between them.
Similarly it can be seen that every point in the risk-profit plane potentially
represents the corresponding characteristics of an investment opportunity,
and every such point can be understood to lie on one particular indifference
curve. It is not necessary to repeat at this point the axiomatic development
of the indifference curve concept, which may be encountered in many parts
of the literature of theoretical economics. Further comments will be made
on the concept in the mathematical analysis later in this chapter.

In the same way as in analogous applications, the slope of the indifference curve in Figure 2 represents the individual's subjective marginal
rate of substitution between the quantities described by the arguments in
the utility function, or the axes of the indifference plane, in this case risk and
profit.

In the case of the concave indifference curves represented here, the
marginal rate of substitution between risk and profit is increasing on any

given indifference locus as successively higher-risk and higher-return investments are envisaged. In the present case the marginal rate of substitution of risk for profit is defined as the increase in desired profit necessary to compensate, in the mind of the investor, for an incremental increase in risk. Finally, it will also be clear, for reasons analogous to those adduced in other applications of the indifference curve concept, that any point on indifference curve II is preferable to any point on indifference curve I. Indifference locus II offers higher profits for a given risk than indifference locus I, or lower risks for given profits. Analogously, an investment project described by the coordinates at point D in Figure 2 would be preferred to projects A and B.

The application of these concepts to our present problem can be seen by considering point C in Figure 2. As this point is on the same indifference curve as A and B and lies on the profit axis, or has a zero risk coordinate, it can be taken as indicating the zero risk profit that would be precisely as attractive to the investor as the risk and profit opportunities offered by projects A and B. The profit at point C, in other words, is the certain profit for which the investor would be willing to exchange A or B. In this sense C is referred to as the certainty equivalent of A and B.

Consider in more detail now the comparison between A and C. Let the profit associated with A be described by π in the same way as in the foregoing valuation equations, and let the profit associated with C be described by π^*. Also, invoking our earlier analysis of the owner's required rate of return or capitalization rate function, let the rate at which the investor would be prepared to capitalize the profits at A, given the risk associated with them, be described as before by ρ. In the valuation of the profits at C, on the other hand, these being the certainty equivalent profits, the only meaningful capitalization rate to apply is a suitably defined riskless rate of interest. We can refer to this as r. With these definitions and relationships in hand, we can refer to the valuation of the income stream in the following terms, as an alternative to the expressions contained in Equations (2-5) and (2-6):

$$V^* = \int_0^\infty \pi^* e^{-rt}\, dt \tag{2-7}$$

or, on the same assumptions as before,

$$V^* = \frac{\pi^*}{r} \tag{2-8}$$

In this expression V^* may be referred to as the certainty equivalent economic value of the profit expectation.

An Alternative Model

The certainty equivalent approach to income stream valuation can be conceptualized in other ways also. We shall refer to one further method very

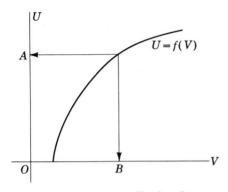

Figure 3. Hypothetical utility function

briefly for the light it throws on an alternative approach to the investment decision maker's utility function. We shall expand our treatment of the case in Chapter 5. Imagine now that, instead of thinking in terms of a utility function described over the two arguments of profit (π) and risk (σ) as in the foregoing case, utility is considered to be simply a function of the wealth or value outcomes resulting from investment opportunities. Invoking the economists' traditional assumption of the diminishing marginal utility of money or wealth, the utility function as now envisaged may be written as

$$U = f(V) \tag{2-9}$$

where V is a measure of wealth and where the function is assumed to be positively sloped and concave downward. Figure 3 indicates the function on which the following comments are based.

Consider now the profit function incorporated in the preceding analysis and the range of possible values of π, having regard to the assumed dispersion of the random component in the function. It may be the case that different assumptions from those previously adopted might well be made regarding the possible dispersion of the profit outcomes about their expected value. The possible profit outcomes may be described, for example, in terms of a probability distribution assigned on the basis of the decision maker's or owner's best judgmental estimates. If, now, a discrete probability distribution of this form were taken, each possible profit outcome in the distribution could be capitalized at a time discount factor equal to the risk-free rate of interest. When this is done the capitalized values thus obtained will appear in the form of a probability distribution of values. Then at this point the analysis is in possession of (1) a function showing the utilities of differing value outcomes (see Figure 3), and (2) a probability distribution of value outcomes. The two sets of data can then be combined in the following manner to calculate what might be referred to as the expected utility:

$$E(U) = \sum_i p_i(V_i)U(V_i) \tag{2-10}$$

or, more fully,

$$E(U) = \sum_i U(V_i)p_i(S_i r^{-1}) \qquad (2\text{-}11)$$

where $\sum_i p_i = 1$. The second term in parentheses represents the present capitalized value, discounted at a risk-free rate of interest r, of each possible profit outcome in the underlying probability distribution of outcomes. In other words V_i is equal to $S_i r^{-1}$ where S_i is the ith possible profit outcome and the term in parentheses is a convenient notational expression of the more familiar form S_i/r.

The expected utility of the investment project is the sum of the products obtained by multiplying the utility attaching to each possible capitalized value by the probability that that particular outcome will occur. (It can be mentioned at this point that the treatment of utilities in this fashion does not involve the analysis in the difficulties of classical cardinality. The arguments at this particular point can be explored in the literature indicated in footnote 1 below. For the present we simply state that it is adequate for the discussion in hand to work with a suitably described ordinal utility scale.)

In this way the expected utility of an investment commitment is obtained. It should be noticed, moreover, that such an estimate is a certainty equivalent estimate in a significant respect. First, it will be recalled that the probability distribution of possible value outcomes was obtained by discounting the possible range of future values at a risk-free capitalization rate. We have thus derived a time-adjusted probability distribution of outcomes. The capitalized values thus obtained will clearly be higher than those which would have been obtained if the future possible outcomes had been discounted at a higher capitalization rate: if, for example, instead of using the risk-free discount rate we had used some estimate of the risk-adjusted required rate of return, such as ρ in our previous analysis. It will be recognized on reflection, therefore, that the distribution of present values obtained by the procedure now being discussed has simply adjusted the future expectations to take account of the pure time value of money, or of what has been called in theoretical economics the individual decision maker's rate of time preference, without any adjustment for risk at all. To this point the distribution of possible profit outcomes has simply been reexpressed in terms of the present capitalized values of those outcomes.

But it is precisely the adjustment for risk that is being accomplished when the probability distribution of present values of outcomes is married, in the manner indicated, to the decision maker's utility function. The probabilities in the argument do themselves inherently describe the degree of risk in the investment, and the issue as to whether the investment is economically worthwhile or acceptable can then be settled in the following way: Taking the computed expected utility of the investment as obtained in Equation (2-10), the certainty equivalent money value (CE) may be obtained by inverse transformation from the utility function, assuming the function is of the single-valued form already indicated. Precisely,

$$CE = f^{-1}(U)_{U=E(U)} \qquad (2\text{-}12)$$

At an expected utility of A in Figure 3, the certainty equivalent money value would be B. The question at issue is, then, whether the certainty equivalent money value is or is not greater than the amount of capital funds it might be proposed to commit to the investment.[1]

Summary of Valuation Approaches

Rather than multiply analytical possibilities unnecessarily at this early stage, we note that we thus have three approaches to the valuation of income, taking account of the degree of risk or uncertainty surrounding the income expectations: (1) the risk-adjusted required rate of return or capitalization rate approach, utilizing the capitalization rate function of $\rho = a + w\text{Var}(u)$ as shown in Figure 1; (2) the capitalization of certainty equivalent expectations at a risk-free discount factor, where the certainty equivalents of future possible outcomes are read from the indifference curves in the argument plane obtained from a two-argument utility function. In the preceding case these were taken as profit and risk, π and σ, as posited in

---

[1] The notion of "certainty equivalent" has appeared in many places in theoretical economics. See, for example, Friedrich Lutz and Vera Lutz, *The Theory of Investment of the Firm*, Princeton University Press, Princeton, N.J., 1951, chap. 15; Alexander A. Robichek and Stewart C. Myers, *Optimal Financing Decisions*, Prentice-Hall, Inc., Englewood Cliffs, N.J., 1965, pp. 79f.; William S. Vickrey, *Metastatics and Macroeconomics*, Harcourt, Brace & World, Inc., New York, 1964, pp. 69–70. On the matter of the utility function and the relevant mathematical analysis a large literature also exists. The following, and the references there cited, may be consulted: William J. Baumol, *Economic Theory and Operations Analysis*, 2d ed., Prentice-Hall, Inc., Englewood Cliffs, N.J., 1965, chap. 22; Robert Schlaifer, *Introduction to Statistics for Business Decisions*, McGraw-Hill Book Company, New York, 1961, pp. 3–63; R. G. D. Allen, *Mathematical Economics*, Macmillan & Co., Ltd., London, 1959, chap. 19; James M. Henderson and Richard E. Quandt, *Microeconomic Theory: A Mathematical Approach*, McGraw-Hill Book Company, New York, 1958, pp. 8–20; Eugene M. Lerner and Willard T. Carleton, *A Theory of Financial Analysis*, Harcourt, Brace & World, Inc., New York, 1966, chap. 6; Donald E. Farrar, *The Investment Decision under Uncertainty*, Prentice-Hall, Inc., Englewood Cliffs, N.J., 1962, pp. 11f. For a very useful development of the certainty equivalent and utility function ideas as applied to the firm's capital budgeting problem, see Harold Bierman and Seymour Smidt, *The Capital Budgeting Decision*, 2d ed., The Macmillan Company, 1966, pp. 168–170 and chaps. 15 and 16.

Equation (2-2) and developed in Figure 2; and (3) the confrontation of a time-adjusted distribution of present values with a utility of money values function, posited in Equation (2-9) and exhibited in Figure 3.

In the construction of optimization models of the business firm as a whole, as distinct from the analysis of separate investment projects, it is preferable to rely mainly on the first of these three approaches and to work with a risk-adjusted capitalization rate. But the function we shall be dealing with shows the capitalization rate as dependent on the degree of risk in the enterprise, as indicated by the variance of possible profit outcomes. It is clear, therefore, that this required rate of return function should be able to be interpreted as a logical precipitate of the decision maker's utility function, described over the same variables of risk and profit. In this way the insights of utility thought forms are incorporated into the analysis. The way in which the investor's capitalization rate or required rate of return will respond to differences in the degree of risk will depend on his subjective marginal rate of substitution between risk and profit. And this, in turn, will depend on the precise form of his utility function or on the manner in which the parameters in the function determine the acceptable substitutability between the respective variables.

It has been noted already that the form of the indifference curves in Figure 2 is determined by the nature of the utility surface inherent in the function $U = f(\pi,\sigma)$. It might be noted now that, against the background of the same utility function, the required rate of return function which is linear in the variance in Figure 1 will be concave in the standard deviation in Figure 2. The details of this proposition will be explored at length in the following sections of this chapter. The analysis of the matter of uncertainty that we have selected and our use of a risk-adjusted capitalization rate will be seen subsequently to be relevant also to our use of the concept of the business firm's "cost of capital."

Some Mathematical Properties of the Argument

The foregoing argument has posited at different points that connections exist between uncertainty, utility, indifference relations, and an investor's capitalization rate or required rate of return. It is necessary now, as a logical foundation for the work ahead, to demonstrate precisely the nature and significance of these connections. Specifically it needs to be shown first that the form of the indifference relation between risk and profit is the logical precipitate of the form of the utility function; and second, that the form of the capitalization rate function is the logical precipitate of the form of the indifference relation.

Let us consider this problem initially in the most general terms.[2] We posit a utility function of the type

$$U = f(\pi, \sigma) \qquad (2\text{-}13)$$

Taking the total differential of the function and writing f_1 and f_2 as the partial derivatives of U with respect to π and σ respectively yields

$$dU = f_1 \, d\pi + f_2 \, d\sigma \qquad (2\text{-}14)$$

[2] The analysis of utility in this chapter is capable of more than one interpretation. In its most general form the function as written in Eq. (2-2) describes the utility derived from the investment in the firm as depending directly, in a deterministic relation, on the expected value of the profit outcome, which we have defined as π, and the standard deviation of the expectation, σ. In the general form, therefore, π and σ refer to the known or assumed parameters of the underlying probability distribution of profits. More complex forms of the utility function could of course be assumed, with different possible specifications of the risk argument. Such a general interpretation is different, however, from the the approach widely discussed in the literature. Most frequently the utility function is defined over a single variable, such as profit or the rate of return. Since the variable in question is conceived of as a random variable, it is possible to transform the utility function $U(R)$ into an expression defining the expected utility, $E[U(R)]$, as a function in the moments of the underlying probability distribution of the random variable R. In this way the utility attaching to the project or activity under discussion is conceived of as depending directly on the possible values of the profit or returns and not directly on the separable arguments of expected profit and risk as in our general case. If, for example, a utility function were posited of the form $U = \alpha\pi - \beta\pi^2$, a quadratic function in profits regarded as a random variable, the expected utility could be expressed as the expected value of this function, or as $E(U) = \alpha E(\pi) - \beta E(\pi^2)$. This reduces to the form $E(U) = \alpha\mu - \beta\mu^2 - \beta\sigma^2$, given the appropriate two-parameter form of the probability distribution of profits, where μ refers to the expected value of that probability distribution, and σ refers to its standard deviation. Equations of higher degree describing more complex utility functions, together with the corresponding higher moments of the relevant probability distributions of profits, may be handled in a similar fashion. See the discussion in Paul A. Samuelson, "General Proof That Diversification Pays," *Journal of Financial and Quantitative Analysis*, vol. 2, no. 1, March, 1967, and references cited there. It would be meaningful to interpret the utility analysis in this chapter in similar terms. In such a case, Eq. (2-2) and all similar expressions and manipulations should be understood as expressions in the expected utility, rather than the total utility. Equation (2-24) is directly analogous to the example given above, recalling that for economy of notation we have written the expected profit as π. A similar expected utility interpretation may be made of the posited utility function in Eq. (2-3), $U = \alpha\pi - \beta\sigma^2$. For a discussion of a similar form see D. E. Farrar, *The Investment Decision under Uncertainty*, Prentice-Hall,Inc., Englewood Cliffs, N.J., 1962, p. 31. In the general case discussed in this chapter the indifference curves in the π-σ plane as shown in Fig. 2 are to be interpreted as loci of constant total utility. If the alternative or expected utility interpretation of the utility function is adopted, the indifference curves, the form of which now depends on the form of the underlying probability distribution, become loci of constant expected utility. In any event, the differentiability characteristics remain as indicated, with corresponding interpretations of the marginal rate of substitution between the arguments in the function and the concavity of the indifference relation.

Equation (2-14) is saying that an incremental change in utility is made up of the incremental change in profit times the responsiveness of U to a change in profit (or the partial derivative of U with respect to profit) plus the incremental change in risk times the partial derivative of U with respect to risk. If the same kind of proposition were put in terms of finite differences in π and σ, the final incremental variation in U would have to take account also of a product term such as $\Delta\pi\,\Delta\sigma$. But invoking the usual infinitesimal assumptions of the differential calculus and proceeding to the limiting variation, the total differential or total variation in U can be understood to have the meaning indicated in Equation (2-14).

If, now, attention is focused on such simultaneous variations in π and σ as will leave unchanged the total value of the utility derived from the profit and risk combination, then dU in Equation (2-14) may be set equal to zero, and the following result emerges by transposition of the right-hand side of the equation:

$$\frac{d\sigma}{d\pi} = -\frac{f_1}{f_2} \qquad (2\text{-}15)$$

In other words the derivative of risk with respect to profit is equal to the negative of the ratio of the partial derivatives of the utility function. But the derivative shown on the left-hand side of Equation (2-15) is recognizable as the slope of the indifference curve in Figure 2. It describes the rate of change of risk subjectively permitted by the investor for a given change in profit, such as will leave him in as favorable a position as before or make him indifferent between his old and his new positions.

The slope of the indifference curve having been established, it is a straightforward matter to test for its convexity or concavity by taking the further derivative of Equation (2-15). This appears as follows:

$$\frac{d^2\sigma}{d\pi^2} = -\frac{1}{f_2{}^2}\left[f_2\!\left(f_{11} + f_{21}\frac{d\sigma}{d\pi}\right) - f_1\!\left(f_{12} + f_{22}\frac{d\sigma}{d\pi}\right)\right] \qquad (2\text{-}16)$$

In this expression f_{11} and f_{22} represent respectively the second partial derivatives of the utility function with respect to profit and risk. Similarly, f_{12} represents the second-order cross-partial derivative obtained by first taking the partial derivative of U with respect to σ and then taking the partial derivative with respect to π of the resulting expression. A similar interpretation attaches to f_{21}, the value of which, it is known, will equal f_{12}.

The seemingly complex form of Equation (2-16) follows from the fact that we are taking the *total* derivative of Equation (2-15). This accounts for the presence of the $d\sigma/d\pi$ terms in parentheses on the right-hand side of Equation (2-16). Consider, for example, $f_{21}(d\sigma/d\pi)$. This is part of the total expression, contained in the first parentheses, which represents the *total* derivative of f_1 with respect to π. Since we are here dealing with a general function of unspecified form in the two arguments π and σ, it must be remembered that in the expression f_1 the π and σ arguments must both be understood as functionally related to each other. To take the total derivative of f_1, therefore, we proceed to take the partial derivative of f_1, with respect to π (thus the f_{11} term) and then the partial derivative with respect to σ (thus the f_{21} term). But focusing now on the f_{21} term, we realize that we did not set out to get the derivative with respect to σ but rather the derivative with respect to π. Therefore the f_{21} term must be multiplied by $d\sigma/d\pi$ to complete the journey, applying the familiar chain rule of the differential calculus. The complete expression in Equation (2-16) may be obtained by a similar successive application of the rules of the calculus, and need not be explained in detail. The general nature of the procedure was referred to briefly here because this kind of analysis will occur in subsequent parts of our work.

If we now substitute the value of $(d\sigma/d\pi)$ in Equation (2-15) into Equation (2-16) the following results are obtained:

$$
\begin{aligned}
\frac{d^2\sigma}{d\pi^2} &= -\frac{1}{f_2{}^2}\left(f_2 f_{11} - f_1 f_{21} - f_1 f_{12} + \frac{f_1{}^2 f_{22}}{f_2} \right) \\
&= -\frac{1}{f_2{}^3}\left(f_{11} f_2{}^2 - 2 f_1 f_2 f_{12} + f_{22} f_1{}^2 \right)
\end{aligned}
\tag{2-17}
$$

It is recalled that the objective of the present argument is to throw light on the possible concavity or convexity of the indifference curves, or to determine the sign of $(d^2\sigma/d\pi^2)$. If the sign of the right-hand side of Equation (2-17) is positive, the indifference curves are convex downward, and if the sign is negative, the indifference curves are concave downward, as posited in Figure 2. Let us leave Equation (2-17) for the present and consider further the characteristics of the utility function.

At this stage we are considering a utility function of the general form shown in Equation (2-13). It is posited only that utility is a function of the twofold arguments of profit and risk, though it will be necessary for concreteness to specify later the precise form of the function on which, it is supposed, economic behavior proceeds. Recognizing now that the utility function may take on any of many possible forms, the question may legitimately arise whether the function tends to a definable maximum or minimum value. Consider, for example, the total differential of the utility function as described in Equation (2-14), assuming the function is continuous with continuous first derivatives. If, for a given increase in the magnitudes of the arguments π and σ, the function is tending toward a maximum value, the second-order differential, or d^2U, must be negative. This means that for the specified changes in profit and risk the total utility of the combination is increasing at a decreasing rate.

The second-order differential is described by writing the total differential of the first-order differential in Equation (2-14). It follows that

$$d^2U = \frac{\partial(dU)}{\partial\pi} d\pi + \frac{\partial(dU)}{\partial\sigma} d\sigma \qquad (2\text{-}18)$$

whence

$$d^2U = (f_{11} d\pi + f_{12} d\sigma) d\pi + (f_{21} d\pi + f_{22} d\sigma) d\sigma$$

or

$$d^2U = f_{11} d\pi^2 + 2f_{12} d\pi d\sigma + f_{22} d\sigma^2 \qquad (2\text{-}19)$$

For a utility function which tends to a maximum value, then, the value of the right-hand side of Equation (2-19) must be negative. It can be shown, moreover, that this condition implies also that the maximum conditions on a two-variable function may be specified more fully as follows:[3]

$$f_1 = 0 \qquad f_2 = 0 \qquad (2\text{-}20a)$$
$$f_{11} < 0 \qquad f_{22} < 0 \qquad (2\text{-}20b)$$
$$f_{11}f_{22} - (f_{12})^2 > 0 \qquad (2\text{-}20c)$$

The condition in inequality (2-20c) is stating that for a maximum or extreme value of the function the value of the determinant of the matrix of second-order partial derivatives of a two-variable function must be positive. The necessary and sufficient conditions for a minimum value of a two-variable function are the same as those specified in conditions (2-20a–c), with the exception that the direction of the inequality signs in condition (2-20b) should be reversed. We shall return to these full-maximization conditions below.

From the second-order differential in Equation (2-19) the following second total derivative can be written by transposition:

$$\frac{d^2U}{d\pi^2} = f_{11} + 2f_{12}\frac{d\sigma}{d\pi} + f_{22}\left(\frac{d\sigma}{d\pi}\right)^2 \qquad (2\text{-}21)$$

The same proposition could also have been derived by dividing Equation (2-14) throughout by $d\pi$, and then proceeding to take the derivative of the result so obtained. If, now, the value of the expression $(d\sigma/d\pi)$ is substituted from Equation (2-15) into Equation (2-21), it follows that

$$\frac{d^2U}{d\pi^2} = f_{11} - \frac{2f_{12}f_1}{f_2} + f_{22}\left(\frac{f_1}{f_2}\right)^2 \qquad (2\text{-}22)$$

[3] See R. G. D. Allen, *Mathematical Analysis for Economists*, Macmillan & Co., Ltd., London, 1950, chaps. 14 and 19, and Taro Yamane, *Mathematics for Economists*, Prentice-Hall, Inc., Englewood Cliffs, N.J., 1962, chap. 5.

This, it is recalled from the derivation, enables us to state that for a two-variable function which tends to a maximum value the right-hand side of Equation (2-22) must be negative. Taking this condition and multiplying throughout by the positive magnitude $f_2{}^2$, such as will prevent any change in the inequality sign, it follows that the condition may also be expressed as

$$f_{11}f_2{}^2 - 2f_1 f_2 f_{12} + f_{22}f_1{}^2 < 0 \qquad (2\text{-}23)$$

But the expression on the left-hand side of inequality (2-23) is exactly the same as the term in parentheses in Equation (2-17). Taking cognizance of this fact and seeking again for the sign of Equation (2-17), and thus the second derivative of the indifference curve, it is now seen that this will depend on the sign of f_2. If this is negative, then the sign of $(-1/f_2{}^3)$ in Equation (2-17) is positive, and the sign of $d^2\sigma/d\pi^2$ will be negative. In that event the indifference curves will be concave downward. In short, if the form of a risk aversion utility function is such that for increases in the values of the arguments it tends to a maximum, the indifference curves implicit in the function, and here shown in the π-σ plane in Figure 2, will be concave downward.

At this point the logical properties of any number of different utility functions could be generated. We take only one such function having general risk aversion characteristics:

$$U = \alpha\pi - \gamma\pi^2 - \beta\sigma^2 \qquad (2\text{-}24)$$

For all values of the risk measure σ, the marginal utility of risk, or the partial derivative of the function with respect to σ, is negative, indicating consistent risk aversion. The marginal utility of profit is positive, however, for all profit values below $(\alpha/2\gamma)$. This, of course, is suggesting that the function in Equation (2-24) has a definable maximum value, as may be confirmed by applying the relevant conditions in (2-20a–c), whence the second-order conditions are as follows:

$$f_{11} = -2\gamma < 0$$
$$f_{22} = -2\beta < 0$$
$$f_{11}f_{22} - (f_{12})^2 = 4\beta\gamma > 0$$

Given the maximum conditions, then, it follows from the previous analysis that a range of possible profit outcomes can be specified such that the indifference curves, similar to those shown in Figure 2, will be positively inclined and concave downward. We shall return to this functional form again below.

But what can be said of the utility function specified in Equation (2-3) as the illustrative form with which we shall work in the ensuing analysis? It is seen from the function $U = \alpha\pi - \beta\sigma^2$ that the marginal utility of profit is not assumed to diminish as in the preceding case. The situation is thereby avoided of being in a position where the marginal utility of profit has become negative. But this could equally well have been avoided by specifying some asymptotic form on the profit argument. Of rather more interest, the simple utility function with which we are working clearly does not have a definable maximum value, since it can be confirmed that the determinant of the matrix of second-order partial derivatives, as specified in condition (2-20c) above, vanishes.

We wish to hold to the general proposition, however, that the form of the indifference curves as already examined is dependent on the form of the utility function, and to proceed with the general assumption of risk aversion with which we began. The assumption needs to be maintained that the stance of the investor or decision maker is such that our previous definition of increasing marginal rate of substitution between risk and profit holds. We wish to continue working, in other words, with the familiar concave-downward indifference curves. In this case, therefore, we consider the following demonstration of the positive slope and the negative sign on the second derivative of the indifference curve, thus establishing the posited concavity:

$$U = \alpha\pi - \beta\sigma^2$$
$$dU = \alpha\,d\pi - 2\beta\sigma\,d\sigma$$
$$\frac{d\sigma}{d\pi} = \frac{\alpha}{2\beta\sigma}$$
$$\frac{d^2\sigma}{d\pi^2} = \frac{1}{4\beta^2\sigma^2}\left[-2\alpha\beta\left(\frac{d\sigma}{d\pi}\right)\right]$$
$$= \frac{1}{4\beta^2\sigma^2}\left(-\frac{2\alpha^2\beta}{2\beta\sigma}\right)$$
$$= -\frac{\alpha^2}{4\beta^2\sigma^3}$$

The Capitalization Rate Function

The analysis to this point has thus established that the form of the owner's or decision maker's indifference relation is the logical precipitate of the form of the underlying utility function. It can now be shown that the form of the capitalization rate function is similarly the logical precipitate of the form of the indifference relation or the utility function. For this purpose we revert to Equations (2-2), (2-3), and (2-4) above, reproduced here as Equations (2-25), (2-26), and (2-27):

$$U = f(\pi,\sigma) \tag{2-25}$$
$$U = \alpha\pi - \beta\sigma^2 \tag{2-26}$$
$$\rho = a + w\mathrm{Var}(u) \tag{2-27}$$

From the total differential of the utility function in Equations (2-25) and (2-26) we derive, in the same manner as before,

$$\frac{d\pi}{d\sigma} = \frac{2\beta\sigma}{\alpha} \tag{2-28}$$

whence it follows that

$$d\pi = \frac{2\beta\sigma}{\alpha} \, d\sigma \tag{2-29}$$

Taking also the basic valuation equation $V = \pi/\rho$, it follows from the total differential that

$$dV = \frac{1}{\rho} \, d\pi - \frac{\pi}{\rho^2} \, d\rho \tag{2-30}$$

If we now focus on a given valuation level and consider the nature of the variations in π and ρ consistent with the maintenance of that level, we may set Equation (2-30) equal to zero and derive from it the following relations:

$$d\pi = \frac{\pi}{\rho} \, d\rho$$

and

$$d\pi = V \, d\rho \tag{2-31}$$

Substituting Equation (2-31) in Equation (2-29) yields

$$d\rho = \frac{2\beta\sigma}{\alpha V} \, d\sigma \tag{2-32}$$

Taking the indefinite integral of Equation (2-32) gives

$$\rho = \frac{\beta}{\alpha V} \, \sigma^2 + C \tag{2-33}$$

Equation (2-33) is then the desired expression for the capitalization rate ρ as a function of the risk argument σ. This function appears as a concave-upward function in the standard deviation as a measure of risk, or linear in the variance. Looked at from another point of view the derivation of Equation (2-33) is saying that an increase in the degree of risk confronting the investor will, if nothing else changes, diminish his total utility, or the utility he associates with an existing level of earnings. In order, therefore, to raise him again to as favorable a utility position as he previously enjoyed, an increase in earnings must occur in order to offset, or compensate for, the increased degree of risk. It is the relation between the higher level of required earnings and the value it is desired to maintain that is here referred to as the capitalization rate. Thus we may continue to rely on the form of the capitalization rate function shown in Figure 1, and it is rewritten from Equation (2-33) as

$$\rho = a + w\sigma^2 \tag{2-34}$$

where a equals C and w equals $\beta/\alpha V$. It is seen, moreover, that the coefficient of the risk argument in Equation (2-34) is dependent on the values of the α and β parameters in the utility function as previously argued.

While the case does not need to be argued at length, it can similarly be shown that a definable form of the implicit capitalization rate function may be derived from the alternative utility function referred to in the preceding discussion:

$$U = \alpha\pi - \gamma\pi^2 - \beta\sigma^2 \qquad (2\text{-}35)$$

By taking the same steps of differentiation, substitution, and indefinite integration, the reader may confirm that a relation of the following form is obtained:

$$\sigma^2 = \frac{\alpha V}{\beta}\,\rho - \frac{\gamma V^2}{\beta}\,\rho^2 - C \qquad (2\text{-}36)$$

Differentiating Equation (2-36) with respect to ρ yields

$$\frac{d\sigma^2}{d\rho} = \frac{\alpha V}{\beta} - \frac{2\gamma V^2}{\beta}\,\rho \qquad (2\text{-}37)$$

and setting Equation (2-37) equal to zero establishes a maximum value of σ^2 at a ρ value of $\alpha/2\gamma V$. The concavity is established by the negative sign on $d^2\sigma^2/d\rho^2$. For specified values of ρ, in other words, the function described in Equation (2-36) is a monotonically increasing function, and can be shown to have a monotonic, single-valued inverse. The implication follows that the capitalization rate is a monotonic convex function of the variance of the income expectation. Using the same axes as in Figure 1, the function is convex downward, and again the parameters of the function have been seen to derive from the magnitudes of the parameters on the arguments in the utility function.

We conclude, then, bringing together the beginning and end of the analysis, that a linkage has been established between the degree of uncertainty in the income expectations on the one hand and the rate at which it will be capitalized on the other. It is this linkage we have in mind when we work in the remainder of this book with a risk-adjusted capitalization rate. It might be noted, by way of anticipation, that we shall later transform the capitalization rate function into a function in the coefficient of variation of the firm's net income stream. This can be done only after we have examined the ways in which that ultimate measure of risk is affected by the degree of financial leverage in the firm, or the manner in which it solves its financing problem, or the combination of owner and nonowner sources of capital it adopts.

We may note, moreover, that while the uncertainty and utility analysis of this chapter has explored the basic issues of the valuation of income streams, we have left unexplored two vital questions. These have recently claimed a good deal of attention in the literature and must clearly be taken into account when we extend the analysis to consider the money capital supply functions confronting the firm. They relate, first, to the way in which an individual's assessment and valuation of an income stream, even though it be conceived in terms of the basic conceptualization we have considered, may be affected or amended by the place which that firm's securities occupy in the individual's total portfolio of securities; and second, to the way in which the demands and supplies of individuals in the securities markets interact to determine the market values of the firm's capital securities, and thereby the effective cost of the money capital available to it. We may refer to these items as the *portfolio problem* and the *market problem* respectively. We shall refer to them again in Chapter 4.[4]

---

[4] The important developments in these directions may be consulted principally in the following and in the references there cited: William F. Sharpe, "Capital Asset Prices: A Theory of Market Equilibrium under Conditions of Risk," *Journal of Finance*, vol. 19, pp. 425–442, September, 1964; John Lintner, "Security Prices, Risk, and Maximal Gains from Diversification," *Journal of Finance*, vol. 20, pp. 587–615, December, 1965; W. F. Sharpe, "Reply," *Journal of Finance*, vol. 21, pp. 743–744, December, 1966; Alexander A. Robichek and Stewart C. Myers, "Valuation of the Firm: Effects of Uncertainty in a Market Context," *Journal of Finance*, vol. 21, pp. 215–227, May, 1966. For alternative developments of problems akin to those we are dealing with, see J. Hirshleifer, "Investment Decision under Uncertainty: Applications of the State-preference Approach," *Quarterly Journal of Economics*, vol. 80, pp. 252–277, May, 1966, and references cited; and José Encarnación, Jr., "Constraints and the Firm's Utility Function," *Review of Economic Studies*, vol. 31, pp. 113–120, April, 1964.

3

The
Enterprise
Decision
Nxeus

The general objective of enterprise management was described in our introduction as the optimization of the economic position of the owners of the firm. This was understood as the maximization of the economic value of the owners' investment, and in the context of the corporation it may be interpreted as the maximization of the market value of the shares of common stock. It was suggested, moreover, that what might previously have been called the purely financial function (raising money capital at the times and in the quantities it is needed, obtaining it from the cheapest or best or most convenient sources, investing it in the firm's activities, and controlling and accounting for it) cannot in fact be understood or discharged in isolation from a larger nexus of forces. These latter, when taken together, determine an optimum economic position of the firm, and the optimization problem was seen as a problem of attaining an optimum enterprise structure.

The Firm's Financial Statements

In the present chapter we shall look more closely at those operating and planning decision problems of the firm which lead to such structural optima. In doing this we are interested first in their financial implications and second in the ways in which their outcomes are reflected in the summary financial statements. These latter are the balance sheet, which describes in money value terms the position of the firm as of a specified date or at a given moment of time, and the income statement, which summarizes the flows of revenues and costs during the preceding period of time. The relevant accounting period may cover any length of calendar time convenient for the

TABLE 1

Balance Sheet

Assets		Liabilities	
Current assets		Current liabilities	
Cash	xxx	Accounts payable	xxx
Accounts receivable	xxx	Short-term debt	xxx
Inventory	xxx	Long-term capital sources	
Fixed assets	xxx	Debt	xxx
		Preferred stock	xxx
		Owners' equity	
		Common stock	xxx
		Earned-surplus	xxx
Total assets	xxx	Total liabilities	xxx

management's analysis and interpretation of business developments, but it may here be taken to be one year. The discussion of the balance sheet and income statement format will provide a basis and a motivation for the subsequent construction of the analytical model of the firm. The empirical categories that the subsequent economic theory will be required to use will be developed here, and something of their mutual dependence and relations will be discussed.

The pro forma financial statements underlying our discussion are set out in Tables 1 and 2.

It will be clear immediately that our discussion will not be concerned

TABLE 2

Income Statement

Total sales		xxx
Less Variable factor costs	xxx	
Fixed factor costs	xxx	
Total operating costs		xxx
Net operating income		xxx
Less Interest on debt capital		xxx
Income before tax		xxx
Less Income tax liability		xxx
Net income		xxx
Less Preferred stock dividends	xxx	
Common stock dividends	xxx	
Total dividends		xxx
Retained earnings		xxx

primarily with accounting conventions, or with the arguments for preferred accounting forms in the presentation of financial position and operating statements. Rather, the classification of statements and the arguments based upon them will be those best designed to serve the purposes of the economic analysis we have in view.[1]

The Balance Sheet

Consider the balance sheet first. Leaving aside for the present the procedures of double-entry bookkeeping which ensure that this position statement will in fact balance, with total assets shown as the same amount as total liabilities, the following four summary statements can be made.

First, the total of the assets side of the balance sheet indicates the total investment that has been made in the firm. In one sense, meaningful for economic and financial analysis, the firm can be described as an aggregation of assets.[2] The asset accounts describe the ways in which the money capital funds available to the firm have been invested or committed to activities, with the objective of generating an income stream and thereby economic values for the owners of the firm. Assets, therefore, generate income. This is the most basic notion of enterprise activity and management. But in the matter of logical priorities and relationships, the causation runs from the availability and acquisition of money capital, to commitment to assets, to the generation of income streams, to the realization of economic values. In the logic of optimization analysis, income is prior to value. The value of an investment depends upon, and is determined by, the level, time shape, and other characteristics of the income stream it can be expected to generate. We have already seen the importance of considering the risk or uncertainty characteristics of an income stream, as well as its expected value.

Second, the *structure* of the assets side of the balance sheet indicates the *structure* of the investment that has been made in the firm. The understanding of the meaning of the structure of the investment follows from what has already been said. It takes up the notion that in any given economic en-

[1] Detailed treatments of matters not discussed in the text may be found in the following selections from a very extensive literature: Myron J. Gordon and G. Shillinglaw, *Accounting: A Management Approach*, Richard D. Irwin, Inc., Homewood, Ill., 1964; Jerome B. Cohen and Sidney M. Robbins, *The Financial Manager*, Harper & Row, Publishers, Inc., New York, 1966; J. Fred Weston and Eugene F. Brigham, *Managerial Finance*, 2d ed., Holt, Rinehart and Winston, Inc., New York, 1966; Robert W. Johnson, *Financial Management*, 3d ed., Allyn and Bacon Inc., Boston, 1966; and, for an economist's view in short compass, Paul A. Samuelson, *Economics*, 6th ed., McGraw-Hill Book Company, New York, 1964, chap. 5.

[2] This notion was the starting point of N. S. Buchanan's important but rather too neglected work *The Economics of Corporate Enterprise*, Holt, Rinehart and Winston, Inc., New York, 1940, p. 15.

vironment there conceivably exists more than one way in which the available money capital can be put to work in an income-earning enterprise. Each of the available investment alternatives can be looked upon as a potentially achievable combination of assets, and the balance sheet shows which of the alternative combinations has in fact been selected and put to work in the firm. This, in turn, immediately raises a twofold question that will concern us at some length: First, is it possible to conceive of criteria to betermine whether any particular combination of assets can be regarded as the optimum combination, having regard to the set of alternatives available; and second, can it be decided whether the management's decisions, which are reflected in the combination of assets described in the balance sheet, were in fact optimizing decisions?

Third, the total of the liabilities side of the balance sheet indicates the total money capital employed in the firm. It follows, of course, that as the total of the liabilities precisely equals the total of the assets, we must simply be looking at the same thing from two different points of view when we transfer our attention from the assets side to the liabilities side of the balance sheet. In a sense this is true. But an important spectrum, of considerable analytical significance, is brought into focus by commanding the alternative points of view we now propose.

The total investment made in the firm must equal the total capital employed in the firm (taking the accounts at book value and leaving aside for the present the possible divergence of economic values from book values as a result of variations in income-earning ability). But focusing attention on the description of capital employed sharpens the awareness of two significant facts: First, the availability of money capital constitutes a constraint on the investment decisions of the firm and establishes the optimization process in the firm as one of *constrained* optimization; and second, we are here concerned with the availability and use of *money* capital, and by this we are alerted to a distinction that will play a large part in our subsequent theoretical models. The distinction that comes into view at this point is that between real capital assets on the one hand and money capital on the other.

The significance of this distinction lies precisely in its relevance for the relation between the theory of production and the theory of capital. In short, we shall note in what follows that in order to understand this relation, and to incorporate with it a robust theory of finance, real capital will have to be incorporated as a variable in the enterprise production function, but money capital will not. To imagine that an integrated body of production-capital-finance theory can be built by regarding money capital as a production factor, coordinate with other factors of production, is to run analysis into a blind alley and a theoretical morass. This will be argued more clearly and fully in what follows. Money capital is not a factor of production in the sense of the technological production function that forms the groundwork of our analysis. It is rather a constraint variable, which influences the manner in which available money funds should be used to acquire the factors of production the firm desires to employ.

The capital factors in the firm are the various asset facilities in which it is necessary to invest in order to provide the units of operating capacity that are required to establish and maintain the productive process. Money capital may be used for the provision of such asset facilities. But it may equally well be used for the provision of other short-lived and current assets, including liquidity, which appear on the assets side of the balance sheet. The precise relation or correspondence between money capital and real capital is therefore of a complex nature, and our analysis has not at this point provided the necessary tools with which we shall have to work in the examination of it. At this point, only this clear relation can be noted: The liabilities side of the balance sheet describes the various sources from which money capital has been obtained, and the assets side of the balance sheet describes the uses to which the money capital has been put.

Fourth, it follows from the foregoing that in the same way that a corresponding set of questions were raised regarding the assets side of the balance sheet, the following can now be asked with respect to the liabilities side: First, is it possible to erect criteria for determining whether a particular combination of money capital sources is in fact an optimum combination; and second, can it be decided whether the decisions of the management that gave rise to the particular combination of liabilities that exists were actually optimizing decisions?

Thus the principal message of the balance sheet is a message regarding the structure of the firm, the structure of its investments on the one hand and the structure of its financing methods on the other. In the most general sense, the overriding desideratum against which the alternative structures of assets and liabilities are to be assessed is that the enterprise structure chosen, and that maintained in the changing context of economic environment and planning, should conduce consistently to the maximization of the economic value of the owners' investment in the firm. In the usual sense of the accounting data recorded by the firm, the assets will be shown in the balance sheet at their historic cost value, subject to the deduction of accumulated depreciation from the gross cost value of fixed assets; and the liability accounts will record the actual amount of money capital or funds made available to the firm from the various sources indicated. Alternatively, it would be perfectly reasonable, for economic-planning purposes, to construct a balance sheet in which the assets held by the firm were shown at liquidation or realization values, indicating, perhaps, their economic value in alternative uses, and therefore the opportunity costs of continuing to employ the assets in the firm. If, in such a case, the realization or the replacement value of the assets were greater than their historic cost value, a balance sheet incorporating such higher values would also be required to show a capital surplus in the capital accounts on the liabilities side, representing the larger effective value of the capital committed to the firm.

In fact, however, whether the asset investments are valued at the accountant's historic cost figures or at some revaluation level, the important thing for the present is that the indications of structural significance advanced in the foregoing analysis continue to hold. And our main objective in this preliminary statement is the understanding of this set of enterprise structural characteristics. In many parts of the ensuing analysis we shall be interested in asset and liability structures at actual historic figures, because we shall be concerned with the wisdom or otherwise of varying the relative amounts of debt capital and equity capital employed in the firm, measuring these values in terms of the actual number of dollars committed. But while this is so, our criterion for determining such optimum relationships will be the economic or capitalized value of the ownership, even though such a value will not appear on the firm's financial statements. On the other hand, instances will occur in which a pro forma balance sheet, usable for economic-planning purposes, must be drawn up on the basis of the liquidation values of the assets in order to decide whether certain disinvestments and redirection of capital employment should be made by the firm. The level of argument will in each case be clear from the context, and in Tables 1 and 2 above, therefore, a pro forma outline emphasizing general relationships was used, rather than illustrative data on one or the other of the different bases.

Of course, the enterprise structure that appears to be the optimum one can vary from time to time. It is in precisely the planning and operating adjustments to change that the skill and effectiveness of enterprise management reside. The balance sheet of the firm describes the position of the firm as of a moment in time. In that sense it is a static or stationary document. But it is a tool of dynamic analysis when it is recognized that the optimum structure it describes will itself be subject to change as the economic environment changes, as variations occur in the firm's own endogenous determinant functions, or as the pressures of various constraints bear on the enterprise with greater or lesser severity.

It is only in a very restricted sense, therefore, that we could agree with Boulding when he suggests that "the simplest theory of the firm is to assume that there is a 'homeostasis of the balance sheet' — that there is some desired quantity of all the various items in the balance sheet, and that any disturbance of this structure immediately sets in motion forces which will restore the status quo."[3] The status quo, it can be replied, and the nature of the homeostasis process itself may change. Moreover, as Boulding himself

---

[3] Kenneth E. Boulding, *A Reconstruction of Economics*, Science Editions, Inc., New York, 1962, p. 27.

points out in his valuable analysis of these concepts, the homeostasis principle, which "is clearly only a very first approximation to a theory of the organism, . . . says nothing about what determines the equilibrium state itself,"[4] or in our terms, what determines the optimum structure of the firm at any particular time.

The Management Functions

For these reasons the task of enterprise management can be regarded as subsisting on two distinct and separable levels of economic significance. First, there is the task of optimum structural planning, which will be our main province of analysis in the remainder of this book; and second, there is the task of the short-run functioning and management of the firm in accordance with the planning structures and processes previously laid down.

Structural Planning

The first of these tasks takes up the question of enterprise decisions at what we referred to previously as "sequential decision-making points," or successive periodic planning dates, at which the enterprise is examined for optimum structural characteristics. At such successive points, decisions will conceivably be taken to bring into existence that size and structure of activity which best serve the economic optimization objectives of the owners. This, it will be seen, may involve adding new projects to the enterprise or changing, expanding, or deleting existing activities. The enterprise structural analysis will therefore envisage the possibilities of partial disinvestment of the existing firm as well as new investments of varying amounts and kinds.

The second of the two enterprise management tasks, that of controlling the short-run functioning of the firm within the limits and in accordance with the requisites of the established scale or structure, will not be our principal concern in this book. But a brief note might be taken of one aspect of the problem at this point, namely, the periodic cash flows generated by the firm. Valuable light can thereby be thrown on the income statement, with whose output data we shall be very much concerned.

Before considering even the summary propositions relevant at this point, however, we might note, with reference to our more basic methodological position, that the perspective we thereby adopt implies that the structural or planning decision of the firm is logically, as well as temporally, prior to the operating decisions and to the functioning of the firm in the interplanning date period. More important, a methodological implication of this

---

[4] *Ibid.*, p. 33.

perspective affects our view of the theory of the firm. It is now implied that the theory of scale or structure should logically precede the theory of equimarginal optimizing in the short-run situation, and a fairly radical recasting and reorientation of what the theory of the firm should be trying to do are accordingly required. It is precisely because the theory of the firm has traditionally started from the short-period optimization problem, and then added on the notion of a long-run cost curve as a less than perfectly integrated appendage, that no adequate integration of production theory and microcapital theory has been able to be achieved.[5]

If there is a logical and temporal priority of the enterprise structural planning in practice, then certainly the empirical relevance of microeconomic theory will be inhibited until the logic and relationships and causal determinants are sorted out in the same order, and with appropriate thoroughness, on the theoretical level.

Management in the Short Run

From the perspective of the short-run flow of values, the functioning of the firm can be described in balance sheet language by saying that the production, selling, and revenue-generating activities are reflected in a successive transformation of assets.

Imagine that at the inception of a business enterprise an inflow of cash from external sources is held in liquid form on the assets side of the balance sheet. The sources from which the cash has been obtained will be described on the liabilities side of the balance sheet. These will necessarily include some equity accounts, since an enterprise is not normally able to raise loan

---

[5] Detailed references to the many texts competently reproducing the received tradition in the theory of the firm need not be given. C. E. Ferguson's *Microeconomic Theory*, Richard D. Irwin, Inc., Homewood, Ill., 1966, is referred to only because it treats very elegantly the general area described in its title, but gives only some nine pages to long-run cost problems at the end of its chapter on the Theory of Cost. It proceeds in terms of the usual long-run envelope curve concept, following the elaboration of short-run relationships. The best treatment of the long-run planning problem in the textbook literature is the extensive discussion of it in Kalman J. Cohen and Richard M. Cyert, *Theory of the Firm: Resource Allocation in a Market Economy*, Prentice-Hall, Inc., Englewood Cliffs, N.J., 1965, chap. 8. In their book Cohen and Cyert rely heavily on the kind of production function analysis advanced in the work of Vernon L. Smith to which we referred in Chapter 1. In the reconstruction of the theory of the production and capital of the firm which has to be accomplished, Smith's work must be recognized as one of the landmarks of the achievements to date. We shall rely on some of its thought forms in what follows in later chapters of our own work, though our specification of the logical content of the production function and other crucial determinant relations will differ from Smith's. To this extent we shall endeavor to achieve also an objective with which earlier work has not in general been concerned: i.e., the elaboration of a theory of finance in coordination with the theories of production and capital.

or debt capital from creditors unless there already exists some equity funds in the business to constitute a cushion of security for the creditors. The security thereby provided is of two kinds. First, the prior existence of equity capital and the asset investment to which it is committed will normally provide an income stream out of which the periodic interest on loan capital can be paid; and second, the asset counterpart of the equity funds will, depending on their true economic values, contribute to the liquidation values available to the providers of loan capital in the event that the firm should encounter financial difficulties. The prior existence of equity capital, or owners' funds, determines the extent of the borrowing ability of the firm. To the extent that it does borrow, the firm may thereby be said to be "trading on the equity," or to be engaging in financial leverage. In any event the newly established firm we have just described will hold a pool of cash which it may now proceed to invest in the envisaged productive processes, against which it holds liability accounts to the same total amount.

Now the activation and management of the enterprise process may be regarded in one aspect as the management of the cash flows through the business in such a way as to generate an optimum income stream and dividend distribution for the owners. But it is this internally generated flow of cash through the business that is reflected in the successive transformation of assets. At the initial stage, cash may flow out of the firm's cash pool to purchase inventories and fixed assets of varying durabilities and for the payment of variable costs of production. By this means an initial investment in an asset called "cash" on the balance sheet is transformed into assets called "fixed assets" and "inventories." To emphasize the point at issue, when cash flows out to pay the costs of the services of variable factors of production, the asset transformation at this stage is from cash into inventories of work in progress or inventories of finished commodities. In due course the commodities produced will hopefully be sold, and the inventory assets are thereby transformed into an asset called "accounts receivable." Subsequently, if debtors pay their accounts as they become due, a further asset transformation will take place from "accounts receivable" back into cash.

Thus the internally generated cash flow has traveled full circle, though the size of the cash flow back into the cash pool at the end of the circular process will not match exactly the size of the initial cash flow out of the cash pool. There are basically two reasons for this. First, part of the cash outflow will have been invested in assets whose durability or expected economic life extends over more than one accounting period and whose total cost will therefore not be included in the costs, and therefore in the selling prices, of goods produced and sold in the same period. Such costs will be spread in some appropriate pro rata fashion over the goods produced during the entire economic (or at least depreciable) life of the asset. This, of course, introduces us to the phenomenon of periodic depreciation charges, to which we shall return. Second, the return cash flow will be higher than the cash outflow properly attributable to the cost of goods sold by a margin set by the management and thought to be adequate to compensate the providers of capital for the use of their funds.

In one sense, then, the periodic management of the enterprise can be thought of as the task of maintaining an optimum timing and process of asset transformation. In another sense it is the optimum management of the size, timing, and periodicity of the cash flows through the business. Or thirdly it is the management of the underlying income-generating process reflected in asset transformations and cash flows. These are the financial flows that determine the size, periodicity, and general risk characteristics of the income stream, on the expectation of which the money capital funds were originally committed to the firm.[6]

Our concern, however, is not with the enterprise cash flows as such, nor with the budgeting and other operating procedures by which the cash flows and the underlying productive activities can be planned and traced. Our concern, rather, is with the nature of the firm's investment in assets within the framework of which the circular flow of income occurs, with the financing of that investment, and with the size and stability of the resulting income generated for the owners of the firm. Let us look briefly, therefore, at the pro forma income statement shown in Table 2 above.

The Income Statement

Again, as was the case with the balance sheet, the income statement is depicted not primarily with respect for accounting conventions, but in the manner in which it will be useful for the ensuing economic analysis. It might be helpful at this point to compare the income statement items with the general form of Equation (1-1) and the accompanying discussion. The equation is reproduced here without the time subscript notation:

$$\pi = pQ - \sum_i b_i X_i - rD \qquad (3\text{-}1)$$

The equation states that the income available to the owners is the residual of the total sales revenue minus all factor costs of production, and minus also the interest income paid to the providers of debt capital. The sales rev-

---

[6] The accounting and finance literature referred to in footnote 1 in this chapter contains adequate descriptions of the manipulation of the accounts in such a way as to exhibit the enterprise cash flows in detail, and offers guidance for the construction of such management tools as flow of funds statements. A sophisticated analysis of the matter may be consulted in James E. Walter, *The Investment Process,* Harvard University Press, Cambridge, 1962, pp. 367f. Illuminating also is Robert K. Jaedicke and Robert T. Sprouse, *Accounting Flows: Income, Funds and Cash,* Prentice-Hall, Inc., Englewood Cliffs, N.J., 1965.

enue item in Equation (1-1) is reflected in the first entry in the income statement, and the factor costs in the equation are reflected in what have been labeled total operating costs in the income statement. If it were assumed for purposes of analysis that no income tax liability exists and if the question of the division of the income stream between dividends to the different classes of owners and retained earnings were deferred for the time being, the residual income designated π in the equation would be reflected in the "net income" item in the income statement.

The remaining entries in the income statement will be self-explanatory, but a comment might be made on the division of operating costs into variable factor costs on the one hand and fixed factor costs on the other. The former, or variable costs, are understood to be the total periodic (say annual) costs of acquiring the necessary services of those factors of production whose durability does not extend beyond the period in which their services are provided. The wages of hourly paid labor is an obvious example. The fixed factor costs represent the total annual cost of providing the requisite amount of the services of those capital assets whose durability does extend beyond the period in which their services are being currently provided. Recalling our discussion of the corresponding point in Chapter 1, the fixed factor costs shown in the income statement must therefore include those allowances for the depreciation of durable assets that are necessary to maintain their original investment value, and thus hopefully their income-earning ability, intact. It was seen that this measurement of depreciation may be different from that generally adopted by accounting conventions, and the income statement in Table 2 might to this extent again be considered an economist's planning tool rather than an accountant's historic record. Conceptually, however, they come to essentially the same thing.

It might be mentioned at this point also that in the remainder of this book, unless indicated to the contrary, the ownership of the firm will be assumed to be wholly in the form of common stock, and no preferred stock will be deemed to exist. Nothing will thereby be lost in generality, and an economy and clarity of analysis will result.

As in the case of the balance sheet, we are again interested principally in the *structure* of the income statement, meaning thereby (1) the proportionate division of the total operating costs between the rewards to factors of production of differing kinds and durabilities, and (2) the division of the net operating income between the rewards paid to the providers of debt capital and the residual earnings or rewards available to the owners of the firm. Each of these structural aspects will be seen to bear directly on the question of the optimum structure of the enterprise as a whole, and the consequent valuation and optimization of the owners' economic position.

As a final matter of definition in connection with the income statement we note the connotative distinction between the net operating income on the one hand and the net income on the other. The former will be looked upon as a measure of the total income-generating ability of the total investment in the firm, irrespective of how that total investment might have been financed. The net income is the true residual income of the owners, and whatever the total income-generating ability of the firm's investment might be, the size and, as we shall see later, the stability of the net income will depend very materially on how the investment has been financed, by creditors' funds or owners' funds respectively. The point and some of the analytical potentialities of this distinction will be intuited if a comparison is made between two firms with similar sales revenues and comparable operating structures, yielding comparable net operating incomes but differing in the financing methods they have employed. In such a case, when the total income is divided between the providers of capital, the economic positions of the owners of the respective firms could appear very differently in the relevant aspects of size and stability. We shall return to this important proposition later in the chapter that follows.

Given the structure of the income statement, our interest extends also to the stability of the sales revenue which it is expected the enterprise will be able to generate. It is the stability or otherwise at this point that underlies the fluctuation of the random term included in our earlier analysis and depicted in Equation (2-1). Since the historic income statement is designed to show the flow of money revenues and costs during the accounting period preceding the date on which the balance sheet is prepared, it is to be expected that the sales revenue may differ from the level that the enterprise operations were planned to produce.

In our present work we shall be employing the balance sheet and income statement relationships as an aid in optimum enterprise planning and in understanding the causal determinants and criteria that describe the optimization conditions. We shall therefore be interested in the ways in which different possible management assumptions regarding the instability or variance of sales revenue, and of the firm's total income-generating ability, may ripple through to determine the corresponding instability or variance attaching to the expectations of the residual owners' income. For it was this latter, we suggested in the preceding chapter, which really constituted the independent variable in the functional relation determining the owners' required rate of return, or capitalization rate, or the rate at which their income expectations should be capitalized to determine the economic value of their investment in the firm.

The Decision Nexus

This analysis of the position statement, the income process, and the money flows in the firm can now be employed as a background to the discussion of the enterprise decision nexus. For purposes of the remainder of our analysis we shall conceive of the enterprise decision problem as made up of three interdependent components: first, the production problem; second, the investment problem; and third, the financing problem. The connotation of each of these aspects of the total optimization objective, and something of the content of the analytical trilogy that results from the recognition of them, will already have emerged from the foregoing arguments. We shall pause at this stage simply to draw together the threads of the discussion and summarize the conceptual groundwork we have established.

First, the production problem of the firm is concerned with deciding upon the optimum level of output, or the optimum level and combination of outputs in a multiproduct firm, and with the optimum combination of input factors of production with which, given the state of technological knowledge and the implied technological possibilities in the production function, the contemplated output should be produced.

Second, the investment problem is concerned with deciding upon the optimum amount and combination of investments in real and monetary assets that are necessary to sustain the productive process as envisaged and provide the amounts of input factor capacities required by the firm.

Third, the financing problem is concerned with deciding upon the optimum combination of financing sources that should be used to finance the investments in assets necessary to maintain, at their interdependent optimum values, the size, structure, and operating processes of the firm.

It is then the management's decisions in the simultaneous solution of these interdependent problems which are reflected in, and determine the structure of, the balance sheet and the income statement. The solution to the production problem, for example, will be reflected in the revenue flow in the income statement and in the structure of operating costs, depending on the division of factor use between variable and durable input factors. So far as investment in real assets is required to provide fixed factor capacities, the solution to the production problem will be reflected also in the corresponding asset section of the balance sheet. Looking at the same question from another perspective, the solution to the investment problem will be reflected in the structure of the assets side of the balance sheet, and so far as relevant depreciation charges are involved it will be reflected also in the operating cost structures in the income statement.

Finally, the solution to the financing problem will be reflected principally in the liabilities side of the balance sheet. To the extent that it gives rise to a division of the total income stream between the different providers of capital, the financing solution will be reflected also in the relevant section of the income statement.

4

Partial Optimization:

Sources Of Money Capital

The perspective we now possess on the structure and planning of the firm might well give rise to (1) descriptive studies of asset and liability forms and to (2) more detailed analyses of pragmatic decision alternatives. But detailed discussions of asset items and financing sources on a point-by-point basis are beyond the scope of our main objective. Such a digression at this early stage could convey the impression that optimum values of asset and liability items can be isolated from other elements of the firm's structural decision problem; and progress toward the necessary integrated economic and financial analysis could thereby be inhibited. A clear understanding of financial management procedures is desirable for the full apprehension of our own rather different objectives, and detailed discussions may be referred to in the literature already cited.

In this and the following chapter we shall use the empirical categories we have established, and the awareness of the economic issues behind them, to consider the ways in which asset and financing decisions might generate forces that bear upon the optimum economic position of the firm. But a full understanding of the causation determining investment and financing optima must wait until we have developed the more robust models of the following economic analysis.

Leverage in Structural Planning and Income Stability

We examine first the stability of the enterprise income flow, the induced effects on the earnings position of the residual owners, and the implications these may have for the economic valuation of their investment. We leave aside for the present the question of what it is that determines in toto the patterns and pressures of consumer demands in the commodity markets of the economy, and what it is, therefore, that determines the variances, or possible cyclicality, of the sales revenue of the firm. Certainly an estimate of the underlying economic forces, tastes, market structures, substitutes and complementary commodities, elasticities, and other factors bearing on revenue possibilities must be made on behalf of the firm. And certainly a set of some such estimates will influence the judgment of the management regarding the viability of what might otherwise be regarded as an acceptable, or perhaps optimum, structure of the firm. But we do not enter at this point the question as to how in detail such estimates and judgments are to be made.

We take it as granted, then, that the sales revenue of the firm as shown in the income statement may vary. The question now at issue is how such variations may in turn determine a calculable degree of instability in the income of the residual owners. The question, it will be seen, must be answered in two stages. First, the fluctuations in sales revenue will give rise to induced and relatively magnified fluctuations in the net operating income, a relationship we shall refer to as operational leverage; and second, the fluctuations in net operating income will give rise, in turn, to further magnified fluctuations in net income, a relationship referred to as financial leverage.

Clearly, the first-stage magnification, or operational leverage, is due to the presence of fixed operating costs in the enterprise structure, such that total operating costs in the income statement do not vary proportionately with sales. And similarly, the second-stage magnification, or financial leverage, is due to the presence of fixed financing costs, such that the net income in the income statement cannot vary in direct proportion with net operating income. As the latter varies, a larger or smaller proportion of it will perforce be siphoned off to pay the fixed income accruing to the providers of debt capital, leaving a varying proportion of a varying income as the residual available for the owners. In the light of our earlier structural analysis, it will be noted that operational leverage, due largely to the fixed costs caused by the presence of depreciable assets in the firm, is a phenomenon reflected in the structure of the assets side of the balance sheet. Similarly, financial leverage, due to the fixed financial costs caused by the presence of capital funds supplied by creditors, is a phenomenon reflected in the liabilities side of the balance sheet.

Operational Leverage

The analysis of operational leverage may be investigated in numerous parts of the literature in conjunction with the so-called break-even chart analysis with which it is frequently associated.[1] It is sufficient to state at present only the following points. If the firm's decision makers confront the advisability of bringing into existence an enterprise of a size and structure that has apparently optimum characteristics, they will be in a position to estimate the variance of their sales expectations at the normal production level envisaged. Taking account, then, of the fixed operating costs implicit in the enterprise structure contemplated, an estimate can be made of the variance of the firm's net operating income.

Consider now the equation

$$O = R - F - bR \tag{4-1}$$

where O refers to net operating income, R to total sales revenue, F to fixed costs of production, and b is the variable-cost ratio designating variable costs as a ratio of total sales revenue. If it is assumed that the variable-cost ratio b is constant, the total variable-cost function bR will be linear. It is conceivable, of course, that the variable-cost ratio itself is a function of the level of operations of the firm, and the variable-cost function may then be of a general nonlinear form $b(R)R$. Adopting, for purposes of clarity, the linearity assumption, the income equation may be written

$$O = (1 - b)R - F \tag{4-2}$$

Applying expected value operators and recognizing that F does not vary, we have

$$E(O) = (1 - b)E(R) - F \tag{4-3}$$

and

$$\text{Var}(O) = (1 - b)^2\text{Var}(R) \tag{4-4}$$

Equation (4-4) indicates the relation between the variance of the sales revenue and the variance of the net operating income expectation. Thus for a given structure of operating costs and a given variance in the revenue expectations, the variance in the net operating income will be negatively related to the firm's variable cost ratio b.

Of more immediate moment, however, is not the absolute size of the

[1] Again the literature already cited may be consulted, in addition to Douglas Vickers, "On the Economics of Break-even," *The Accounting Review*, vol. 35, pp. 405–412, July, 1960, reprinted in Hector R. Anton and Peter A. Firmin (eds.), *Contemporary Issues in Cost Accounting: A Discipline in Transition*, Houghton Mifflin Company, Boston, 1966, chap. 20. Attention might be paid to the discussion in the last-mentioned reference of the irreversibility and nonlinearity of the functions in the break-even analysis.

measures of variance we are dealing with here, but the corresponding measure of the proportionate fluctuation in the respective variables. Taking the relation $\mathrm{Var}(O) = (1 - b)^2 \mathrm{Var}(R)$ and reading σ as the standard deviation, or positive square root of the variance, we have

$$\sigma_o = (1 - b)\sigma_R \qquad (4\text{-}5)$$

In words, the standard deviation of the probability distribution of net operating income is, for any given dispersion of the probability distribution of sales revenue, again negatively related to the variable-cost ratio.

Taking now the relative standard deviation, or the so-called coefficient of variation, of the variables of interest, we have

$$CV_R = \frac{\sigma_R}{E(R)} \qquad (4\text{-}6)$$

and

$$CV_o = \frac{\sigma_o}{E(O)} \qquad (4\text{-}7)$$

Substituting Equations (4-3) and (4-5) in Equation (4-7) yields

$$CV_o = \frac{(1 - b)\sigma_R}{(1 - b)E(R) - F} \qquad (4\text{-}8)$$

We may now compare Equations (4-6) and (4-8), remembering that the latter is the proportionate variation in net operating income for a given sales expectation and a given enterprise structure. Equation (4-8) divided by Equation (4-6) yields

$$\frac{(1 - b)\sigma_R}{(1 - b)E(R) - F} \cdot \frac{E(R)}{\sigma_R} = \frac{(1 - b)E(R)}{(1 - b)E(R) - F} > 1 \qquad (4\text{-}9)$$

Thus it can be seen that the relative variation of the net operating income will be larger than the relative variation of sales revenue as shown in inequality (4-9) and, more importantly, that the increase in the relative variation will be directly proportional to the amount of fixed operating costs F in the firm. It is precisely this induced effect of the larger or smaller fixed costs of production that constitutes the operational leverage of the firm. It is this phenomenon that we referred to in our initial discussion as the magnification of fluctuations in the variable of interest.

Financial Leverage

In the same way, it would be possible to develop a comparable expression for the relative variation of the net income of the firm and to show that the degree of magnification of the residual owners' income was dependent on

the interposition of fixed financial charges between the net operating income
and the net income. The resulting phenomenon, which has been referred
to as financial leverage, could be described, in ways similar to the foregoing, as the relationship between the coefficient of variation of net income
and the coefficient of variation of the underlying earning ability of the firm,
or its net operating income. In this way we should have derived symmetrical
explanations of the two-stage leverage effect, operational leverage and financial leverage, in terms of which, it was said at the beginning of the discussion, the overall instability of the residual income earned for the owners
is to be related to the fundamental instability in the firm's sales or gross
revenue expectations.

The phenomenon of financial leverage, bearing directly as it does on the
firm's use of borrowed money capital, or on the financial structure as expressed in the debt-equity ratio, can be seen to be related also to the choice
by the firm of optimum financing methods. Without repeating the foregoing
leverage analysis in different terminology simply to fit the present financial
case, it will be useful for what follows to consider the following alternative
argument. It will be seen that the financial leverage ratio, or the debt-equity
ratio, may in some sense serve as a measure or a partial determinant of the
riskiness of the owners' income position and thus also as a partial determinant of the owners' required rate of return or capitalization rate.

TABLE 3

Earning Ability of Corporation A

Total assets	$1,000	
Dept capital	200	(Interest rate 5%)
Equity capital	800	
Financial leverage ratio	¼	

	Internal Rate of Return			
	5%	**10%**	**15%**	**20%**
Net operating income	$50	$100	$150	$200
Interest on debt	10	10	10	10
Income before tax	40	90	140	190
Tax (50%)	20	45	70	95
Net income	20	45	70	95
Rate of return on equity	2.5%	5.6%	8.7%	11.9%

Consider three corporations of the same size, operating in the same industry and the same general economic environment, having similar operating structures, and earning the same rate of return on their total investment. This latter, or the internal rate of return, may be expressed as the percentage of net operating income to the total capital employed, or total

TABLE 4

Earning Ability of Corporation B

Total assets	$1,000	
Dept capital	500	(Interest rate 5%)
Equity capital	500	
Financial leverage ratio	1	

	Internal Rate of Return			
	5%	**10%**	**15%**	**20%**
Net operating income	$50	$100	$150	$200
Interest on debt	25	25	25	25
Income before tax	25	75	125	175
Tax (50%)	12.5	37.5	62.5	87.5
Net income	12.5	37.5	62.5	87.5
Rate of return on equity	2.5%	7.5%	12.5%	17.5%

assets at work in the firm. Imagine, however, that the only structural difference between the corporations is that they have adopted the differing financing structures indicated in Tables 3, 4, and 5. These three tables show condensed income statements for the three firms A, B, and C, on the assumption that the internal rate of return is 5, 10, 15 and 20 percent respectively.

The figures in the tables are of course in no sense thought to be realistic; they are employed only to indicate the general direction of the causal relations involved. Up to this point, for example, nothing has been said concerning the fact that the firm will conceivably be required to pay a higher rate of interest on its debt capital as its financial leverage or debt-equity ratio increases. A nod in the direction of realism is made in Table 5 by supposing that the rate of interest on the debt has risen from 5 to 6 percent in response to the increase in the leverage ratio. More will be said on this point in subsequent contexts.

With a view to clarifying the financial leverage effects in the briefest space, relevant data from Tables 3, 4, and 5 are summarized in Table 6. In this table Corporations A, B, and C are referred to as low, medium, and high leverage respectively.

Several summary propositions may be adduced from the data in Table

TABLE 5

Earning Ability of Corporation C

Total assets	$1,000			
Dept capital	800 (Interest rate 6%)			
Equity capital	200			
Financial leverage ratio	4			

	Internal Rate of Return			
	5%	10%	15%	20%
Net operating income	$50	$100	$150	$200
Interest on debt	48	48	48	48
Income before tax	2	52	102	152
Tax (50%)	1	26	51	76
Net income	1	26	51	76
Rate of return on equity	0.5%	13%	25.5%	38%

6. First, in both the low-leverage and medium-leverage corporations the rate of return on equity is 2.5 percent when the internal rate of return on total capital employed is 5 percent. This follows from the fact that the internal rate of return is precisely the same as the rate of interest being paid on the debt capital. When borrowed funds are put to work in the firm at the rate of return indicated, in other words, they are not earning any returns over and above the contractual interest rate to which they are entitled, and no surplus earnings are therefore available to accrue to the residual owners. Only if the latter should be the case can the equity owners be said to receive the benefits of financial leverage.

But even in the present situation where no change in the owners' income occurs from a leverage effect, the owners' overall economic position could in fact be worsened if the potential instability introduced into their income expectations by the debt-equity ratio should induce an increase in the equity capitalization rate and a consequent reduction in the capitalized value of their investment. The example before us shows clearly how such effects may emerge. If the internal rate of return should be 5 percent while the rate of interest on borrowed funds should be, say, 6 percent, as in the case of the high-leverage corporation in the table, the contractual interest on the debt would absorb part of what would otherwise be the residual income of the owners, and the rate of return on the equity could fall to a very low level.

TABLE 6

Summary of Financial Leverage Relationships

Degree of Leverage	Rate of Return on Equity for Indicated Internal Rates of Return			
	5%	10%	15%	20%
Low	2.5	5.6	8.7	11.9
Medium	2.5	7.5	12.5	17.5
High	0.5	13.0	25.5	38.0

	Percentage Variations in Rate of Return on Equity for Indicated Changes in Internal Rates of Return		
	Internal Rate of Return Changing from		
	10% to 5% = −50%	10% to 15% = +50%	10% to 20% = +100%
Low	−55	55	112
Medium	−66	67	133
High	−96	96	192

Second, in those instances in which the internal rate of return is greater than the interest rate on the debt, the rate of return on equity will be greater where the degree of financial leverage is greater, or where the debt-equity ratio is higher. This is shown in the last three columns of the first part of the table.

Third, for any given proportionate change in the internal rate of return, the existence of the leverage effect will give rise to a magnified change in the rate of return on the equity capital. Consider the last two columns of the lower section of the table. Increases of 50 and 100 percent in the internal rates of return caused larger rates of increase in the rate of return on equity in each of the low-, medium-, and high-leverage corporations. Even more important, the degree of magnification of residual rates of return is seen to increase as the financial leverage ratio increases. But of course the same magnification effect can work in reverse if the underlying income-generating ability of the firm should fall. The reverse effect is depicted in the first column of the lower section of the table.

Implications of Leverage for Economic Values

The purpose of this discussion, however, has not been the mere demonstration of the leverage effect as such. But having now a sharper apprehension of the instabilities and uncertainties imposed on the firm by the relevant structural decisions, we can consider directly the implications for the owners' capitalization rates and their economic values.

Consider first, for this purpose, the relative variation of the residual income. Referring to the income statement in Table 2, we derive the following expression:

$$N = O - M \tag{4-10}$$

In this equation N refers to net income, and O and M refer respectively to net operating income and the total interest on the debt capital employed by the firm. Applying expectational operators,

$$E(N) = E(O) - M \tag{4-11}$$

Again, proceeding as before on the basis of Equation (4-10),

$$\mathrm{Var}(N) = \mathrm{Var}(O) \tag{4-12}$$

and

$$\sigma_N = \sigma_o \tag{4-13}$$

where the last two equations are expressions in the variances and standard deviations respectively. The coefficient of variation of net income may then be written as $\sigma_N/E(N)$, or

$$V_N = \frac{\sigma_o}{E(O) - rD} \tag{4-14}$$

where rD now represents the total interest on debt capital. This is obtained by multiplying the total debt outstanding, D, by the average rate of interest on the debt, r.

The Capitalization Rate Effect

Leaving the expression for V_N in the form of Equation (4-14), we investigate now its significance for the owners' economic position. For this purpose we call on Equation (2-34), which established our basic postulates regarding the dependence of the form of an individual's capitalization rate function in the presence of uncertainty on the form of his underlying utility function. The relevant expression is reproduced here as

$$\rho = a + w\sigma^2 \qquad (4\text{-}15)$$

where the variables are as previously defined. We shall proceed for the present to discover what further light can be thrown on the valuation problem by the individual risk-averter's attitude to the income-earning possibilities of the firm.

In the preceding discussion of the implications of financial leverage the coefficient of variation of the net income was taken as the measure of the degree of risk in the owners' economic position. It would be useful, therefore, if the capitalization rate function in Equation (4-15) could be transformed from a function in the variance to a function in the coefficient of variation. Again, though the issue is clear, it will be useful to clarify the economic meaning behind it. It follows from Equation (4-15) that

$$d\rho = 2w\sigma \, d\sigma \qquad (4\text{-}16)$$

From the definition of the coefficient of variation, $V_N = \sigma/E(N)$, it follows that for any given level of income expectations the magnitude of V_N will change in the following manner for different degrees of variability or dispersion of the probability distribution of the expectations:

$$dV_N = \frac{1}{N} \, d\sigma$$

whence

$$d\sigma = N \, dV_N \qquad (4\text{-}17)$$

Substituting Equation (4-17) in Equation (4-16) yields

$$d\rho = 2w\sigma N \, dV_N$$

or

$$d\rho = 2wN^2 V_N \, dV_N \qquad (4\text{-}18)$$

by substitution of $\sigma = V_N N$. If we now take the indefinite integral of Equation (4-18),

$$\rho = wN^2 V_N^2 + C \qquad (4\text{-}19)$$

On the basis of Equation (4-19) the conclusion is reached that if the level of income expectations is taken as given, the capitalization rate will vary with the coefficient of variation in accordance with the relation

$$\rho = a + sV_N^2 \qquad (4\text{-}20)$$

In Equation (4-20) the wN^2 term in Equation (4-19) is written as s, and C is written as a, to preserve comparison between this expression and the initial form of the function in Equation (4-15). The capitalization rate function is thus nonlinear in the coefficient of variation and concave upward, as may be seen by taking the first and second derivatives of the function in the usual manner.

Reflecting on our earlier discussion and invoking the measure of the coefficient of variation of the net income in the form in which we derived it in Equation (4-14), the substitution of this value into Equation (4-20) yields an alternative expression for the capitalization rate function:

$$\rho = a + s\left(\frac{\sigma_o}{E(O) - rD}\right)^2 \tag{4-21}$$

Thus it would appear, as might have been intuited from the earlier discussion of financial leverage, that a definable relation exists between the amount of debt in the capital structure of the firm and the owners' capitalization rate. We can note, moreover, that the transformations we have effected enable us to use, as the determinant variables in the capitalization rate function, the standard deviation of the firm's net operating income stream as distinct from net income on the one hand, and the extent of debt financing on the other.

The Scale Effect

Before the validity of these effects can be concluded, however, the analysis requires additional scrutiny. For it should be recalled that the financial leverage analysis thus far has been confined to the case in which, at the same time as the results of variations in the debt-equity ratio were examined, the total capital employed in the firm was assumed to remain unchanged. This still leaves open the very important question as to how increases in the amount of debt capital employed may affect the risk position of the owners, and thereby their capitalization rate, when the increase in debt involves also an increase in the total capital employed in the firm. It is this latter and more complex case with which we shall be principally concerned in the following chapters, and it will be profitable, therefore, to confront the question posed at this point. Unfortunately, it will be seen that the answer is not unambiguous, but the clarification of the reasons why this is so will itself throw valuable light on our subsequent problems.

Let us consider the capitalization rate function in Equation (4-21) from the point of view of the management decision makers within the firm and and imagine that an increase in debt capital is contemplated. If such an increase in debt will also increase the total capital employed (rather than constitute a substitution of debt for equity capital), an increase in net operating income may be expected to result, and this may or may not also be accompanied by a change in the variance of the underlying earning ability of the firm. An important reason why the variance of the operating income may change is related to the possibility that the increased availability of money capital may induce a substitution of real capital for other factors of production, giving rise to a different optimum combination of factor inputs, a different level of fixed operating costs, and a new equilibrium at a different point on the firm's production function. We have noted in earlier contexts that the increased availability and use of money capital may induce a new degree of capital deepening in the firm, altogether apart from the degree of capital widening that may also result. We do not have in hand at this stage of our analysis sufficient conceptual apparatus to examine all the possibilities in detail, and this must wait until we have developed the economic theory behind our optimization model. But significant light can nevertheless be thrown on the basic question at issue.

For this purpose we first differentiate Equation (4-20) with respect to debt. The rate of change of the capitalization rate is shown as

$$\frac{d\rho}{dD} = 2sV_N\frac{dV_N}{dD} \tag{4-22}$$

The direction of the change depends on the sign of dV_N/dD, or the way in which the increase in debt affects the relative variability of the owners' residual income. To test for this effect we take the expression $V_N = \sigma_o/[E(O) - rD]$ and differentiate with respect to D:

$$\frac{dV_N}{dD} = \frac{[E(O) - rD]\frac{d\sigma_o}{dD} - \sigma_o\left[\frac{dE(O)}{dD} - r\right]}{[E(O) - rD]^2} \tag{4-23}$$

It might be expected that an increase in the total capital employed in the firm would increase the absolute variance of the income expectation (though this will not necessarily follow), giving a positive value to the first term in the numerator of Equation (4-23). But even if this were so, the overall effect on the sign of the equation would depend also on the magnitude of the second term. For the expression in the final brackets can be looked upon as the marginal productivity of the new capital employed in the firm minus the marginal cost of the additional debt. (We shall subsequently drop the present simplifying assumption that the interest rate is invariant with respect to the amount of debt and incorporate the more realistic suggestions made in this connection in the earlier discussion of financial leverage.) It is to be expected that in the normal case this net marginal productivity of the new money capital will be positive. Taking together, then, the separate terms in the numerator of Equation (4-23), the effect on the relative variability of the net income will depend on how the increase in debt affects both the expected value and the variance of the total net operating income.

At this point the assumption might conceivably be made by the management that in whatever way the scale effect of the increase of capital may affect total expected earnings, the relative variability of the earnings will remain unchanged. In other words,

$$\frac{\sigma_o}{E(O)} = k \qquad (4\text{-}24)$$

where k is a constant. Substituting this relation in the expression of V_N we can write $V_N = kO/(O - rD)$, where the expectational operator is eliminated for notational convenience. Differentiating this last expression with respect to debt yields

$$\frac{dV_N}{dD} = \frac{(O - rD)k\frac{dO}{dD} - kO\left(\frac{dO}{dD} - r\right)}{(O - rD)^2} \qquad (4\text{-}25)$$

whence

$$\frac{dV_N}{dD} = \frac{rkO - rkD\frac{dO}{dD}}{(O - rD)^2} \qquad (4\text{-}26)$$

The sign on the right-hand side of Equation (4-26) will be positive, and the coefficient of variation of net income will increase with an increased use of debt (given, as in the present case, a constant relative variation of the total income stream), as

$$O > D\frac{dO}{dD} \qquad (4\text{-}27)$$

where O refers, as throughout this analysis, to the net operating income of the firm.

This condition may well be satisfied in general, as might be inferred from considering the meaning of the derivative in the inequality. As previously indicated, this is the marginal productivity of the incremental debt capital and may be expected, in the normal case, to be of the same general order of magnitude as the marginal interest cost on the debt. The right-hand side of inequality (4-27), therefore, may be expected to be of the same order of magnitude as the firm's total interest burden on its debt. In such a case, and if the positivity condition in inequality (4-27) is established, the relative variability of the owners' income will increase as does the use of debt capital. Reading this result back into Equation (4-22), the increase in debt has a positive effect on the equity capitalization rate.

But of course there is no necessity to this effect. On the other hand the increased employment of debt capital may lead to a reduction in the coefficient of variation of the owners' income, and this will in fact occur if the increase in the capital employed causes such a change in the level and variability of the total earnings expectation as to cause, in turn, a sufficient reduction in the coefficient of variation at the net operating income level. While this may not be the case usually encountered in enterprise optimization activities, it is nevertheless true that the full effects of the changes under discussion do depend on the complete relations in Equation (4-23), and the magnitude of the effect from a change in debt to a change in the owners' risk position does depend upon all the magnitudes in the equation.

Of course in the case in which the increment of debt is accompanied by a reduction of the equity capital at work in the firm due, say, to a dividend distribution to the common stock holders out of accumulated retained earnings, there is no increase in the total capital employed in the firm and no reason why the net operating income should rise. In that event the numerator in Equation (4-26) reduces to rkO, the relevant positivity condition is established, and the owners can be expected to raise their capitalization rate in response to the increased use of debt. For in such a case there has been an increase in the debt-equity ratio of the kind examined in the arithmetic of Tables 3 through 6.

While this conclusion holds in the general conditions posited in connection with it, it is still possible that some marginal change in the net operating income characteristics of the firm may occur following a change in the debt-equity ratio, even though the total capital employed remains the same. This could follow if the change in the capital structure were associated with, or indeed induced the management to adopt, a set of investment projects and productive activities that implied perhaps both a lower intrinsic risk (in their gross-revenue-generating ability) and a lower rate of return.

The most important conclusion to draw from the analysis, however, is that the change in the residual owners' risk position is ambiguous with respect to increases in both debt capital and the total capital employed, and that the analysis is not rescued from the ambiguity by the assumption that the relative variability (the coefficient of variation) of the net operating income stream remains unchanged. In the respect in which we are now interested in it, such an assumption does not necessarily remove the scale or size effect from the impact that the change in debt capital has on the residual owners' risk position, as argued from Equations (4-25) and (4-26). It remains true that for comparable capital structures, indicated by comparable debt-equity ratios, the ownership shares of large corporations *may* be valued at a lower capitalization rate (higher value per dollar of earnings) than those of smaller corporations. The only point that can be made unambiguously, on the basis of the assumptions of risk aversion that we have posited, is that, *ceteris paribus*, a higher debt-equity ratio for any given capital usage can be expected to be associated with a higher equity capitalization rate.

The Valuation of Equity Ownership

With this background there is no need to pursue the taxonomy further. We recall that the purpose of the analysis is to place in the hands of the firm's management, or to incorporate in our explanatory models of the firm at an appropriate point, an equity owners' capitalization rate function, the form of which is related to empirically meaningful variables. It is at this point, however, that an inventory should be taken of the propositions we have thus been able to adduce. Methodologically, a chain of causation has been traced from the basic assumption of an individual investor's risk aversion, and the implied form of his utility function, through the determinants and implications of risk, to the specifications, *ceteris paribus*, of his risk-adjusted capitalization rate. If it were possible to assume generalized risk aversion in the market for corporate securities, or on the supply side of the money capital market, the analysis to this point could be taken as disclosing the underlying logic in the theory of the value of the firm or in the determination of the firm's cost of money capital.

It was pointed out at the end of Chapter 2, however, that two important logical steps now intervene between the point we have reached and the specification of the firm's equity capitalization rate function. These we characterized earlier as referring to the portfolio problem on the one hand and the market problem on the other. The relevance of the first of these two matters can be put briefly as follows. While the nature and the impact of a risk averter's valuation procedure will be precisely as we have outlined it, the price at which he is prepared to acquire and hold an equity security will depend not only on its own separable risk characteristics as already analyzed, but on the contribution which that security makes to the return and the overall riskiness of the total portfolio of securities of which it is a part. And this, it is shown in the literature we have referred to, will depend not only on the variance of the returns on the specific security (if variance is assumed to be an acceptable index of risk) but also on the covariances between that security and the rest of the portfolio. The ways in which the individual's solution of the portfolio problem will affect the demand for a particular firm's ownership security and the rate at which that firm's earnings will be effectively capitalized, or its capitalization rate function determined, cannot, therefore, be uniquely specified a priori. It can only be said that the capitalization rate that an individual will apply to a firm's security will depend on what we may call that security's effective risk dimension, but that the estimate of that risk dimension may depend on its place in any of many possible security portfolios.

The second of the questions that now call for attention, or what we have referred to as the market problem, is again embedded in our underlying risk-aversion-valuation analysis. But again it is possible to say only the following. If generalized risk aversion on the supply side of the money capital market is assumed, the market value of ownership securities, per dollar of income, will tend to be lower in higher-risk securities. The underlying causation is of the kind examined in our basic analysis, but the value of a firm's securities, and therefore the effective capitalization rate at which the money capital market is valuing its income, will depend on the changing pressures of supply and demand in the market. It can be posited only that, in the absence of undue imperfections, the market mechanism will maintain comparable yields on comparable risk securities.

We leave aside, however, the more detailed analysis of the points just raised. For purposes of our present discussion we assume that in general the underlying forces of risk aversion will reflect themselves in the manner indicated in the equity capitalization rate applicable to the firm. From the point of view of the firm's optimization decisions, therefore, we can summarize the analysis as follows, based on the equation system developed in the preceding sections of this chapter. First, the capitalization rate is a concave-upward function of the relative variability of the residual owners' income. Second, for any given level of total capital employed, this relative variability is a positive function of the debt capital at work in the firm. Third, although there is some ambiguity, increases in capital employed may moderately depress what would otherwise be the effects of debt changes on the capitalization rate. This depressive effect is due to the presence of the negative term in the numerator of Equation (4-26) or (4-23), even though the magnitude of the negative term may not be sufficient to determine the sign of the equation.

We may accordingly take the capitalization rate function from the form in which it stands in Equation (4-20), namely, $\rho = a + sV_N^2$, where V_N is the coefficient of variation of the owners' net income stream, and write it in general terms in some such form as

$$\rho = a - b(K + D) + c\left(\frac{D}{K}\right)^2 \tag{4-28}$$

where K and D respectively represent the equity capital and the debt capital employed in the firm, and the first term in parentheses in the equation therefore represents the total capital employed. It should be noted, however, that in Equation (4-28) the constant term will not now represent the riskless rate of interest as in the initial form of the capitalization rate function. By way of interpretation it can be said that $(a - bK)$, given that D is equal to zero, would indicate the rate at which the owners' residual income would be capitalized if only equity capital were at work in the firm. If the function were written as $\rho = a - bD + c(D/K)^2$, the constant term a could then be directly interpreted as the capitalization rate applicable to the net earnings of a pure equity capital structure.

More generally, the function may be written as

$$\rho = \rho(\theta, M, L) \tag{4-29}$$

where θ represents the coefficient of variation of the firm's total net operating income stream, M the total capital employed, and L the leverage, or debt-equity ratio. The rate of change of the capitalization rate with respect to an increase in the debt-equity ratio may be written as

$$\frac{d\rho}{dL} = f_L + f_\theta \frac{d\theta}{dL} + f_M \frac{dM}{dL} \tag{4-30}$$

where the subscripted variables respectively indicate the partial derivatives of the function with respect to L, θ, and M. In Equation (4-29) M, the total capital employed, and L, the debt-equity ratio, are connected via D, the amount of debt capital, so that the derivative dM/dL, for example, follows from the chain rule $(dM/dD)(dD/dL)$.

In parts of our subsequent work we shall wish to examine the changes in the equity capitalization rate as changes occur in the amount of debt capital employed in conjunction with a given amount of equity capital. In that case $d\rho/dD$ will be understood as deriving from Equation (4-29) as follows:

$$\frac{d\rho}{dD} = f_\theta \frac{d\theta}{dD} + f_M \frac{dM}{dD} + f_L \frac{dL}{dD} \tag{4-31}$$

In any event we now have before us in Equation (4-29) the general form of the firm's capitalization rate function, on the basis of which estimates of empirical parameters can be made. Conceptually, the results derived in such a form can then be incorporated in the optimization models we shall develop and in the firm's planning and optimization procedures.[2]

Alternative Financing Structures

The foregoing analysis furnishes us with all the implications it is necessary to draw, for present purposes, from the structure of the firm's income statement. It has provided us with a linkage between the structure of that statement and the possible instabilities of the earnings figures it reports at the different levels of operation, net operating income and net income respectively. It has provided a linkage also between the structure of capital sources used and the implied degree of risk in the economic position of the owners. It will be appropriate now to look a little more deeply at this same

[2] It is not necessary for present purposes to multiply instances of empirical work. Relevant procedures, hypotheses, and results may be inspected in Ronald F. Wippern, "Financial Structure and the Value of the Firm," *Journal of Finance*, vol. 21, pp. 615–633, December, 1966, and references cited.

set of relationships, this time from the viewpoint of the structural character-istics of the liabilities side of the balance sheet. It will be seen that addition-al light can thereby be thrown on the question as to what, under varying assumptions and with varying degrees of realism, constitutes the optimum structure of liabilities, or the optimum usage of different sources of money capital funds.

Again, however, the same qualification must be made as we invoked in a previous context. Since we are here considering the relation between dif-ferent financing sources, in isolation from the question of how and where and with what combination of factors the money capital is to be invested in the firm, we are at best able to describe a partial or first-approximation set of optimization conditions. We shall see subsequently that interdependent relations exist between availability of and demand for money capital on the one hand and the factor combinations employed, and thus the structure of the productive enterprise, on the other.

Moreover, the nature of our present work does not require us to stop and consider the details and institutional characteristics related to the pro-vision of funds from all the liability sources indicated in the balance sheet. Full discussions abound in the technical literature already referred to. The availability of funds from trade creditors in the form of accounts payable will be commented on again subsequently, and for purposes of the present discussion no distinction will be made between short-term and long-term debt. In fact, in order to bring out the essential principles involved in choos-ing the optimum financial leverage, or the optimum debt-equity ratio in the firm, we shall imagine the capital structure to be made up in the first in-stance of a combination of homogeneous debt and homogeneous equity. Subsequently, this assumption will be relaxed, and while all the firm's equi-ty must in the nature of the case remain homogeneous (the equity being taken as voting ownership capital and it having been agreed previously to abstract from preferred stock capital), we shall envisage the employment by the firm of heterogeneous forms of debt capital. This will enable us to con-sider two further and interesting phenomena: first, the possibility that the firm may practice monopsonistic discrimination against its suppliers of debt capital; and second, the possibility that in so doing the firm may be able to affect the relative elasticities of supply of debt and equity capital respec-tively, and thereby influence directly the choice of optimum capital struc-ture.

Debt Capital Supply Function

Consider first the supply of debt capital to the firm. The terms on which creditors will make funds available will depend on several aspects of the structure and operating characteristics of the enterprise, foremost among them the following: first, the so-called asset cover of the firm's debt, or the ratio of total assets to total debt or fixed assets to total debt, indicating the possible availability of realizable money values that would constitute a cushion behind the debt in the case of financial difficulty or in the event of bankruptcy and liquidation; second, the earnings cover on the debt, or the ratio between the total earnings available to pay the interest on the debt (the net operating income) and the actual debt interest liability; third, and standing behind the factors already mentioned, the important but intangible fact of the creditors' confidence in the general efficiency of the management of the firm; and finally, which in a significant sense gathers up the effects of the matters already referred to, the degree of stability or instability in the firm's total income stream. The earnings stability was referred to in an earlier discussion as indicated by the coefficient of variation of the net operating income stream, and we may take this ratio as a measure of the general risk exposure of the creditors.

Taking together the factors mentioned in the preceding paragraph, we might summarize by saying that the willingness of the creditors to supply money capital funds is described by the following debt cost function:

$$r = r\left(V_o, \frac{D}{K}\right) \tag{4-32}$$

In this equation r represents the average rate of interest on the firm's total debt, V_o refers to the coefficient of variation of the earnings stream available to cover the interest on the debt, and D/K, the debt-equity ratio, indicates the relative strength of asset values and, implicitly, the size of the income stream standing behind the debt.

Equation (4-32) might be compared with Equation (4-29), where the matter of risk was similarly incorporated in the specification of the equity owners' capitalization rate function, or the cost of equity capital. In the latter case the risks in view were ultimately those associated with the instability of the residual net income stream, while in the case of debt capital the relevant risks are those associated with the instability of the net operating income stream.

In the debt cost function of Equation (4-32) it follows, from the same kind of considerations as contained in our earlier risk analysis, that in the general case

$$\frac{\partial r}{\partial V_o} \geq 0 \quad \text{and} \quad \frac{\partial r}{\partial (D/K)} \geq 0$$

In our present analysis we shall require information about the way in which changes in the amount of debt capital employed in the firm will affect the average rate of interest on the debt. In the context immediately below we shall be seeking for partial equilibrium theorems concerning the optimum debt-equity ratio for a given total capital employment, though subsequently, as indicated in our consideration of the cost of equity capital, we shall be seeking for the optimum amount of debt to employ in conjunction with a given amount of equity. At the latter point we shall be envisaging increases in the total capital employed *pari passu* with increases in the debt. In any event it follows from Equation (4-32), again writing D/K as L, that

$$dr = \frac{\partial r}{\partial V_o}dV_o + \frac{\partial r}{\partial L}dL \qquad (4\text{-}33)$$

whence

$$\frac{dr}{dL} = \frac{\partial r}{\partial V_o}\cdot\frac{dV_o}{dL} + \frac{\partial r}{\partial L} \qquad (4\text{-}34)$$

and

$$\frac{dr}{dD} = \frac{\partial r}{\partial V_o}\cdot\frac{dV_o}{dD} + \frac{\partial r}{\partial L}\cdot\frac{dL}{dD} \qquad (4\text{-}35)$$

In the immediate context, in which the total capital employed is understood to remain constant as the debt capital changes (thus focusing sole attention on changes in the debt-equity ratio), the income-earning characteristics of that total capital can also be deemed to remain unchanged, and the level of net operating income and the coefficient of variation of that income stream will remain as they were before. In that case the first term on the right-hand side of Equation (4-35) vanishes, and the remaining term expresses the change in the average cost of debt as dependent on the change in the leverage ratio induced by the change in debt capital employed by the firm.

The Optimum Financing Structure:
A Partial Equilibrium Solution

Bringing together now the equity cost function and the debt cost function, as in Equations (4-29) and (4-32), we can combine our income statement and balance sheet analysis and seek for the criteria of optimum capital structure, at least on the partial equilibrium level to which we are confined by our present context. We examine first the analytically simplest case in which we abstract from changes in both the debt cost and equity costs as the capital structure changes. No realism attaches to this particular case, but it will establish the technique of the argument in its simplest form.

In the case before us, successive substitutions of debt for equity capital will have been carried to the optimum extent when the degree of leverage in the capital structure is such as to maximize the rate of return being earned on the equity capital in the firm. In all our arguments to this point we have considered the relationships between the income statement and balance sheet items as shown in the books of the firm, and in the matter of the capital structure we have accordingly been envisaging the actual amount of equity funds committed to the firm and shown at their balance sheet values. For the time being we continue to measure the capital accounts at book value. It follows that in our equity and debt cost functions of Equations (4-29) and (4-32) the capital values, as in the debt-equity or leverage ratio, for example, are taken at book values. This, it will be recalled, follows from the logic of the relationships adduced from the financial leverage discussion in Tables 3 through 6. We shall subsequently incorporate in the analysis the market values of the capital securities and note in particular the significance of the market value, or economic value, of the owners' investment.

We consider, then, the optimization of the rate of return on the book value of the owners' investment for increases in financial leverage. We define our maximand as

$$\frac{\pi}{K} = i = \frac{O - rD}{K} \qquad (4\text{-}36)$$

where all variables are defined as previously. Taking the general differential equation from Equation (4-36) yields

$$di = f_o\, dO + f_r\, dr + f_D\, dD + f_K\, dK$$

where the subscripted symbols represent the partial derivatives of (π/K) with respect to the variables indicated. In particular it follows that

$$di = \frac{1}{K} dO - \frac{D}{K}\, dr - \frac{r}{K}\, dD - \frac{\pi}{K^2}\, dK \qquad (4\text{-}37)$$

Now at the solution conditions that satisfy the maximum value of the rate of return on equity, the value of the total differential in Equation (4-37) must be equal to zero. Since we are considering capital structure changes for a given total capital employment and a given total income, moreover, the expression containing dO can also be set equal to zero. Again, if the interest cost is assumed to remain fixed as the use of debt increases, dr is also equal to zero. Making these substitutions in Equation (4-37), multiplying throughout by K, and rearranging yields

$$\frac{\pi}{K}dK + r\, dD = 0 \qquad (4\text{-}38)$$

reading the right-hand side of the equation as zero.

In the present case, however, where debt is being progressively substituted for equity, dK is equal to $-dD$. Equation (4-38) can therefore be rearranged to read

$$\frac{\pi}{K}dD = r\, dD \qquad (4\text{-}39)$$

From this it follows that the optimum degree of financial leverage will be that at which the rate of return on equity is equal to the rate of interest on the debt. Further rearrangement of Equation (4-39) yields the result

$$O - rD = Kr \qquad (4\text{-}40)$$

whence

$$r = \frac{O}{K + D} \qquad (4\text{-}41)$$

This implies that the interest rate on the debt, the rate of return on total capital employed, and the rate of return on the equity are all equal to one another.

This is, of course, an anomalous and empirically untenable conclusion and follows only because of the unrealistic assumption that neither the cost of debt nor the cost of equity increases in response to the riskiness of the respective security holders' positions. The case actually holds within it no equilibrating mechanism at all, and the most it can say is that the firm would be advised to employ 100 percent of the cheapest source of capital funds available. But the case does point up the weakness of certainty model theorizing in this context, and it establishes an analytical technique we can use without extensive comment in what follows.

A Second Approximation

As a step toward realism, consider again the general differential Equation (4-37) and let us suppose that the debt cost function is as specified in Equation (4-32). Then Equation (4-37) can be rearranged as before to read

$$\frac{\pi}{K} = r + D\frac{dr}{dD} \qquad (4\text{-}42)$$

If now we suppose that the total interest liability of the firm increases as debt capital increases, partially because the debt itself rises in volume and partially because the cost per unit of debt rises, we can conceive of the marginal cost of borrowing debt capital as follows:

$$m = \frac{d(rD)}{dD} = r + D\frac{dr}{dD} \qquad (4\text{-}43)$$

If this expression is now substituted into Equation (4-42) it emerges that in the case contemplated the optimum degree of financial leverage will be that at which the rate of return on equity is equal to the marginal cost of borrowing, or π/K equals m. This, of course, is to be expected from a priori economic reasoning. For as long as the cost of equity capital is not changing, the average and the marginal costs of equity are equal, and the optimization condition we have derived is simply saying that the optimum allocation of the firm's demand for capital over alternative capital sources will be such as to equate the cost of each capital source at the margin.

Elasticities of Debt and Equity Capital Supply Functions

The analysis points, therefore, to the more robust optimization conditions implicit in the simultaneous use of the equity cost function of Equation (4-29) and the debt cost function of Equation (4-32). The notion of optimum capital structure for any level of capital employment becomes meaningful now, however, only if we redefine our maximand. Our interest here is in generating for the owners the maximum attainable economic value per dollar of equity investment committed to the firm. Our maximand therefore appears as V/K, and using previous notation this may be written as

$$\frac{V}{K} = \frac{O - rD}{\rho K} \tag{4-44}$$

Employing a similar technique to that used above, the general differential equation may be written as follows:

$$d\left(\frac{V}{K}\right) = \frac{1}{\rho K}dO - \frac{D}{\rho K}dr - \frac{r}{\rho K}dD - \frac{\pi}{\rho K^2}dK - \frac{\pi}{\rho^2 K}d\rho \tag{4-45}$$

This differential equation may be written in a reduced form by setting $d(V/K)$ and dO equal to zero, multiplying throughout by ρK, setting dK equal to $-dD$ for the same reasons as previously, and rearranging terms. It follows that

$$\frac{\pi}{K}dD = r\,dD + D\,dr + \frac{\pi}{\rho}d\rho \tag{4-46}$$

whence

$$\frac{\pi}{K} = r + D\frac{dr}{dD} - \frac{\pi}{\rho}\frac{d\rho}{dK} \tag{4-47}$$

Given this result, Equation (4-47) can be transformed by multiplying and dividing by r and K at the points indicated in the following expression:

$$\frac{\pi}{K} = r + r\left(\frac{D}{r}\frac{dr}{dD}\right) - \frac{\pi}{K}\left(\frac{K}{\rho}\frac{d\rho}{dK}\right) \tag{4-48}$$

It will be recognized that the first term in parentheses in Equation (4-48) is the elasticity of the cost of debt with respect to changes in debt capital, and similarly the second term in parentheses is the elasticity of the equity cost with respect to the concomitant changes in equity capital. We write these elasticity expressions as E_D and E_K respectively. Equation (4-48) then appears as

$$\frac{\pi}{K} = i = r + rE_D - iE_K \tag{4-49}$$

or, by transposition,

$$i = r\left(\frac{1 + E_D}{1 + E_K}\right) \tag{4-50}$$

Given, in other words, a positive responsiveness of the respective capital costs to changes in the capital structure, or to changes in the capital holders' risk positions, the optimum employment of debt and equity capital may be defined in terms of a discoverable relation between the rate of return being earned on the equity, i, and the rate of interest being paid on the debt, r. This relationship is in turn described by, and is dependent upon, the elasticities of the respective capital supply or capital cost functions.

In the general case the elasticity of the debt cost with respect to debt changes, E_D, may be expected to be positive, and the elasticity of the equity cost with respect to equity changes, E_K, may be expected to be negative. Relatively less equity means relatively more risk for the equity holders. It follows from Equation (4-50), therefore, that so long as the absolute value of E_K is less than unity, the value of the expression in brackets is positive and greater than unity. The optimization condition thereby indicates the general order of the extent to which the rate of return on the equity can be expected to be greater than the interest rate being paid on the debt, a direction of relationship our general a priori on risk aversion would lead us to expect.

It might be useful to note also the following points in connection with the optimization condition in Equation (4-50). First, it will be clear that in the general case, and in recognition of the risk aversion characteristics we have assumed throughout, the return on the owners' investment will exceed the rate of interest being paid on the debt capital. In Equation (4-50) i will be greater than r. Now the optimum capital structure condition is indicating that there is a limit to which the ratio of i to r can fall, depending on the elasticities of the capital cost functions. As the financial leverage and the risk measure increase, both the elasticities will increase; and the more rapid the increase in either or both the elasticities, the sooner will the ratio of i to r be brought to its critical value. At this point no further substitution of debt for equity will be profitable from the owners' point of view. The lower, therefore, will be the optimum debt-equity ratio.

The question of the sufficiency condition on the foregoing solution can be seen by first differentiating Equation (4-44) with respect to D. It can be left as an exercise for the reader to show that by this method the same solution condition as in Equation (4-50) may be derived. But such an exercise will emphasize, more clearly perhaps, that any degree of substitution of debt for equity at all will be advantageous only so long as the first derivative thus obtained is positive. That is to say, it will be beneficial for the owners to increase the leverage ratio only so long as a "greater than" inequality can replace the equation sign in Equation (4-50).

But this, of course, leaves quite open the possibility that no use of debt at all might be advisable. This would be very forcibly the case if there existed reason to believe that, for any debt at all, the absolute values of either of the elasticity measures in the equation were prohibitively high. But by the same token, if the initial conditions are such that the use of at least some debt is indicated and if the positivity condition on the first derivative of Equation (4-44) is satisfied, it follows that our optimization condition in Equation (4-50) satisfies a maximum leverage and maximum advantage result. If we hold to the previous assumption of concave-upward debt and equity cost functions consistent with the assumed risk aversion utility functions presupposed at the beginning, the general nature of the conditions we have discussed in this argument can be expected to hold.

The Relevance of Market Values

Before examining the further implications of the elasticity concepts we have thus opened up, it will be helpful from the standpoint of our subsequent work to consider briefly some propositions as to optimum capital structure in terms of relationships between the market values of debt and equity securities. When this is then set against our earlier analysis in terms of the actual dollar investment by the owners, using, as just indicated, the notion of the relation between the owners' economic values and their book values, a clearer linkage will be provided between our own analysis and certain significant discussions in the recent literature.[3]

In this argument the following notation will be employed: V, π, and ρ will refer, as before, to the market value, profits, and capitalization rate applicable to the owners' equity.

B, F, and r will refer to the market value, interest earnings, and market yield on the debt capital of the firm.

W, O, and k will refer to the total capitalized value W of the net operating income of the firm O, and the relationship O/W will provide a measure of k, the effective rate of capitalization at which the total earnings of the firm

---

The literature referred to has stemmed mainly from the article by Franco Modigliani and Merton H. Miller, "The Cost of Capital, Corporation Finance and the Theory of Investment," *American Economic Review*, vol. 48, pp. 261–297, June,1958, reprinted in Ezra Solomon (ed.), *The Management of Corporate Capital*, The Free Press of Glencoe, New York, 1959. See also the related "Comments" by J. R. Rose and David Durand, *American Economic Review*, vol. 49, pp. 638–669, September, 1959; Merton H. Miller and Franco Modigliani, "Some Estimates of the Cost of Capital to the Electric Utility Industry, 1954–57," *American Economic Review*, vol. 56, pp. 333–391, June, 1966; Ezra Solomon, *The Theory of Financial Management*, Columbia University Press, New York, 1963, and "Leverage and the Cost of Capital," *Journal of Finance*, vol. 18, pp. 273–279, May, 1963; Alexander A. Robichek and Stewart C. Myers, *Optimal Financing Decisions*, Prentice-Hall, Inc., Englewood Cliffs, N.J., 1965; Alexander Barges, *The Effect of Capital Structure on the Cost of Capital*, Prentice-Hall, Inc., Englewood Cliffs, N.J. 1963; William Beranek, *The Effect of Leverage on the Market Value of Common Stock*, The University of Wisconsin Press, Madison, Wis., 1964; J. Fred Weston, "A Test of Cost of Capital Propositions," *Southern Economic Journal*, vol. 30, pp. 105–112, October, 1963; Eugene M. Lerner and Willard T. Carleton, *A Theory of Financial Analysis*, Harcourt, Brace & World, Inc., New York, 1966.

are being valued in W. The variable W will accordingly appear also as the total market value of the firm's capital securities. It will be clear, on reflecting on our discussion of the balance sheet and income statement, that W may be taken to refer also to the total market valuation of the total asset investment of the firm, considered as a continuing and going concern. The following relations are implied in the foregoing definitions.

$$V = \frac{\pi}{\rho} \qquad \pi = \rho V \qquad (4\text{-}51)$$

$$B = \frac{F}{r} \qquad F = rB \qquad (4\text{-}52)$$

$$W = \frac{O}{k} \qquad O = kW \qquad (4\text{-}53)$$

If at any point in time a set of security values and income statement items are observed and described as in the foregoing list, the following summary or definitional statements may be made:

$$k = \frac{O}{W} = \frac{F + \pi}{W} \qquad (4\text{-}54)$$

whence

$$k = \frac{rB}{W} + \frac{\rho V}{W} \qquad (4\text{-}55)$$

From Equation (4-55) the overall capitalization rate, which may be referred to as the average cost of capital, is seen to be a weighted average of the cost of debt and equity capital respectively, r and ρ, where each such capital cost is weighted by the relative importance of the corresponding capital in the total market value of the corporation's securities.[4]

---

[4] At this point, it might be noted, a troublesome proposition has been introduced into the literature, notably in the initial paper by Modigliani and Miller referred to in the preceding footnote and taken up by others of the authors referred to there. This is the postulate that under certain *ceteris paribus* conditions, referring mainly to the absence of taxes and to assumed perfection in the securities markets, the average cost of capital to the firm, here written as k, can be regarded as a constant. If this position is taken, interest can be centered in the following deduction from the definitions in the text: $\rho = (O - F)/V$, whence it can be shown that $\rho = k + (k - r)B/V$. Now if it is assumed that k is constant, and this postulate is insisted upon (possibly on the basis of some assumed securities market arbitrage such as Modigliani and Miller also envisaged) in the face of a rising cost of debt function, it can be shown that institutional arrangements may well exist that require, logically, a diminishing rate of increase in the equity cost function as the leverage ratio B/V increases, and ultimately, for a very high leverage ratio, the equity cost function may even decline. The unsatisfactory state of the literature which depends on these positions is summarized elegantly in Robichek and Myers, *op. cit.* We therefore confine our attention to the development of the different and, it is thought, more productive perspectives indicated in the text. A further discussion is contained in Douglas Vickers, "Elasticity of Capital Supply, Monopsonistic Discrimination and Optimum Capital Structure," *Journal of Finance*, vol. 22, pp. 1–9, March, 1967.

The question now is similar to that previously confronted in a different context. Is it possible, from the viewpoint of the definitional framework based on the market valuations of securities, to indicate solution conditions describing the optimum capital structure of the firm? For this purpose we may consider again Equation (4-55), this time in the form

$$kW = rB + \rho V \tag{4-56}$$

The general differential equation derived from this expression may be written as follows:

$$k \, dW + W \, dk = r \, dB + B \, dr + \rho \, dV + V \, d\rho \tag{4-57}$$

Now it may be imagined that a capital structure could be said to be optimum if it involved those amounts of debt and equity capital, at those debt and equity costs, which permitted the maximization of the total market value of the enterprise, here interpreted as the total market value of the firm's capital securities.[5] If we consider an optimization condition in these terms on the basis of differential Equation (4-57), we may set both dW and dk equal to zero, for at the maximum attainable value of W the optimization condition is satisfied, and at the debt-equity structure that brings this about no changes in W or k will be envisaged.

Making these substitutions and replacing dV by $-dB$ as debt is substituted for equity (given the level of total capital employed and therefore the level of total income), Equation (4-57) may be transformed as follows:

$$\rho \, dB = r \, dB + B \, dr + V \, d\rho \tag{4-58}$$

whence

$$\rho = r + B\frac{dr}{dB} - V\frac{d\rho}{dV} \tag{4-59}$$

---

[5] A note on terminology will be useful at this point. The literature which adopts the perspectives from which our text is now developing new partial equilibrium theorems usually refers to the total market value of the firm as meaning the total market value of the firm's capital securities. We have therefore adopted the same terminology for clarity at this point. But it will be clear from the general orientation of this book, and become doubly meaningful in the subsequent development of the optimization models, that for us the total value of the firm means the total value of the ownership of the firm. We therefore refer to this latter measure consistently — in the text at this point and in all other contexts — by the symbol V. We shall also argue consistently and simply that this value is what it is because the net income available for the owners is what it is, and is being capitalized at a required rate of return that takes account of the owners' attitudes to the risks inherent in the residual earnings stream. An alternative line of argument which derives the market value of the ownership, using the symbols at this point in our text, as a residual value defined by W-B, may be consulted in the literature cited in footnote 3 of this chapter.

By multiplying and dividing, at the points indicated, by r and ρ, Equation (4-59) may be transformed as follows:

$$\rho = r + r\left(\frac{B}{r}\frac{dr}{dB}\right) - \rho\left(\frac{V}{\rho}\frac{d\rho}{dV}\right) \qquad (4\text{-}60)$$

Again, analogously with Equation (4-48), the first term in parentheses in Equation (4-60) contains the elasticity of the debt cost with respect to changes in debt capital, and the second term in parentheses contains the elasticity of the equity cost with respect to the concomitant changes in equity capital. Referring to these elasticities as E_r and E_ρ respectively, the optimization solution condition we are seeking resolves, analogously with Equation (4-50), to

$$\rho = r\left(\frac{1 + E_r}{1 + E_\rho}\right) \qquad (4\text{-}61)$$

The difference between Equation (4-50) and Equation (4-61) is that the first indicates an optimization condition in terms of a ratio of i/r on the one hand and elasticities E_D and E_K, on the basis of book value measures, on the other. Equation (4-61) presents analogous propositions in terms of ρ/r, employing the equity capitalization rate rather than the rate of return on the book value of the equity, and E_r and E_ρ, or elasticities couched in terms of market valuations rather than book values of securities.[6]

If we examine either of the elasticity or earnings rates ratios, it is seen that it is necessary, for a tenable specification of an optimization condition, that the value of E_K (or E_ρ) be of absolute value less than unity (given the expectation, consistent with our initial risk aversion assumptions, that its value will be negative). Taking Equation (4-61), for example, if this condition is not satisfied, the right-hand side of the equation takes on a negative value, a nonsense result in the context of the conditions necessary for a minimum value of k or a maximum value of W. But this statement itself leads to two observations: First, the absolute value of the E_ρ measure can be expected to take on such large values only when the leverage ratio is quite high and when equity costs react very sharply to changes in the relative importance of the amount of equity at work in the firm; and second, the solution condition specified in this context in terms of elasticities suggests that the optimum capital structure as here envisaged (minimum k) will in fact occur before such a high leverage ratio is reached.

[6]We shall return to the interpretation of this equilibrium condition in Chapter 10 after we have developed sufficient tools of analysis to see its significance in the context of the *optimum optimorum* structure of the firm.

This last condition can be seen most readily as follows. Equation (4-58) can be written in the following form:

$$\rho = r + B\frac{dr}{dB} + V\frac{d\rho}{dB} \qquad (4\text{-}62)$$

The first two terms on the right-hand side of Equation (4-62) describe the marginal direct cost of borrowing, or, referring to Equation (4-52), $d(rB)/dB$. The final term on the right-hand side of Equation (4-62) contains the rate of increase in the equity capitalization rate as debt capital is increased. As previously argued on the assumption of risk aversion in the securities markets, this can in general be expected to take on a positive value. Thus the same equilibrium conditions that satisfy the requirement of minimum k also give us the condition that ρ must be greater than the marginal direct cost of borrowing. But granted that this marginal cost of borrowing must exceed the average interest rate on the debt r, the solution conditions also imply that ρ will be greater than r. Importing this conclusion back into Equation (4-61), the solution condition of ρ greater than r requires that the expression in parentheses must have a positive value. This, however, is effectively bounding the capital structure to a debt-equity ratio at which the absolute value of E_ρ must be less than unity.

Elasticities and Monopsonistic Discrimination

More important for our present purposes than the estimation of *de facto* magnitudes involved in the foregoing relationships is the nature of the logical causation implicit in them. Take, for example, the elasticity relationship just envisaged. It is not necessary to digress to the problem of its empirical estimation to see clearly the following significance. If, on the basis of Equation (4-61) or (4-50), the managers of a firm can so discriminate against the suppliers of debt funds—for example by specifying terms, covers, covenants, etc., attaching to parcels of debt — as to prevent the average cost of debt capital from rising as rapidly as might otherwise be the case, they will be successfully practicing what we shall refer to as monopsonistic discrimination. By doing so they will effectively be holding down the elasticity of the debt cost function. If this is accomplished, then for any given equity cost function and its implicit elasticities at various capital structures the terms in parentheses Equations (4-50) and (4-61) will tend to be held to lower values, and a larger amount of low cost debt may be able to be introduced into the capital structure before the critical i/r or ρ/r relation is reached. To the extent that this can be accomplished by the kind of discrimination we have referred to, corresponding benefits will accrue to the equity owners, whose economic position we are seeking consistently to optimize.

The question of monopsonistic borrowing has not been thoroughly examined in the economic-financial literature, nor integrated into the factors determining the firm's optimizing decision.[7] It might be of interest, therefore, to recall that Hicks made the point two decades ago that

> each particular borrower thus finds himself confronted with a sort of "supply curve for loan capital." . . . There is no reason to suppose that this curve will be perfectly elastic . . . . This consideration introduces into the theory of interest questions analogous to those which have been discussed by writers on Imperfect Competition . . . . Thus the complications of the financial structure of firms seem to be largely due to attempts at discrimination on the capital market.

And although Hicks moves his analysis at that point to different issues, he perceptively remarks that "we must not allow these matters to slip our minds altogether."[8]

[7] Some consideration is given to the question in Albert G. Hart, *Anticipations, Uncertainty, and Dynamic Planning*, The University of Chicago Press, Chicago, 1940, and in Sune Carlson, *A Study on the Pure Theory of Production*, published in Stockholm, 1939, republished by Augustus M. Kelley, *Reprints of Economic Classics*, New York, 1965. A fuller and interesting geometrical treatment appears in Eli Schwartz, "Theory of the Capital Structure of the Firm," *Journal of Finance*, vol. 14, pp. 18–39, March, 1959.
[8] J. R. Hicks, *Value and Capital*, Clarendon Press, Oxford, 1946, p. 144.

5

Partial Optimization:

Asset Investments

The discussion in the preceding chapter of the sources of money capital available to the firm was related directly to the structure of the liabilities side of the balance sheet and to the stability of the income-earning ability as reflected in the income statement. We shall consider in this chapter some aspects of the assets side of the balance sheet, or of the solution to the firm's investment problem that lies behind the income-earning process. As in the case of the liabilities, or sources of money capital, we shall not be concerned here primarily with detailed accounting classifications or with institutional arrangements. Again, technical financial and business literature abounds in this area. On the contrary, our concern again will be with the logical issues involved in determining whether investment in particular assets is economically worthwhile; whether criteria are available for deciding which assets or subset of assets from among those involved in potential investment opportunities form an optimum set of investment commitments; and how any such investment commitments may, in conjunction with the existing structure of the firm and its income-generating potential, conduce toward the consistent objective of optimizing the economic position of the owners.[1]

---

[1] The detail passed over in the text, as well as some excellent discussions in the area of capital budgeting, may be found in the following selections from an extensive literature: Harold Bierman and Seymour Smidt, *The Capital Budgeting Decision*, 2d ed., The Macmillan Company, New York, 1966; A. J. Merrett and Allen Sykes, *The Finance and Analysis of Capital Projects*, John Wiley & Sons, Inc., New York, 1963; Ezra Solomon (ed.), *The Management of Corporate Capital*, The Free Press of Glencoe, New York, 1959; J. Fred Weston and Eugene F. Brigham, *Managerial Finance*, 2d ed., Holt, Rinehart and Winston, Inc., New York, 1966; Robert W. Johnson, *Financial Management*, 3d ed., Allyn and Bacon, Inc., Boston, 1966; James T. S. Porterfield, *Investment De-*

Analogously with our remarks regarding the items on the liabilities side of the balance sheet, the following observations on possible investments in assets can at best point toward a partial or first approximation set of optimization conditions. For we are not yet in a position to say anything of a thoroughgoing nature regarding the way in which the firm's decisions on investment in assets are linked with its decision regarding the optimum combination of productive factor inputs. And it is finally the input factor requirements that determine the need for, and the optimum structure of, the firm's investment in assets.

The remarks in this chapter on asset investments will therefore take up only some of the main headings under which this subject area has been traditionally discussed. Our objective is that of providing at this stage a tentative application of some of the thought forms we have already developed and also of clarifying the principal points of departure for our subsequent work. Certainly it is a shallow approximation, if not a complete betrayal of the empirical relevance of microeconomic theory, to endeavor to tie the elements of the optimization problem together in any such manner as the following: "Each proposed investment has associated with it a proposed source of financing. . . . It is the combined cash flows of the project and its funds source that are relevant to the acceptance decision."[2] Quite to the contrary, we shall argue that the attempt to tie specific financing operations to specific investment commitments is the precise theoretical maneuver best calculated to sidetrack the hoped-for integration of analysis. For the availability of funds at any time will not be independent of the structure of fund sources already being used by the firm, nor of the economic characteristics of the investments already made, and about to be made, by the firm.

But the temptation for theoretical analysis to associate specific financing and specific investing seems to have been very strong, and has marred some of the best work on the financing of the firm. Thus Beranek, following an earlier lead of H. V. Roberts, argues firmly:

Normally a firm is confronted with several borrowing alternatives. Therefore, the small project's payoffs would be adjusted to reflect *each* alternative financing proposal. Hence, for a given project we would have as many adjusted payoff streams as borrowing alternatives for financing the project. A combination of a project and a financing proposal we shall call a *project finance*. Its purpose is to assure the analyst that the effects of the proposed financing of the proposed project are fully

---

cisions and Capital Costs, Prentice-Hall, Inc., Englewood Cliffs, N.J., 1965; William Beranek, *Working Capital Management*, Wadsworth Publishing Company, Inc., Belmont, Calif. 1966; G. David Quirin, *The Capital Expenditure Decision*, Richard D. Irwin, Inc., Homewood, Ill, 1967.
[2] Porterfield, *op. cit.*, pp. 70–71.

reflected in the payoffs to be discounted . . . . We must prepare a project-finance combination which reflects each of these sources in combination with the given project.[3]

Again, the path-breaking work of Smith is marred by an ambiguity in this matter, and his attempt to achieve what he refers to as "a unified theory of production and investment" falters at this point.[4] The seriousness of Smith's failure to grasp and develop clearly the relevance of finance theory to production and investment theory will become clearer in what follows, as the dependence of parts of our own work on some of his insights and theoretical constructs is recognized.

In a word, then, we have thus emphasized one particular direction of development taken by the analysis of the firm's optimization problems in order to place in the sharpest possible relief the following postulate. The total supply of money capital funds available to the firm must be looked upon as constituting a pool of investable resources, the supply conditions of which are described by the equity and debt capital cost functions we have already employed. The magnitudes of the determinant variables in these functions depend, it has already been seen, on the expected values and risk characteristics of the income streams of the firm, and indirectly, therefore, on the nature of the investments being made. The way in which the availability and cost of capital are to be introduced into the problem solving is to regard the supply of money capital funds as a constraint variable, to be specified and incorporated as part of a larger constrained optimization model. Then the ways in which the pressure or severity of the money capital availability constraint will influence the firm's planning solution outcomes will depend on the forms of the supply functions as already envisaged, and on the levels at which they confront the firm in the external capital market. Further development of the issue at this stage, however, would be premature. It is sufficient to say that for the present we shall speak of investment in specific assets without trying to tie in with it any specific financing, and we shall return to the investment-financing relationship in the following chapters.

The Asset Forms

Given the partial and incomplete nature of the optimization propositions that we can deduce from this initial look at the assets side of the balance sheet, we can nevertheless consider some of the factors determining the amounts that might be held in different asset forms. Reference to the

[3] William Beranek, *Analysis for Financial Decisions*, Richard D. Irwin, Inc., Homewood, Ill., 1963, p. 128. Italics in original.
[4] Vernon L. Smith, *Investment and Production*, Harvard University Press, Cambridge, Mass., 1961, pp. vii, 163.

pro forma balance sheet in Chapter 3 indicates that for structural analysis the total asset investment may be divided into two main sections: first, current assets containing varying degrees of liquidity, the principal categories among which are cash (including near-cash items such as short-term marketable securities in which temporarily surplus cash has been invested), accounts receivable, and inventories; and second, the fixed assets, sometimes referred to as capital assets. (The latter term, however, may be misleading, by tending to conceal the fact that money capital is required to finance investment in liquid funds, in the same way as it is needed to finance investment in fixed assets.)

An essential difference in asset forms is found in the fact that among the fixed assets of the firm are those assets whose durability, or expected economic life, extends over more than one accounting or operating period. It is the phenomenon of varying durabilities among the fixed assets that gives rise to the difficult problem of accounting properly for the assets' periodic depreciation.

Current Asset Investments

It is beyond our present scope to give a detailed analysis of the forces determining the desirable amounts of the firm's investments in cash, receivables and inventories.[5] On the basis of our discussion in Chapter 3 of the circular flow of values through the enterprise (the cash flow reflection or counterpart of the successive transformation of assets), the average permanent size of the firm's investment in cash will depend on the efficiency with which operating management is supervising and controlling the underlying cash flow forces: credit sales and collections, discounts and time payment terms, deployment of temporary cash surpluses, etc. It will be clear that underinvestment in cash (too low an average permanent cash or near-cash balance, particularly if this is associated with less than effective periodic cash flow budgeting) and overinvestment in cash are both undesirable. Underinvestment in cash may lead to liquidity strains and even, if the timing of the cash inflows and outflows diverges seriously and unexpectedly when temporary borrowing facilities are not available, to financial embarrassment, technical insolvency, or bankruptcy proceedings. Overinvestment in cash may also be a result of inefficient operating management, but the effect may be disguised by the comfortable liquidity cushion it provides.

In short, efficient management of the investment in cash can make an important contribution to the overall objective of optimizing the owners' economic position. But the liquidity crisis that may result from too little

---

[5] Valuable detailed discussions are available in Beranek, *Working Capital Management*, and *Analysis for Financial Decisions*.

cash is not as well disguised as the suboptimum overinvestment in cash, which diverts too much of the firm's investable resources away from more directly income-generating forms.

The forces determining the firm's necessary and optimum investment in cash can be subsumed under the general heading of the transactions motive, or the need to hold a certain amount of cash in relation to the size of the periodic transactions being financed. At certain times cash may be accumulated also in anticipation of capital investment outlays, or such infrequent operations as debt retirement, and (hopefully more frequently) dividend distributions. In the case of the business firm, accordingly, the size of the cash requirements can be expected to bear some definable relation to the total gross sales of the firm, taking the latter as an indication of the firm's level of operations. The higher the level of operations the larger will be the cushion of cash required to take care of the discontinuities between the timing of operating cash inflows and outflows.[6]

The firm's investment in receivables, similarly, will depend on its volume of sales, given the complex of operating forces determining its credit granting and collections policies. The structure of debtors' payments habits, the stability of sales, the time lags of payments behind sales, the stability of credit arrangements and terms of sales — all such factors will contribute to the relation between sales and the investment in accounts receivable. And again, as with the more liquid assets, we note that the capital funds necessary to finance the firm's investment in receivables must be part of the total funds described on the liabilities side of the balance sheet. Moreover, increases or decreases in fund requirements for this purpose must similarly affect the manner in which the firm's total money capital availability constraint can also make funds available for fixed assets and other investments.

Finally in connection with the firm's investment in current assets, it can be imagined also that the average permanent holdings of inventories of various kinds — raw materials, work in progress, and finished commodities — will be similarly related in some definable fashion to the level of operations of the firm.[7] Again the same kind of pressures on available money

---

[6] See Paul Davidson, "Keynes's Finance Motive," *Oxford Economic Papers*, vol. 17, pp. 47–65, March, 1965; William J. Baumol, "The Transactions Demand for Cash: An Inventory Theoretic Approach," *Quarterly Journal of Economics*, vol. 66, pp. 545–556, November, 1952; James Tobin, "The Interest Elasticity of Transactions Demand for Cash," *Review of Economics and Statistics*, vol. 38, pp. 241–247, August, 1956; Johnson, *op. cit.*, pp. 118–119; and William J. Frazer, "Firms' Demands for Money: The Evidence from the Cross-section Data," *Federal Reserve Bulletin*, vol. 53, p. 16, January, 1967.

[7] A large literature exists on inventory investment and management policies. For an introduction see Beranek, *Working Capital Management*, chaps. 5 and 6, and William Baumol, *Economic Theory and Operations Analysis*, 2d ed., Prentice-Hall, Inc., Englewood Cliffs, N.J., chap. 1, and references cited in both these sources.

capital supplies will emanate from this source also. In connection with these various demands on capital resources for investment in cash, receivables, and inventories, nothing definitive can be said on an a priori basis regarding the form of all the associated demands for money capital functions. As with many of the functions we have discussed and shall be introducing as we proceed, these must be subject to empirical estimation by the firm's decision makers for incorporation into a generalized optimization decision nexus. But some a priori suggestions as to probable forms can be made.

It might be imagined, for example, that the transactions demand for cash will be a monotonically rising but concave-downward function of the volume of output or level of operations of the firm. Particularly is this likely to be the case if the firm is producing and selling in an imperfectly competitive environment and if its total sales revenue is increasing in less than direct proportion with its sales volume. If the sales revenue is taken as the determinant variable in the demand for cash, the general form of the demand function just suggested may be posited, since it is unlikely that the need for cash to cover liquidity requirements due to the irregularities and discontinuities in cash flows will increase proportionately with the volume of total revenue.

Under certain plausible assumptions as to the nature of the cash flows it can be shown that the transactions cash requirements may increase proportionately with the square root of the level of sales.[8] This proposition is analogous to the corresponding statement frequently made with reference to the optimum size of investment in inventory as changes occur in the level of sales. Here again the demand for funds for inventory investment may be envisaged as described by a monotonically rising, concave-downward function. It will be useful to look at this a little more closely, and indicate how the solution outcome of the model may be affected by varying degrees of competition in the inventory commodity markets.

At the detailed operational level, or at a lower level of particularization than we are primarily concerned with in the general theses of this book, we can look at the demand for inventory stocks in the following terms. We shall employ the following notation:

S = firm's annual volume of commodity sales
P = purchase price per unit of inventory
Q = optimum order quantity, or size of each inventory purchase order
i = rate of interest on funds invested in inventory stocks
a = fixed costs per annum of ordering inventory
b = variable ordering costs per inventory order

It follows that the number of inventory stock purchases during the

<hr>

[8] See Baumol's "The Transactions Demand for Cash: An Inventory Theoretic Approach."

year will be given by S/Q. If the assumption is made that inventory stocks are depleted at a uniform rate during the year, the average stock on hand will be one-half the amount acquired at each purchase date, or $Q/2$. At a unit purchase price of P, the average value of the investment in inventory will be $PQ/2$, and at the indicated interest rate, the annual carrying cost of this investment will be given as

$$Ca = \frac{iPQ}{2} \qquad (5\text{-}1)$$

Given the number of times inventory is purchased during the year, the total annual ordering cost of inventory may be described as

$$C_o = a + \frac{bS}{Q} \qquad (5\text{-}2)$$

The total annual costs of the inventory investment can thus be regarded as the sum of the carrying costs and ordering costs:

$$C = a + \frac{bS}{Q} + \frac{iPQ}{2} \qquad (5\text{-}3)$$

Differentiating Equation (5-3) with respect to the order quantity to ascertain the purchase size that minimizes the total annual inventory costs, it follows that

$$\frac{dC}{dQ} = -\frac{bS}{Q^2} + \frac{iP}{2} \qquad (5\text{-}4)$$

This expression yields, for minimum total cost,

$$Q = \sqrt{\frac{2bS}{iP}} \qquad (5\text{-}5)$$

It follows that the optimum size of each inventory purchase, and thus the average stock of inventory, varies directly as does the square root of the firm's total sales volume, given the levels of the parameters in the model. That the inventory order size indicated here yields a minimum total cost is confirmed by the usual second-order conditions, which can be seen by taking the second derivative of Equation (5-3).

If now it were the case that the purchase price per unit of inventory commodity were a function of the quantity purchased, say a declining function owing to the availability of quantity discounts from the purchase price, we may specify, for illustrative purposes, a price function of the general form $p = \alpha - \beta Q$. The total annual inventory cost now appears as

$$C = a + \frac{bS}{Q} + \frac{ip(Q)Q}{2} \qquad (5\text{-}6)$$

Differentiating with respect to order size then yields

$$\frac{dC}{dQ} = -\frac{bS}{Q^2} + \frac{i}{2}\left(p + Q\frac{dp}{dQ}\right) \tag{5-7}$$

If Equation (5-7) is set equal to zero and rearranged to yield the usual optimization condition, the following relation is obtained:

$$Q^3\frac{dp}{dQ} + pQ^2 = \frac{2bS}{i} \tag{5-8}$$

We may introduce into Equation (5-8) the price function posited above and derive the following expression:

$$\alpha Q^2 - 2\beta Q^3 = \frac{2bS}{i} \tag{5-9}$$

Equation (5-9) may then be solved for Q by the usual mathematical methods.

Alternatively, Equation (5-9) may be rearranged to read

$$Q^2(\alpha - 2\beta Q) = \frac{2bS}{i} \tag{5-10}$$

and this may be rewritten in a seemingly more complex form as

$$Q^2(\alpha - \beta Q - \beta Q) = Q^2\left(p + Q\frac{dp}{dQ}\right) = \frac{2bS}{i} \tag{5-11}$$

Equation (5-11) may then be written in the equivalent form

$$wQ^2 = \frac{2bS}{i} \tag{5-12}$$

where the term in parentheses in Equation (5-11) is written as w. But if the selling price function of the inventory commodity is declining in the manner posited, w may be taken as describing the marginal revenue function relative to the selling price function the seller is offering and against which the buyer is optimizing. At the solution value of the order quantity, this marginal revenue magnitude will of course be less than the unit selling price.

Solving Equation (5-12) for Q yields

$$Q = \sqrt{\frac{2bS}{iw}} \tag{5-13}$$

The optimum order quantity, and thus the optimum inventory stock, is seen to be related in the same manner to the variables previously indicated, and negatively related to the size of w. But the size of w depends on how sharply the inventory purchase or selling price function declines. For rapid declines, or for a large absolute value of β in the price function, the smaller will be the value of w. The larger therefore will be the solution value of Q. In a word, inventory stock will be higher, the better or more attractive the price discounts for quantity purchases.

The Working Capital Requirements

Our purpose in generating the foregoing inventory investment model was not primarily to consider its operational details as such. Reverting to our prior propositions on current asset investments, our main concern has been to indicate the manner in which a priori awareness of the principal relations involved, together with appropriate empirical investigations and testing on the part of management, may lead to a specification of the way in which the requisite funds for investment in current operating assets may be determined. It will be sufficient for our own purposes in subsequent chapters, provided the general nature of the causal determinants is understood, to specify a positive functional relation between the level of the firm's operations and its current asset requirements. It will be convenient, moreover, without impairing the generality of the analysis, to recognize also that as the level of operations increases, a larger amount of funds may become available to the firm from the current liabilities section of the balance sheet. This effect may be most directly observable if part of the increased inventory requirements at higher output levels is in fact financed by carrying a larger average amount of accounts payable on the balance sheet. In that case creditors will be contributing more funds to the business, leaving a smaller net increase in investable fund requirements to be provided from cash flows, either internally generated or obtained from additional external sources.

If we bring together the functional relations between changes in output levels on the one hand and increases in both current assets and current liabilities on the other, we can rearrange the balance sheet in a condensed form as follows:

TABLE 7

Assets (or capital fund requirements)	
Current assets	xxx
Less Current liabilities	xxx
Net working capital requirements	xxx
Fixed assets	xxx
Total assets	xxx
Liabilities	
Permanent capital fund sources	xxx

It now appears on the basis of Table 7 that the permanent capital fund sources of the firm, or what we have referred to in previous discussions simply as debt and equity capital respectively, can be regarded as required for two principal purposes: first, investment in the firm's net working capital requirements; and second, the financing of fixed asset investments. Our interest at present centers in the first of the uses, the provision of working capital funds. Reshaping the traditional definition of working capital, which is usually referred to as current assets less current liabilities, we can change the focus of analysis from the requirements side to the financing side of the balance sheet, and describe the firm's working capital as that part of current assets financed from permanent sources.

The form in which the working capital requirements will be incorporated into our subsequent optimization models can be summarized as follows. Taking W as referring to net working capital requirements as shown in Table 7 and writing p_i and Q_i respectively for the selling price and the sales volumes of the firm's product outputs, we have

$$W = f\left(\sum_i p_i Q_i \right) \tag{5-14}$$

This function will in due course be incorporated into a total money capital requirement function, and without specifying the form of the relationship in Equation (5-14) at this time, we can bear in mind the a priori reasons we noted for supposing that some concavity may well appear in actual fact.

Fixed Asset Investments

We must consider finally the firm's investments in fixed assets. It is at this point that the divergence of our work from traditional constructs will be seen to emerge most sharply. In the enterprise optimization model that we shall construct in the following chapters, the firm's demand for, and usage of, fixed assets will be tied in firmly and directly to the form of its production function and to the technological possibilities of substitutions between the factors represented by the arguments in that function. The larger or smaller the degree of capital intensity of the factor capacities being used by the firm, the greater or less will be the necessary fixed asset investments and therefore the money capital requirements of the firm. The existing and usual analysis, on the other hand, allows the firm's demand for fixed assets to emerge indirectly and by implication from its decisions as to the acceptability of the various investment projects presented to it. Little attention has yet been given, in the development of the traditional project analysis, to the question of a possible interdependence between the earnings of the various individual projects, or between the projects on the one hand and the previously existing firm on the other.[9] A good many methodological and statistical difficulties lie in the way of the kind of interdependence analysis that must be envisaged if the project analysis approach to enterprise optimization is to be extended significantly. For this and other reasons that will emerge, we are proposing that a halt be called to the complete reliance on the project or project-set analysis, at least for purposes of optimum enterprise planning.

In its place we suggest that a direct and frontal attack be made on the overall question of what the total structure of the enterprise should be. In this new attack on the optimization problem, the individual project possibilities available to the firm will become more important as determining the range of possible outputs, production techniques or production functions, and input combinations that the decision makers in the firm should consider in moving toward their optimum structural plan. The project possibilities will thus enter the planning analysis indirectly, by influencing the possible forms of the several underlying and determinant functions on which the enterprise planning decision depends. And then, in the implementation of the optimum enterprise plan as adopted, the features that come to light initially as project possibilities will serve as guidelines for the management at the operational level. But to adopt a piecemeal approach and endeavor to build up to an optimum enterprise structure by adding together a set of separate projects is sidetracking economic analysis by starting at the wrong end.

Project Analysis

This having been said, it will be profitable to conclude this chapter with a brief look at the traditional project analysis, principally for the light it will throw on our subsequent and broader argument. The question of economic worthwhileness, or the acceptability of possible investment commitments, has usually been settled by one of two basic decision criteria: (1) Either the present capitalized value of the stream of benefits expected to be generated by the project is calculated and compared with the amount of capital funds it would be necessary to commit to the project; or (2) the implicit rate of return expected to be generated by the project is computed, for comparison with the cost of raising the capital funds to finance the project.[10] To indicate the essential logic of these approaches we employ the following notation:

---

[9] Some attempts have been made to build on the promising beginnings of a more robust portfolio optimization analysis made by Harry M. Markowitz, *Portfolio Selection*, John Wiley & Sons, Inc., New York, 1959. See also Donald E. Farrar, *The Investment Decision under Uncertainty*, Prentice-Hall, Inc., Englewood Cliffs, N.J., 1962, and references there cited.

[10] The literature already cited in this chapter, particularly that in footnote 1, contains a full development of the work done in this direction, and the remarks in our text therefore make no attempt to be exhaustive.

S_t = expected cash flow properly attributable to the project in time period t
n = number of years in the expected economic life of the project
r = firm's cost of capital
i = a riskless rate of interest
k = expected true rate of profit in the project
V = economic value, or present capitalized value, of the project
C = required total capital outlay on the project
S_t^* = certainty equivalent of the project's expected cash flow in time period t

The following formulas and propositions will take up many of the thought forms laid down in Chapters 1 through 3, and these accordingly will not require detailed comment at this stage. We shall pass over the first approximation of the so-called certainty model frequently encountered in the literature and discuss briefly the several ways in which a fully risk-adjusted decision model may be developed. It is necessary, however, to note the fuller definitions of the variables involved.

First, the periodic cash flow S_t is to be regarded as the enterprise net incremental cash flow properly attributable to the project being examined. Logically it is derived by considering the total enterprise cash flow which, it is expected, would be generated if the project under consideration were adopted, and then deducting from this the similarly computed cash flow which would be generated if the project were not undertaken. The connotation of enterprise cash flows was indicated at some length in Chapter 3. Care should be taken, in interpreting and applying the concept to the estimation of a project's net incremental cash flow, to work with the cash flow before deduction of depreciation and financing costs. The reason for this will emerge in what follows.

Second, the firm's cost of capital, here designated r, should be understood as a risk-adjusted discount factor, the kind of variable referred to in our ρ function examined previously, or, in the case where the firm employs a levered capital structure, the weighted average cost of capital also examined previously. In the latter case the separate capital costs incorporated in the weighted average will themselves be risk-adjusted capitalization rates. The risk-adjusted cost of capital is thus an opportunity cost concept, indicating the investors' required rate of return on security holdings having a degree of risk equal to that contemplated in the investment project now in view or in the total enterprise of which the project forms a part.

Third, the required capital outlay on the project, here designated C, must take account of all necessary expenditures that have to be made to bring the project to operational or income-earning condition. It is comprised of three elements: (1) the cost of acquiring the fixed assets necessary to implement the project; (2) the installation expenses necessarily incurred prior to the operational date, and properly attributable to the project; and (3) the value of the firm's incremental investment in current assets which has to be made in order to maintain the project in continuous operation and income-earning condition. To put the investment criterion in one of its forms, the income stream generated by the project must be sufficiently large to give an acceptable rate of return on all the expenditures incurred under these three heads.

The Rate of Profit Criterion

The logic of this project decision model can best be clarified by comparing the total capital outlay on the one hand and the expected stream of net periodic cash inflows on the other. It is important to grasp at this point an important feature of the cash flow argument. In order to be able to say that the project is economically worthwhile, the cash flow stream must be large enough to enable it to accomplish two distinct and logically separable objectives. First, it must provide a sufficiently large contribution to an annual amortization or "return of capital" fund, so that the fund, when reinvested at an appropriate annual rate of growth, will accumulate, by the terminal date of the project, to the amount of the initial capital investment. Second, the cash flow must, in addition, provide an acceptable rate of return per annum on the initial investment in the project. Only if the cash flow stream is sufficiently robust to accomplish both these requirements can the following necessary statement be made at the terminal date of the project: Not only has the desired rate of return been earned on the project throughout its economic life, but the capital value of the initial investment has been maintained intact. It is for this reason that the cash flows incorporated in the model must be computed before the accountant's usual deduction for depreciation. The periodic cash flow S_t should therefore be regarded as made up of (1) a "return-of-capital" component and (2) a "true residual income" component.

Concretely, and employing familiar notation, we may write

$$C = \sum_{t=1}^{n} S_t(1 + k)^{-t} + J_n(1 + k)^{-n} \tag{5-15}$$

where the solution value of k represents the true rate of profit on the project. Alternatively it may be referred to as the project's internal rate of return. Formally, the true rate of profit in the project is that discount factor which will equate the present discounted value of the future expected cash flows to the total capital outlay on the project. The expected liquidation value of the project at its terminal date is referred to as J_n in Equation (5-15). This will in general include at least the nondepreciable portion of the current asset investments included in the total capital outlay on the project.

If for simplicity we assume that this terminal value is zero and that the periodic cash flow is constant, the solution value for k may be written as

$$k = \frac{S}{C} - \frac{S}{C}\left(\frac{1}{1+k}\right)^n \qquad (5\text{-}16)$$

For projects of longer economic lives, or as n in Equation (5-16) increases, the true rate of profit approaches asymptotically the value of S/C. This, in turn, will be recognized as the reciprocal of the project's payoff period. The latter, or C/S, is the number of years it would take for the project's cumulative annual cash flow to aggregate to the initial capital investment.

The Reinvestment Assumption

More problems arise in the interpretation of this model than it is desired or necessary to examine for our present purposes (problems of possible multiple solution values for k, problems in comparing and ranking projects of different economic lives, etc).[11] We shall concentrate at this point on only one issue and be concerned solely with what is known as the reinvestment rate assumption. We do this not only because some lack of clarity frequently surrounds the recognition and interpretation of this assumption, but also because this again provides an important linkage, or contrast, with the different conceptualization in the models that follow. The point at issue can be summarized by saying that the solution value of k in Equation (5-15) or (5-16) can in fact be called a true rate of profit only if a crucial assumption or condition is satisfied. This condition is that the previously indicated "return of capital" components of the cash flow must be able to be reinvested at the same cumulative annual rate of return as k, the rate of profit in the original project.

Consider for the moment that k is in this rigorous sense a true rate of profit. Then the true residual income generated by the investment must be able to be regarded as k percent of the original capital committed to it. Taking kC, therefore, as a measure of the true income component of the cash flow, the balance, or $(S - kC)$, must be regarded as the return-of-capital component available to preserve the original capital investment intact. If such an amount, $(S - kC)$, is reinvested at the end of the first year of the life of the project and accumulated at k percent per annum, its accumulated value at the terminal date of the project will be given by $(S - kC)$ $(1 + k)^{n-1}$. If all such annual reinvestment components were similarly

---

[11] Reference should be made to the fairly full discussions of related points in Bierman and Smidt, *op. cit.*, and in Solomon, *op. cit.*

accumulated, the condition it is desired to attain by the terminal date could be described as

$$C = \sum_{t=1}^{n} (S - kC)(1 + k)^{n-t} \qquad (5\text{-}17)$$

It can be shown by simple algebraic manipulation that the same value of k satisfies both Equations (5-16) and (5-17). If, therefore, there is reason to doubt that the periodic return of capital components of the cash flow can in fact be reinvested at as favorable a rate of return as appears to be earned on the original project, then in order to maintain the capital investment intact the annual return of capital components will have to be larger, the residual income component of the cash flow will accordingly be lower, and the true rate of profit on the project will be lower than was thought to be the case. The amount by which the true estimate of the rate of return must then be reduced will clearly depend on what can be regarded as a reasonable or attainable reinvestment rate assumption.

A Methodological Comment on the Model

It will be recalled from the preparatory conceptualization in Chapter 2 that the economic worthwhileness criteria in the optimization models we are constructing in this book do not depend on a rate of profit computation at all. Rather, we shall speak consistently in terms of capitalized values, or economic values, of alternative decisions or plans or enterprise structures. Moreover, having avoided the individual project approach, the successive annual components of the income streams that are capitalized in our models will not be defined as cash flows before deduction of the return of capital component as in the foregoing. We shall be dealing with a net residual income figure after a suitable allowance for the depreciation of durable assets has already been made. This, of course, raises the question as to how that suitable allowance for depreciation can be assessed. And though it is not appropriate to digress to a development of that point at this stage (for among other things we have not yet developed the necessary theory of optimum asset lives), it is useful to highlight this feature as an important difference, separating the following work from the project analysis we have here under review.[12]

---

[12] The methodological status of professional work in this whole area is best summed up by the titles of two most widely used books on the American and British sides of the Atlantic: Bierman and Smidt, *The Capital Budgeting Decision, Economic Analysis and Financing of Investment Projects,* and Merrett and Sykes, *The Finance and Analysis of Capital Projects.* Both books end their titles with an emphasis on the word "projects." Against this we argue not for a project approach but for a total enterprise structure approach.

But our attitude to the depreciation or return-of-capital question differs from that in the project analysis for a further reason. Our optimization models will be seen to envisage the planning problem of a firm setting out to produce an infinitely renewable income stream, or a flow of income which, subject to capital maintenance, can extend over an infinite time horizon. Our firm, like any going concern, is thus effectively an entity envisaged as having perpetual economic life. Particularly does this acquire enhanced empirical meaning if the firm is established as a legal corporation, in which the ownership is held in the form of nonredeemable or nonmaturing, and therefore effectively perpetual, shares of common stock. Analytically, moreover, the method of adjustment for depreciation and capital maintenance that we shall use in what follows, being based as it is on a theory of optimum asset lives, has the advantage of permitting each asset in the fixed asset section of the balance sheet to be subject to its own appropriate depreciation rate. All such depreciation or capital maintenance allowances based on the values of the optimum structure of assets will thus be deducted from the firm's gross income stream before the economic worthwhileness of the net income stream from the point of view of the owners is assessed.

The Project Value Criterion

We look now at the valuation aspects of the project approach to investment decisions. Using established notation and interpreting the periodic cash flows, and therefore the economic value of the project, as random variables, we have the basic expression

$$E(V) = \sum_{t=1}^{n} E(S_t)(1 + r)^{-t} \qquad (5\text{-}18)$$

If it can be assumed that the successive periodic cash flows are independent of each other, the capitalized value of the project can be interpreted as the weighted sum of a set of random variables, where each such random variable is an element of the cash flow stream and the weights attached to the elements are equal to the discount factor raised to the appropriate power, as in Equation (5-18). In such a special case, the longer the economic life of the project, or the larger the number of elements in the weighted sum, the more confidently we can rely on the underlying mathematical central limit theorem to produce a normal probability distribution of capitalized values of the project. Given, then, normality in the probability distribution of capitalized values and recognizing that we are thereby dealing with a two-parameter distribution, the entire probability distribution of the value of the project could be specified, provided we could specify also the variance of the expectation. Under the special conditions now being discussed, the following relation obtains:[13]

$$\mathrm{Var}(V) = \sum_{t=1}^{n} \mathrm{Var}(S_t)(1 + r)^{-2t} \qquad (5\text{-}19)$$

In many cases, however, it would be unrealistic to rely on the assumption of statistical independence between the successive components of the cash flow stream. In those cases, therefore, it would not be possible to derive information about the expected value and variance of the implied probability distribution of project values by the procedures of mathematical analysis just indicated. If, for example, a given period's cash flow depends on the cash flows achieved in preceding periods, then the successive cash flows can be described by a sequence of conditional probability distributions. In such an event there will be as many conditional probability distributions for a given period's cash flow as there are prior situations or outcomes upon which the given period's cash flow conditionally depends.[14]

Looking over the entire time horizon of the project, we may then build up a number of possible sequences of cash flows over the project life based on the management's assessment of the conditional probabilities involved. It will then be possible, by multiplying together the conditional probabilities for each successive year's outcome, to estimate the probabilities attaching to each possible sequence of cash flows or to indicate the probability that of all the possible cash flow sequences that could result from the project, any specific sequence will in fact be realized. In this way an entire probability distribution of project cash flow sequences may be described. And if each such sequence is then discounted back to its present value, we are again in possession of a probability distribution of capitalized values. The probability attaching to each possible capitalized value will, of course, be the calculated probability attaching to the cash flow sequence from which it was derived.

We leave aside the mathematics of the conditional probability approach just noted and refer the reader for this purpose to the literature already mentioned. It can be indicated also, but again not discussed in detail, that other methods, such as simulation techniques, can be employed to discover the probability distribution of present values inherent in an investment project proposal.[15]

---

[13] For the mathematics of this statement see Beranek, *Analysis for Financial Decisions*, p. 151, and Markowitz, *op. cit.*, chap. 4.

[14] See Beranek, *Analysis for Financial Decisions*, pp. 254f.

[15] See, for example, two articles by John F. Magee in the *Harvard Business Review*, "Decision Trees for Decision Making," July–August, 1964, and "How to Use Decision Trees in Capital Investment," September–October, 1964; also D. B. Hertz, "Risk Analysis in Capital Investment," *Harvard Business Review*, January–February, 1964; also Frederick S. Hillier, "The Derivation of Probabilistic Information for the Evaluation of Risky Investments," *Management Science*, April, 1963; and G. David Quirin, *The Capital Expenditure Decision*, Richard D. Irwin, Inc., Homewood, Ill., 1967.

Risk-adjusted Valuations

We recall now that in the discussion in Chapter 2 of the valuation of the enterprise income stream, the problem was confronted of obtaining a measure of the economic value of an undertaking, or a decision criterion based on economic values, which could be said to be fully adjusted not only for the decision maker's subjective time preference, but also for his subjective attitudes to the degree of risk in the undertaking. It cannot be emphasized too strongly that a thoroughly coherent and logical set of decision criteria must take full account of both these elements of the decision situation: the adjustment for time preference on the one hand and the adjustment for risk on the other. In connection now with the project analysis approach, it can be said in summary that, in the same way as in Chapter 2, there are three distinguishable methods of setting up the decision criteria to take account of both these adjustments.

First, there is the use again of a risk-adjusted discount factor, in this case a fully risk-adjusted cost of capital r, in which event the valuation model in Equation (5-18) applies. The expected value in this equation can then be compared with the proposed capital outlay on the project to determine its acceptability. A difficult logical problem, however, may exist in this method of project evaluation. For in this case the risk-adjustment reasoning may be circular. The capital costs entering into the discount factor, r, are presumably based upon the risk characteristics of the firm as a whole, to which the capital is being supplied. These very enterprise characteristics, however, may themselves be changed by the incorporation into the enterprise of the project whose value is currently being sought. But if the new project should change the total risk of the firm, thus logically pointing to the applicability of a different risk-adjusted discount factor, the true contribution of the project to the valuation of the enterprise may well be different from what it was thought to be when it was first assessed at the decision margin. The logic of this, it would therefore seem, is that a decision model such as that summarized in Equation (5-18) is applicable only when there is reason to believe that the risk status of the firm would not be changed if the particular project or projects under consideration should be adopted.

Hence the difficulties in the decision method just considered point to an alternative procedure. We recall for this purpose the argument underlying the construct in Figure 2 of Chapter 2. In brief, it would be possible to envisage, for each time period during the economic life of the project, an estimate of S_t, the period's cash flow, described by an expected value and a standard deviation as in the figure. Invoking again the indifference loci deriving from the assumed form of the decision maker's utility function, a certainty equivalent S_t^* of the period's expected cash flow could be specified. Having thus made an adjustment for risk in each separate time period, the risk-adjusted or certainty equivalent cash flows can then be reduced to a present capitalized value by discounting at a riskless rate of interest (again as specified more fully in Chapter 2). In this case the decision model assumes the form[16]

$$V^* = \sum_{t=1}^{n} S_t^*(1 + i)^{-t} \tag{5-20}$$

Third, there exists the possibility of discounting the actual cash flow expectations at a riskless rate of interest in accordance with the model

$$E(V) = \sum_{t=1}^{n} E(S_t)(1 + i)^{-t} \tag{5-21}$$

In this case, again analogously with the enterprise argument in Chapter 2, the future expectations are adjusted in Equation (5-21) only for time preference, a riskless discount factor having been employed in the equation. The second stage, or the adjustment for risk, therefore still remains to be accomplished. Hence it can be remarked that in this case we require not only the expected value, in the probabilistic sense, of the possible economic value of the project, but we really require information about the entire probability distribution of economic or capitalized values.

Without repeating argumentation needlessly, we may adduce at this point two implications of our earlier analysis. First, the probability distribution of capitalized values of the project can presumably be obtained in any one of the three ways previously discussed: (1) We may employ deduction from mathematical analysis to show that the expected value and variance of the project depend on the expected values and variances of the cash flow components. This will be particularly applicable in the case where statistical independence between the cash flow components permits the assumption of normality in the probability distribution of capitalized values. In this case the capitalized value is interpreted as a weighted sum of random cash flow components. (2) We may use the techniques of sequential conditional probability distributions in cases where periodic cash flows are conditional on previous periods' outcomes, and by that means we may derive a probability distribution of capitalized values from the probability distribution of cash flow sequences. (3) Finally we may employ techniques of project cash flow simulations. In addition, at any point at which the use of any of these

[16] For a perceptive comment on the relation between the first two models here referred to see Alexander A. Robichek and Stewart C. Myers, "Conceptual Problems in the Use of Risk-adjusted Discount Rates," *Journal of Finance*, vol. 21, pp. 727–730, December, 1966.

techniques requires the reduction of future values to present values, the reduction should be accomplished by discounting the future at a riskless rate of interest.

Using the project valuation procedure of the preceding paragraph, the decision maker will now be in possession of a probability distribution of the capitalized value of each project. The degree of risk in the project is implicitly represented in the dispersion of this probability distribution of values. Appealing, then, to a decision maker's utility function described over the single argument of wealth or economic values, such as exhibited in Figure 3 of Chapter 2, the expected utility of the project can be estimated by marrying the utility function with the probability distribution of value outcomes. The relevant propositions now appear in the following form:

$$E(U) = \sum_i p_i(V_i)U(V_i) \qquad (5\text{-}22)$$

or

$$E(U) = \int_V p(V)U(V)\, dV \qquad (5\text{-}23)$$

Equations (5-22) and (5-23) give alternative expressions for the expected utility of the project.

If the value argument in Equation (5-22) or (5-23) is a net present value, that is, the capitalized values of the project cash flows minus the the necessary capital investment outlay, the investment decision criterion can be put in the form

$$E(U) \gtreqless U(0) \qquad (5\text{-}24)$$

In this case the question is being asked whether the utility expected to result from the project is greater than the utility that attaches to a zero dollar outcome. If, on the other hand, the value argument in Equation (5-22) or (5-23) is a gross capitalized value of the project cash flows, it would be necessary to find what we previously called the certainty equivalent money value of the expected utility of the gross present values:

$$CE = f^{-1}[U]_{U=E(U)} \qquad (5\text{-}25)$$

In this event the investment decision criterion will take the following form:

$$(CE - C) \gtreqless 0 \qquad (5\text{-}26)$$

The question is then being asked whether the certainty equivalent money value is greater than the capital outlay needed on the project. The argument is summarized in Figure 4.

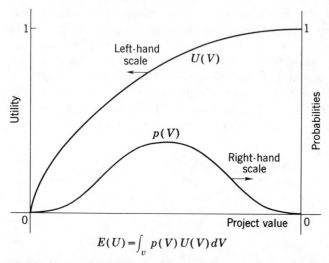

$$E(U) = \int_{v} p(V)\,U(V)\,dV$$

Figure 4. Expected utility of an investment project

The Optimum Set of Projects

Throughout the foregoing discussion, very little has been said about the problem of choosing the optimum set of investment projects from among the larger set of projects submitted to the firm for consideration. Little progress has been made in this direction.[17] But at least we might indicate, on the basis of the preceding analysis, the directions in which such further developments of the traditional project approach can be expected to point.

Let us imagine that in respect of each investment project presented to the firm's management for consideration we can specify (1) its expected true rate of profit, defined in the more careful sense referred to above and taking proper account of what might be the most reasonable reinvestment rate assumption to employ, and (2) a measure of the degree of risk in the project. The risk may be defined, say, in terms of the coefficient of variation (relative standard deviation) of the probability distribution of the economic value of the project, obtained in the same manner as indicated in our immediately preceding paragraphs and described in Figure 4. It would then be possible to conceive of an investment opportunity map, such as shown in Figure 5, where each cross represents the summary characteristics of a particular investment project. The coordinates of the cross refer to the

[17] Refer to the literature cited in footnotes 9 and 15.

project's expected return and measure of risk respectively. The curve OB represents the boundary of the firm's investment opportunity set, indicating the locus of the investment projects that offer the highest available returns for any given degree of risk, or the lowest attainable risks for any given level of returns.

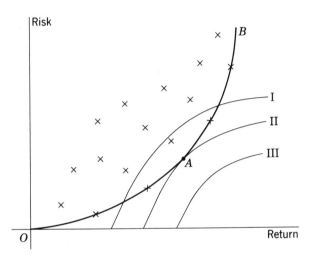

Figure 5. The enterprise investment plan

If, now, an analytical advance could be made (though this is one of the precise points at which, at the present time, a hiatus exists in the analysis) and if the investment opportunity map could be transformed from a map describing the risk and return characteristics of individual projects to one describing the risk and return characteristics of alternative total enterprise structures, the following step could be taken.

Given the decision maker's risk-return indifference map derived from his underlying utility function as previously argued and as shown in Figure 2 of Chapter 2, this can be superimposed on the opportunity map as in Figure 5 to ascertain the decision maker's preferred enterprise plan position. There is no need to reargue at this time the reasons why point A in Figure 5 represents the decision maker's optimum decision point.[18]

A Perspective on Traditional Analysis

It should be recalled that the purpose of the foregoing discussion has not been simply to adumbrate some of the principal logical forms of project evaluation and investment decision making. Our primary objective has

[18] Refer to the corresponding analysis in Chap. 2, and also to Friedrich Lutz and Vera Lutz, *The Theory of Investment of the Firm*, Princeton University Press, Princeton, N.J. 1951, pp. 190f.

been that of indicating the way in which the appearance and structure of the assets side of the firm's balance sheet will emerge as a logical by-product of the management's decisions as to which investment project or projects should be given expenditure approval. Thus we have completed as much of the exposition of the traditional capital budgeting analysis as is necessary for our present purposes.

We can now stand back and regard in fuller perspective the two different sets of piecemeal and partial approaches to the larger question of enterprise optimization that we have examined in this and the preceding chapters. First, we have discussed, in such a way as to develop the logical potentialities of traditional thought forms, the question of the optimum capital structure with which to finance a given level of total capital employment, or total investment in the firm. It was seen that for this purpose it is usually assumed that the level and stability characteristics of the firm's total income stream are also given.

Second, the question was examined as to what capital expenditure projects should be adopted by the firm, thereby envisaging changes, presumably, in the level and risk characteristics of the firm's total income-generating ability. But the latter, the income and risk characteristics of the firm, are the precise variables which, on the financing side of the analysis, the traditional arguments generally assume to be given and fixed. Clearly there is all too often a logical hiatus in the analysis. The traditional analysis, though it has brought the financing question on the one hand and the investment project question on the other to higher levels of sophistication, has not really been moving in the direction of a logical integration of the total determinant forces. An integration of determinant forces such as to explain the mutually consistent, optimizing decision outcomes for the firm as a whole has not been achieved.

For this latter purpose a reorientation of the analysis is required. A frontal attack has now to be made on the mutually determinant decision levels in the firm of (1) the production or enterprise operating structure, (2) the investment or asset structure, and (3) the financing structure. This is what we have called the recognition of the analytical trilogy of the production problem, the investment problem, and the financing problem. On the level of theoretical analysis we have therefore to reconstruct the relevant thought forms and achieve a new integration of the theory of production, the theory of capital, and the theory of finance. We turn to the task of erecting the theoretical framework immediately in the following chapter.

6

Production
And
Capital
Theory:

The
Issues
In
Historical
Perspective

Our work to this point has been designed to accomplish three things: (1) The clarification of the meaning of economic optimization, particularly as understood from the viewpoint of the owners of a corporate business enterprise. It was seen that this must take account of the uncertainties surrounding value expectations and the utilities or disutilities attaching to them. (2) The specification, thus far in a highly adumbrated form, of the planning and operating environment within which the firm's optimization decisions are made. This involved also an examination of the ways in which the decisions are reflected in the financial statements describing the stance of the firm in its economic milieu. (3) The examination of some of the determinant forces lying behind the optimization decision outcomes. This involved a discussion of the probable functional forms in which the underlying forces might be described and incorporated in a robust equilibrium analysis. We have noted, at the same time, some of the ways in which, consistent with the constraints of its own restrictive thought forms, traditional financial analysis might be used to specify some partial equilibrium decision criteria.

Our argument thus far, however, has concentrated principally on what can be called the categories of financial analysis. This has provided a linkage, in terms familiar to the existing literature, between the earlier attempts at equilibrium model building and our own optimization analysis to follow. The concentration on the financial aspects of our problem has indicated also, in a familiar and recognizable form, some of the empirical problems and categories our optimization models must take into account. This, however, has left unexplored a large part of the necessary background of our argument. For we have not yet considered the ways in which the optimization of the firm needs to be embedded firmly in the thought forms and analysis of relevant economic theory. At this, of course, we have cast occasional glances, and even in the initial specification of our problem we envisaged an interconnection between the theories of production, capital, and finance. The task that confronts us now is that of reconsidering and refurbishing some of the building blocks of the theory and putting them in a form directly usable for model-building purposes.

Relevance in Economic Analysis

It will be useful at this initial point to be perfectly clear as to what we intend by the reconstruction and use of relevant economic analysis. We shall consider as examples the employment of labor and capital as factors of production.

From the corpus of neoclassical analysis we can extract the proposition that the employment of labor has been carried to an optimum or equilibrium level when the marginal revenue product per unit of labor is equal to the marginal cost per unit. It might be imagined that a theory of the employment of capital in the firm can be approached in the same way and the problem exhausted by saying that additional units of capital should be employed by a firm so long as the marginal product of capital is greater than its marginal cost.

This, unfortunately, is only part of the truth. Though it has lately entered the financial analysis of the firm, such a proposition all too readily shunts the theory into a logical alley and a rapid dead end. No possibility then exists of defining a genuine enterprise optimum or equilibrium situation. The nature of the logical puzzles that lead to this conclusion, and the theoretical problems implicit in them, can be summarized basically on two levels: first, that of the meaning of the marginal productivity of capital; and second, the adequacy or the validity of the analogy with the theory of labor just adduced.

Capital as a Factor of Production

We take first the question of the employment of capital and its marginal productivity. Here, it will be seen, the crux of the matter lies in the confusion as to what exactly is to be understood as the factor of production whose productivity is in view. When the thought forms of theoretical economics are imported into the financial analysis of the firm, in other words, is it possible or meaningful to speak of money capital as a factor of production and to conceive of its marginal revenue product and its marginal cost in coordinate terms? Our own answer to this question will be firmly in the negative. Money capital is not to be understood as a factor of production. And without an understanding of the meaning of this statement no possibility exists of achieving an integration of the analytical trilogy of production, capital, and finance theories.

Money capital is not a factor of production. Rather, it represents a generalized purchasing power, giving the firm command over the assets and factor services it wishes, or needs, to employ. The terms on which such money capital is available, moreover, constitute one of the most crucial constraints in the context of which the optimization decisions of the firm are to be made. As we have seen already, available money capital may be used for the acquisition of factors of production and for asset investments, including a certain amount of investment in liquidity, quite distinct from what, on a first approach, might be thought to be capital.

The statement of the matter in this perspective leads immediately to several corollary propositions. At least four can be adumbrated at this point, sufficient to establish the methodological ground we are now concerned with. First, if money capital is not a factor of production, it must be necessary for the constructs of theory to do two things clearly. On the one hand they must specify the enterprise production function precisely and consider, against the phenomenon of it, the ways in which the factor usages actually raise a demand for money capital. They must consider also how, as a reciprocal or mutually determinate causation, the availability of money capital in part determines the optimum usages of factors.

Second, the firm's demand for money capital is dependent not only on its usage of real capital, but on the usage of all other productive factors with which anything we might want to refer to as real capital is combined. Analytically, therefore, the demand for money capital cannot be specified independently of the demands for all the factors of production and of the specification of factor combinations employed. A microtheory of capital cannot be specified independently of a microtheory of production.

Third, it now follows that a direct analogy between the productivity characteristics of labor on the one hand and money capital on the other does not exist in any meaningful form. For labor and money capital enter the analytical problem at very different points. One is an argument in the production function; the other is not. The seemingly correlative notions of the marginal productivities of labor and money capital turn out to have rather different kinds of analytical parentage.

Fourth, the foregoing points instance the meaning we propose to attach in this work to the notion of analytical integration. The concept of the margin, for example, is a powerful and indispensable tool of our optimization analysis, and the notions of productivities and costs at the margin will be pervasive. But the mere use of words, or the statement of seemingly symmetrical thought forms, does not necessarily, in and of itself, constitute a relevant, adequately specified, or meaningfully determinate economic analysis. It may be recognized that we have not made the parrot into an economist by training him to say supply and demand, but that he must also say marginal product and marginal cost. But it would still need to be made clear to him that whatever meaning might be attached to the marginal costs and products of productive factors, a vastly different meaning attaches to the marginal costs and productivity of money capital. Though the words may be the same, the concepts import into their different levels of use rather different hinterlands of analytical significance.

An integrated theoretical analysis, then, is concerned not only with a similarity of words or with superficially similar concepts in varying contexts. It is concerned, more importantly, with a radical examination of the interdependent causal relations in the relevant optimization nexus. Economics is a study of causal, determinant relations, and as we have already observed Marshall to say in his comment on Cournot,

> it is necessary to face the difficulty of regarding the various elements of an economic problem . . . as all mutually determining one another. Nature's action is complex; and nothing is gained in the long run by pretending that it is simple, and trying to describe it in a series of elementary propositions.[1]

Mutually Determinate Variables

The thrust of the argument in the preceding paragraphs is to caution against a reasoning by analogy from the product of labor to the product of money capital. The second respect in which, it was noted, a caution needs to be raised exists at a deeper level of analysis than the recognition that labor and money capital are not coordinate factors of production. Here the matter can be stated rather more briefly since it is already implicit in what has been said under the preceding point.

Quite simply we can ask: Do we have a viable theory of the optimum employment of labor if we lay down only the dictum with which we began?

[1] Alfred Marshall, *Principles of Economics*, 9th (variorum) ed., C. W. Guillebaud (ed.), Macmillan & Co., Ltd., London, 1961, pp. ix–x.

Is a theory of factor usage exhausted by erecting the guideline that requires the marginal productivity of the factor to be greater than, or equal to, its marginal cost? Again the answer is patently in the negative. The productivity or the economic worthwhileness of employing a specific factor is interdependent with the comparable considerations with respect to every other productive resource with which the factor is, or might be, combined. The theory of factor worthwhileness is thus inseparable from the theory of the optimum factor combination. The notion of the equality of a firm's marginal revenue and marginal cost is, in suitably defined contexts, a useful and significant optimization condition. But "marginal cost equals marginal revenue" does not in any meaningful sense constitute a theory of the firm. It leaves too much unsaid and conceivably unexplored, notably the relevant implications for the theory of optimum factor combinations on the one hand and the implied distribution of values produced on the other. Similarly, the theory of factor use is not exhausted until something is said of the derivation of factor demands from product demands, and of the potentialities that exist for exploiting the elasticities of substitution between factors in the technological production function.

It follows therefore, in the same way and for the same reasons as before, that the theory of the use of money capital is not exhausted by saying that its marginal cost should be equal, or as nearly equal as is actually achievable, to the marginal revenue productivity of employing it. This again leaves too much unsaid regarding the determinants of the demand for money capital emanating from the product market, the factor markets, the production function characteristics, the potentialities of optimum factor combinations, and the other determinants of the optimum structure of the enterprise.

Thus it emerges that anything that might be called a financial theory of the firm is hardly capable of a very simple, or at least a very short, statement. On this level, as on other relevant levels, the theory of the firm is in no sense exhausted simply by marginal-cost-equals-marginal-revenue thought forms. But unfortunately, this is substantially the point to which the literature on the financial theory of the firm has come. Under the general rubric of the capital-budgeting problem, much valuable thought has been given to the computation of the true rates of return implicit in money capital investments, given the amounts of capital required and given also the periodic cash flows expected to be generated by the investment. On the other hand valuable work has been done in the specification of the cost of capital, given the level of capital requirements, and arguments have ensued as to whether the cost of capital as a decision criterion is or is not dependent on the forms in which capital is raised by the firm (or, in the language of our preceding chapters, on the structure of the liabilities side of the balance sheet).

The logical defects of this stream of theorizing, it will now be clear, lie in the restrictive nature of what were referred to as the "givens" in the preceding statement. It is this very method of theorizing that inhibits the usefulness of much existing work for the description of enterprise optimum structures, or for the determination of optimum structural-planning decisions.

The Theory of the Firm

It is against this background that we can take the analysis back to the starting point and reexamine what should be viewed as the underlying theory of the firm. In doing this we can reconsider the most relevant and useful precipitate of the neoclassical theory and construct logical bridges from economic theory to the pragmatic problem of enterprise planning and management. On the level of microeconomics our concern is with the theory of production and the theory of capital. We shall proceed in the remainder of this chapter by first noting the cleavage in the literature in the treatment of these two bodies of theory, and shall raise the question of the extent to which they have been, or should be, regarded as mutually dependent. It will then be possible to reconstruct the economic theory in the form in which it can best illumine our enterprise problem. Then finally we shall be able to lay down a usable specification of the functional relations that constitute the building blocks in our enterprise optimization model.

It is fortunately unnecessary to stay at length with a statement of the received tradition in the theory of the firm. Its general content will be familiar to readers and may be further inspected in relation to its own determining thought forms in the literature referred to in the note below.[2] For the present we note two of the prominent methodological points which an inspection of the literature quickly reveals.

First, throughout the literature of microeconomics the theory of production and the theory of capital have been developed along lines only tenuously connected. It is only in recent times that there has emerged a significant move toward an integration of these separate bodies of theory, in such a way as to exhibit their mutual dependence. The microeconomics literature, in addressing itself to the theory of the firm, has been preoccupied with a solution to the firm's production, factor use, price, and output prob-

---

[2] The historical development since Marshall's *Principles* is marked out fairly clearly in the following works, and references there cited provide contact with the relevant periodical literature: Joan Robinson, *The Economics of Imperfect Competition*, 1st ed., Macmillan & Co., Ltd., London, 1933; E. H. Chamberlin, *The Theory of Monopolistic Competition*, Harvard University Press, Cambridge, Mass., 1933; G. J. Stigler, *The Theory, of Price*, The Macmillan Company, New York, 1949; Robert Triffin, *Monopolistic Competition and General Equilibrium Theory*, Harvard University Press, Cambridge, Mass., 1949; J. R. Hicks, *Value and Capital*, Oxford University Press, Fair Lawn, N.J., 1946; Kenneth E. Boulding, *Economic Analysis*, 4th ed., Harper & Row, Publishers, Inc., New York, 1966; American Economic Association, *Readings in Price Theory*,1952, and *Readings in the Theory of Income Distribution*, 1951; Richard D. Irwin, Inc., Homewood, Ill., Sidney Weintraub, *Price Theory*, Pitman Publishing Corporation, New

lems, to the virtual exclusion of the questions of capital investment and financing. The most significant exceptions to this generalization will be noted in the following argument.

Second, we note on the methodological level the theoretical stance or standpoint from which the now mature tradition in the theory of the firm has developed. This we shall refer to as the recognition, and the consequent analytical assumption, of the economic uniqueness of the firm. It will be useful to explore the logic of this assumption and development a little more fully.

The last recrudescence of interest in the theory of the firm stems from Sraffa's famous article in 1926.[3] Joan Robinson has acutely commented on its catalytic significance. Dissatisfied with the confusion in theory stemming from "the logical priority of perfect competition," Mrs. Robinson observed that

> no sooner had Mr. Sraffa released the analysis of monopoly from its uncomfortable pen in a chapter in the middle of the book than it immediately swallowed up the competitive analysis without the smallest effort. The whole scheme of analysis, composed of just the same elements as before, could now be arranged in a perfectly uniform manner, with no awkward cleavage in the middle of the book.[4]

Henceforth, it had become clear, a new paradigm of microanalysis was to be adopted. Perfect competition was not only a particular, though seemingly pervasive, assumption that had "somehow trapped" the economists, but if situations of perfect competition were observed in the real world, the analysis and description of them were to be understood as special cases of more general theorems and analytical constructs.

In the same way, now that we are moving toward a more thorough-going integration of capital theory with theories of enterprise optimization and, in particular, toward the incorporation into the micromodel of theories of finance and money capital usage, it will be necessary to consider the classical assumption of perfection, on either side of the product and factor markets and on either side of the money capital market, as a special case of

---

York, 1949 (note the valuable bibliographical notes at the chapter ends in this work)' and *Intermediate Price Theory*, Chilton Company, Philadelphia, 1964; C. E. Ferguson· *Microeconomic Theory*, Richard D. Irwin, Inc., Homewood, Ill., 1966; James M. Henderson and Richard E. Quandt, *Microeconomic Theory: A Mathematical Approach* McGraw-Hill Book Company, New York, 1958; Kalman J. Cohen and Richard M Cyert, *Theory of the Firm: Resource Allocation in a Market Economy*, Prentice-Hall Inc., Englewood Cliffs, N.J., 1965; William J. Baumol, *Economic Theory and Operations Analysis*, Prentice-Hall, Inc., Englewood Cliffs, N.J., 1965.

[3] P. Sraffa, "The Laws of Return under Competitive Conditions," *Economic Journal*, vol. 36, pp. 535–550, December, 1926.

[4] Joan Robinson, *op. cit.*, pp. 3-4.

a more general economic condition. Correspondingly, the assumption of market perfection should not form the starting point of analysis or provide the paradigm. It should be introduced into the analysis at a later point, with a view to considering the nature of the parameters and the forms of the behavior functions that could be expected to be observed if the special case of perfect competition did in fact prevail.

If, moreover, our analysis can thus begin from a recognition of the unique characteristics of the individual firm as an economic entity, our ongoing argument regarding its structural problem and its optimization conditions will influence also the way in which a remedy might be proposed for the other main defect of the theoretical tradition we have noted, namely, the relative neglect of the capital problem. For quite apart from the way in which the particular configuration of market conditions (product differentiation, elasticities, market shares, product substitutabilities, and factor mobilities) confer a uniqueness on the firm and determine the structure of its real capital employment, the same issues spill over and influence also its position in the money capital market. Here they determine, as will be seen, both the structure of money capital employment and the prices of its several components as well as the structure of factor use in the firm.

Money capital is homogeneous. But real capital is a sum of heterogeneous units. And for a firm's decisions regarding the employment of both, individual enterprise demand and supply functions will somehow have to be built. As Lachmann has said, to invest in the firm is to "de-homogenize money capital,"[5] and he warns against the danger to analysis of what he calls an "illegitimate generalization based on the homogeneity hypothesis."[6] Each business firm enjoys a unique location on the demand side of the money capital market, and the form in which the market's supply function confronts the firm must accordingly be uniquely specified. It is doubtful how much progress can be made if our analysis is shackled to assumptions of perfection, or perfect mobility of funds, in the money capital market on the supply side or to the assumption of homogeneous classes of firms on the demand side.[7] Too much of the once-for-allness of the firm-market confrontation is thereby lost. The firm that is imperfectly competitive in the product output market is conceivably, though not of course necessarily, monopsonistic in the capital input market.[8]

[5] L. M. Lachmann, *Capital and Its Structure*, London School of Economics, G. Bell & Sons, Ltd., 1956, p. 36.
[6] *Ibid.*, p. 10.
[7] Cf. Franco Modigliani and Merton H. Miller, "The Cost of Capital, Corporation Finance, and the Theory of Investment," *American Economic Review*, vol. 48, pp. 261–297, June, 1958.
[8] Cf. footnote 7 of Chap. 4 and the suggestions made there regarding the possibility of monopsonistic discrimination by firms on the demand side of the money capital market, and the implications of such behavior for the effective elasticity of supply of money capital.

The conclusion reached by Hart in 1940 that "the theory of the firm ... is perhaps the most thoroughly explored and best-mapped field of economics"[9] should not be permitted to convey the impression that significant theoretical finality had by that time been attained. Nor did Hart's own valuable treatment of anticipations and uncertainty clinch the matter. It was possible for Kuh to begin his elegant essay in 1960 with the statement that "capital budgeting, the task of determining the optimum quantity of assets and their financing, stands out as a central and unsettled problem in the theory of the firm."[10] "The demand for and cost of capital," Kuh argued, needed to be treated "within a consistent maximizing framework." *A fortiori*, therefore, is a new maximizing framework required if we wish to take account in our optimizing solutions not only of the problems of financial structure that Kuh considered, but also of the ways in which these issues impinge, in turn, on the firm's production, output, factor use, and real capital structure decisions.

Capital Theories and the Economics of the Firm

While the development of the economics of the firm has proceeded mainly as in the literature already referred to, there has appeared, beside the mainstream but never really confluent with it, an important line of production-capital analysis. It is to this work by Smithies (1935), Lange (1936), Carlson (1939), Makower and Baumol (1950), Gabor and Pearce (1952 and 1958), Lachmann (1956), and Smith (1959 and 1961) that the model developed in this book owes its most direct intellectual debt, so far as the general question of the theory of the firm is concerned.[11]

---

[9] Albert G. Hart, *Anticipations, Uncertainty, and Dynamic Planning*, The University of Chicago Press, Chicago, 1940, p. 7.

[10] Edwin Kuh, "Capital Theory and Capital Budgeting," *Metroeconomica*, vol. 12, pp. 64–80, December, 1960.

[11] See A. Smithies, "The Austrian Theory of Capital in Relation to Partial Equilibrium Theory," *Quarterly Journal of Economics*, vol. 50, pp. 117–150, November, 1935; Oskar Lange, "The Place of Interest in the Theory of Production," *Review of Economic Studies*, vol. 3, pp. 159–192, June, 1936; Sune Carlson, *A Study on the Pure Theory of Production*, published in Stockholm, 1939, republished by Augustus M. Kelley, New York, 1965; H. Makower and William J. Baumol, "The Analogy between Producer and Consumer Equilibrium Analysis," *Economica*, vol. 17, pp. 63–80, February, 1950; Andre Gabor and I. F. Pearce, "A New Approach to the Theory of the Firm," *Oxford Economic Papers*, vol. 4, pp. 252–265, October, 1952, and "The Place of Money Capital in the Theory of Production," *Quarterly Journal of Economics*, vol. 72, pp. 537–557, November, 1958; Lachmann, *op. cit.;* Vernon L. Smith, "The Theory of Investment and Production," *Quarterly Journal of Economics*, vol. 73, pp. 61–80, February, 1959, and *Investment and Production: A Study in the Theory of the Capital-using Enterprise*, Harvard University Press, Cambridge, Mass., 1961.

No doubt this earlier work contains some false starts and fruitless investigations, but it nevertheless does contain in embryo, and in some cases in a fairly sophisticated stage of development, many of the concepts that we shall turn into building blocks in our own theoretical model. In some of this development, the earlier Austrian notion of the "period of production" interpretation of capital theory continues to hold a fascination. Into that it is not necessary to enter, except to point out one or two of its more relevant features. In the form in which Jevons laid down one of the earliest definitions in the neoclassical theory ("Capital, as I regard it, consists merely in the aggregate of those commodities which are required for sustaining labourers of any kind or class engaged in work"[12]) through Bohm-Bawerk[13] and Wicksell,[14] the theory of capital "was fully developed . . . only for the case of circulating capital."[15] Robbins concluded that "although later on, in his review of Dr. Akerman's book Wicksell developed a solution for the case of capital of varying degrees of durability, it is obvious that this is one of the fields of pure analysis in which most yet remains to be done."[16]

Against this background, Smithies attempted in 1935 to show "that the analysis of the part played by durable goods in the process of production involves no departure from the fundamental theory as expounded by Bohm-Bawerk."[17] To accomplish this he endeavored to concentrate on the "services a durable good renders per unit of time," and, expanding explicitly on the Jevonian concept of capital as "the advances that have to be made to labor," he introduced the notion of the "average period of time for which the labor embodied in a single service is employed." He followed this notion with that of the "delay period," or "the time that elapses between the application of a factor of production and the emergence of the product." The relevance of the point at present is that the same notion appears again in Gabor and Pearce (1958) as the "maturity time," or "the lapse of time between the payment for the first unit of a factor and the commencement of the product flow which it is designed to create."[18] "The maturity time is a new and vitally important dimension of every factor."[19]

This attempted rehabilitation of the concept of the period of production points unfortunately toward the "morass involved in the search for

[12] W. S. Jevons, *The Theory of Political Economy*, 1871, Reprint Kelley & Millman, Inc., New York, 1957, p. 223.
[13] See R. Dorfman, "A Graphical Exposition of Bohm-Bawerk's Interest Theory," *Review of Economic Studies*, vol. 26, pp. 153–158, February, 1959.
[14] Knut Wicksell, *Lectures on Political Economy*, Lionel Robbins (ed.), Routledge & Kegan Paul, Ltd., London, 1934.
[15] Robbins in *Ibid.*, p. xvi.
[16] *Ibid.*
[17] Smithies, *op. cit.*, p. 117.
[18] Gabor and Pearce, "The Place of Money Capital in the Theory of Production," p. 544.
[19] *Ibid.*

average-period formulas" which, Baumol suggests, has consistently trapped capital theorists, or at least those theorists who have argued from a "deceptively simple expression which is applicable only to the analytically uncomplicated stationary point-input, point-output case."[20] But the concern shown for this matter does serve to highlight two of the important problems we shall have to confront and which will have to be defined explicitly in our model: first, the manner in which input factors of more than one-period durability are to be incorporated in the enterprise production function, the latter taking, apart from these matters of definition, something akin to its general neoclassical form; and second, the price per unit at which durable factor services are to find their way into enterprise cost functions and thus contribute to factor use equilibria.

Lange's work referred to above is of the utmost importance for the next advance in the theory of the firm, tending to abolish as it does the barriers to the confluence of production and capital theory. Though Lange acknowledges Smithies' work on the concept of the "delay period," he assumes away most of the problems this concept introduces by explicitly confining his analysis "to the case of circulating capital" and assuming that within such a context the delay periods of all factors may be regarded as fixed. In the course of his analysis, however, Lange does make use of several notions which we shall develop further below. First, money capital and real capital factors are considered as quite distinct, each having different points of relevance to the broader analysis of the firm. Second, since money capital was recognized as a general command over productive resources, the productive resources themselves were recognized as arguments in the production function, but money capital was not.[21] This, we have already argued, is a point at which confusion has existed, and which has inhibited a more fruitful alliance between economic theory and business decision problems. Too often, money capital has been taken as a factor of production. It is not, in the technological sense in which the production function now needs to be understood. And it is to the credit of Gabor and Pearce (1958) that they did confront this particular issue firmly. For them "the exclusion of money capital from the production function is the cornerstone of our approach."[22]

[20] William J. Baumol, *Economic Theory and Operations Analysis*, 2d ed., Prentice-Hall, Inc., Englewood Cliffs, N.J., 1965, p. 421.

[21] Lange, *op. cit.*, p. 178. Lange here refers to "the distinction between money capital and real capital. . . . we prefer to speak simply of money capital as a sum of money invested in the purchase of factors of production and of real capital as a mere alternative term to denote equipment co-operating with labor in production."

[22] Gabor and Pearce, "The Place of Money Capital in the Theory of Production" p. 540. It is worthy of comment that while we thus recognize the relevance of this Gabor-Pearce proposition for sound microeconomic theory, the literature since the time they

Third, though the point was not taken up by Gabor and Pearce, Lange related his notion of the money capital requirement function of the firm to that of the operation of the available money capital supply as a constraint against which the product output and factor combination optimization process worked itself out. The Lagrange multiplier in terms of which the effect of the capital constraint was observable performed a function for Lange similar to that for which we shall employ it in our discussion of the marginal productivity of capital. It was given a similar application, though, significantly, in the context of a production function different from the one we shall adopt, in Smith (1959 and 1961). Thus Lange was able to speak of what he called the marginal productivity of indirect labor and direct labor, an implication that will be reinterpreted in our model as relevant to the optimum combinations of the firm's factors of production.

Carlson's study set out explicitly to "emphasize the bearing of the capital and interest theory on the cost and revenue calculations of a single firm's production,"[23] though most of his analysis is confined to that of enterprise decisions in a single time period. In this so-called monoperiodic optimization analysis, optimum amounts of debt financing in conjunction with a given amount of equity capital are examined. Carlson does, however, consider briefly the "poly-periodic maximization problem,"[24] and his work contains at this stage significant pointers for the subsequent development of our subject. His suggestions on the form of the capital supply function and on the elasticity or, as he says, flexibility of the supply of borrowed funds raise again the notion, previously referred to, of the monopsonistic position of borrowers. Makower and Baumol, in their 1950 paper, raise several other issues directly relevant to our present objectives. In their "Analogy" the price effect and the income effect in consumer analysis are reflected in a "substitution effect" and a "resources effect" in the producer analysis. The treatment in the Makower-Baumol paper of the maximization of an entrepreneur's utility function subject to a money capital constraint will be

---

wrote has in some cases failed completely to comprehend the point. Consider the comment by Donald Dewey in his recent *Modern Capital Theory*, Columbia University Press, New York, 1965, p. 26n.: "In discussing definitions of capital we should probably take note of the approach which holds that capital is not a factor of production at all ... see Andre Gabor and I. F. Pearce, 'The Place of Money Capital in the Theory of Production.'" Certainly in a study of "modern capital theory" such a comment is very wide of the mark, for in Gabor and Pearce as in Lange before them the question is not whether capital is or is not to be viewed as a factor of production. The issue quite simply is whether we apprehend the distinction between real capital on the one hand and money capital on the other. One is a factor of production whereas the other is not. It is to this latter point that the Gabor-Pearce proposition is addressed.

[23] Carlson, *op. cit.*, p. v.

[24] *Ibid.*, p. 118.

reflected in our model, though both our production function and our constraint functions will be differently specified.

Lachmann's work, as already noted, emphasizes the heterogeneous nature (and therefore the varying degrees of economic specificity and complementarity) of units of real capital factors, as against the homogeneous, divisible, mobile nature of money capital. And this conception has, in turn, implications for Lachmann's "Plan-Period-Analysis" of a business firm's reaction to economic change. The process analysis is in his view "a causal-genetic method of studying economic change,"[25] and the important thing is that changes in plans at successive planning dates will be reflected in new optimum structures of capital goods usage, and therefore of factor combinations in the production process. "Production plans," Lachmann concludes, "are the primary object of the theory of capital."[26] In one respect our own optimization model will be concerned precisely with this very same issue: with pursuing the logic of the optimum structures of factor employments, broadened to consider the money capital requirements implicit in alternative production plans and the question of the financing of such requirements. Lachmann's Plan-Period-Analysis might be thought comparable with our own "sequential decision making," intending by the latter the periodic reexamination of the enterprise production, capital, and financing structures and the sequential readjustment of them in the light of changes in decision parameters, aiming consistently at a maximization of total ownership values.

It is in Smith's *Investment and Production* that perhaps the closest conceptual similarity to our optimization model exists. Though it will be necessary to differ from Smith on the questions of the form of the production function, the definition of capital factors and their periodic costs, the form of the money capital requirement function, and consequently the manner of specifying equilibrium factor use combinations, we shall nevertheless employ a similar method of attack on those problems we have in common. These concern basically the maximization of some appropriately defined profit or value function, subject to relevant product output or capital input constraints. Given the similarity of our method to that of Smith, notwithstanding the differences in content, it will be preferable to defer fuller comment on his important work to the appropriate contexts in what follows.

As a final note on the theoretical background of the developments we wish to pursue, it is necessary to examine now the ways in which the cooperation of input factors has been conceived to be relevant to the optimum

---

[25] Lachmann, *op. cit.*, p. 39.

[26] *Ibid.*, p. 54. Note also Lachmann's footnote reference in *Ibid.*, p 50, to Palander's argument regarding the change of capital structures and its significance for the maximization of ownership values.

position of the firm. Precisely, the problem we bring to the fore is that of interpreting capital as a factor of production and, as we have already anticipated, its place in the firm's production function.

The Production Function

To clarify the issues at this point and to indicate the way in which differing conceptions have influenced model construction, it will be useful to consider briefly three quite different lines of attack on the theoretical production function problem. These we attribute, for the sake of brevity and without doing full justice to the authors' presentations, to Scitovsky, Lutz and Lutz, and Gabor-Pearce-Smith respectively. Basically, the economists' production function has been shown in detail to be analogous to the industrial engineers' technical efficiency relations.[27] It describes the technological relationships existing between different amounts and combinations of factor inputs per unit of time and the possible output of product during the same period of time.[28] The relationship may be expressed as

$$Q = f(X,Y,\ldots) \tag{6-1}$$

where Q refers to the quantity of output, and X, Y, ... indicate the different factor inputs. More precisely, these inputs, or as we may now refer to them, these arguments in the production function, will be interpreted subsequently as units of factor services. While the full implications of the statement need not detain us at this point, it will be useful to keep in mind the following distinction. The things that will be understood as the factors of production, and that will have definable unit costs, are not the assets in which the firm invests, but rather the services those assets provide.

In considering the notion of the production function and its relevance for enterprise optima, differences of view have emerged on two levels in economic theory. One, as we have just inferred, has surrounded the question as to how the arguments in the production function are to be defined. The question becomes acute when some of the factors necessitate investments in assets that have a durability extending over more than one operational period. Other factors, which might be referred to as current inputs, necessi-

---

[27] See Vernon L. Smith, *Investment and Production*, chap. 2 *et passim*. See also L. B. Lave, "Engineering Production Functions and Capital-Labor Substitution in Metal Machining: Comment," *American Economic Review*, vol. 56, pp. 872–877, September, 1966, and the "Reply" by E. G. Furubotn. The paper by Lave includes a valuable short bibliography on the production function problem.

[28] The time unit here envisaged is some appropriate and economically significant unit of operational time, and is not to be confused with the stretch of calendar time elapsing between what were referred to above as sequential-planning dates. A plan period will conceivably include any number of operational time units.

tate investments of only a one-period durability, or are themselves completely absorbed in the moment of use. The second difference in theory is concerned with the way in which, if at all, money capital is to be regarded as a factor of production. We have already indicated our own answer to this last point of difference, but it will be appropriate now to consider the issue more fully.

Attempts to integrate capital theory and production theory have foundered whenever the approach has been made via an attempt to recognize money capital as a factor of production. Scitovsky's analysis is noted in what follows only because it occurs in a very articulate manner in a valuable and articulate book:

> The time-consuming nature of production renders capital funds necessary to the operation of the firm. The theory of capital regards these capital funds as a factor of production, similar and additional to the factors of production already considered . . . . In short, all that capital theory does is to add capital funds to the list of productive factors, and interest and dividend payments to the list of cost items.[29]

But difficulties arise when later in the same chapter Scitovsky wishes to cease talking solely of capital as a sum of money, or "the total value of assets," and to recognize "the need for a 'real' interpretation of the concept of capital." At this latter point the money capital fund is regarded as the means of command over the products of other firms, and consideration is given to the difference between the marginal productivity of the money capital and the marginal product of the capital goods in which it is embodied. The question at issue is quite properly that of the relation between the productivity of capital factors on the one hand and the rate of return on investment of money capital on the other.

It would seem, however, that only confusion can follow from an attempt to regard as identical the sets of causal factors determining each of these outcomes. For the rate of return on the investment of money capital depends on the total conjuncture of forces operating in the enterprise in which the investment has been made, and some of the funds represented by the money capital will not be invested in real units of capital equipment at all. They will be required as liquid balances necessary to finance the turnover in the business of current factors of production. Moreover, it would be a mistake to attempt to identify inseparably a particular unit of real capital equipment and a unit of money capital funds, even though particular doses of money capital may in fact be acquired as concomitant with the acquisition of particular items of equipment.

[29] Tibor Scitovsky, *Welfare and Competition*, Richard D. Irwin, Inc., Homewood, Ill. 1951, pp. 201–202.

In the business firm's confrontation with the capital market, the terms
on which sources of capital funds are available at the margin of requirements will depend in part on the structure of sources already in use, and it
is preferable, therefore, to consider the *total* investment of capital, particularly the owners' equity, and the returns available to it, depending on the
total structure and income-generating ability of the business. Then relations
can be established between the employment of a *marginal* unit of money
capital and the induced increment in the value of the firm, taking account of
whatever changes in business structure and income-generating ability may
have been effected by the marginal investment. Holding, then, to the need
to distinguish sharply between the provision of money capital to the firm
and the investment of such funds, or the use to which the funds are allocated
by the firm, we conclude that progress is not likely to be made by regarding
money capital as a factor of production. Rather, the availability of money
capital is more properly to be regarded as a constraint within the context of
which the firm's real resources are acquired and its optimization decisions
made. Given the nature of the economic world, business optimizing is in the
general case constrained optimizing. This attitude is implicit in the early
work of Lange, though, as noted earlier, he confined his analysis to the case
of "circulating capital."

The attitude of Lutz and Lutz to the theoretical problem of the
production function is one of virtual agnosticism.[30] Recognizing, following
Carlson, that when durable goods are introduced into the production
process the firm's operations and decision problems can no longer be considered as simply monoperiodic, they in effect conclude that in such a case
no production function analysis is possible:

> The solution can no longer be found with the aid of constant product
> curves, because time cannot be treated as a factor of production
> coordinate with the inputs . . . . Putting the difficulty in terms of the
> conventional diagram depicting constant product curves, it means that
> we do not know how many units of service of the capital good . . . are
> being combined with the labor or other services in any given short
> period to produce the constant product of that period.[31]

In terms of the firm's accounting procedures, the Lutzes conclude that the
difficulty is the same as that involved in the search for the "true" depreciation method. No such method, they say, exists.

The question of enterprise optimization is taken care of in the Lutz
system by (1) focusing attention on the succession of short periods, (2)

[30] Friedrich Lutz and Vera Lutz, *The Theory of Investment of the Firm*, Princeton University Press, Princeton, N.J., 1951, pp. 6ff.
[31] *Ibid.;* cf. Smith's criticism of the Lutz position in his article in the *Quarterly Journal of
Economics*, vol. 73, pp. 61f., February, 1959.

calculating the quasi rent which equates the marginal revenue and the marginal cost of production in each such period, and (3) evaluating the investment as the present discounted value of the whole series of quasi rents thus determined. In spite of the elegance and intuitive appeal in this procedure, it cannot be said to have achieved the integration of capital and production theory that a properly constructed planning model should provide. Given that we desire to use the production function concept for purposes of periodic structural planning, we do require a system which, unlike that of the Lutzes, does allow us to talk of factor substitutions and optimum combinations, envisaging, in fact, alternative possible patterns of factor durabilities and complementarities. But recognizing this, we still have the problem of defining the fixed factor argument in the production function in such a way as to make economically meaningful the unit cost, per operational time unit, of the services of the fixed factor. This we shall consider in detail below in conjunction with the related problem of the optimum economic life of fixed factors.

The earlier neoclassical theory, prior to the Lutzes' effective agnosticism on the question of the production function, did not specify clearly the differentia between the fixed services and the variable services of inputs. The problem was faced most explicitly, perhaps, in Carlson's *Study*, though here it was for the main part assumed away in his almost exclusive emphasis on the monoperiodic analysis. "The distinction between durable and non-durable productive resources is therefore of no concern here. It may be postponed to the study of poly-periodic production."[32] Against this generally unsatisfactory state of affairs and in revolt against the Lutz departure, Smith proposed a significant reinterpretation of the firm's technical production possibilities. Building on earlier work in so-called stock-flow market analysis by Clower and Horwich,[33] Smith developed a "stock-flow production function."[34] Smith's specification, which is also implicit in the Gabor-Pearce papers referred to,[35] is of first-rate importance in the development of

---

[32] Carlson, *op. cit.*, pp. 12–16.

[33] See the references in Smith, *Investment and Production*, p. 99n, notably R. W. Clower, "Business Investment and the Theory of Price," *Proceedings of the 28th Annual Conference of the Western Economic Association*, 1953, and "An Investigation into the Dynamics of Investment," *American Economic Review*, vol. 44, pp. 64–81, March, 1954; and G. Horwich, "Money, Prices and the Theory of Interest Determination," *Economic Journal*, vol. 67, pp. 625–643, December, 1957.

[34] Smith, *Investment and Production*, chap. 3, p. 62.

[35] Gabor and Pearce, "The Place of Money Capital in the Theory of Production," p. 541. We shall not refer to these authors' development further, as it suffers, as already indicated, from their attempted rehabilitation of the Austrian period-of-production notion, via the Smithies concept of "delay periods" and their own "maturity times." We have already noted that the Smith production function analysis has begun to find its way into the textbooks in Cohen and Cyert, *Theory of the Firm, op. cit.*, pp. 138f.

the theory of the firm:

> In any unified theory of production and investment . . . one imagines
> the typical firm confronted with a variety of substitutable inputs,
> ranging all the way from inputs whose consumption is immediately and
> directly associated with current production, through replaceable and/or
> maintainable durable inputs whose "consumption" embraces many
> production periods, to highly durable capital goods such as pipelines,
> transmission cables, and buildings. The production function relating
> these various classes of inputs must necessarily be at the technological
> core of the theory of investment.[36]

Granted, then, that a fuller specification might be made of current and
variously durable inputs to production, and granted the logical possibility
of describing the substitutability between them and the optimum combinations of inputs that might, on some criteria, be found to exist, this still leaves
open the question of defining the inputs of durable factors in such a way as
to make their "costing" to the productive process economically meaningful.
It is in this last connection that we shall differ from Smith's analysis. For
him, emphasis should be placed on the presence of physical equipment as
such, production of any kind not being able to take place without physical
equipment in some quantity and form. Then the specification of the
"current cost" of "maintaining the presence of a unit of equipment in
production" (the current cost being "the constant outlay stream that has a
present value equal to that of all future cost outlays . . ."[37]) includes three
components: (1) an annual proration of the investment cost of the equipment, (2) an annual interest charge on the capital cost, and (3) the associated
maintenance, servicing, and obsolescence charges, "all of which are required
as 'logistic' support for a unit of equipment."[38] In this way Smith defines
the flow price or flow cost of the durable input to the process. If account is
properly taken of the cost magnitudes involved at each of these points, the
flow cost of durable inputs is directly analogous to the unit cost of current
inputs, and isocost or isooutlay contours can conceivably be built up from
the relations between the various types of inputs. Such isooutlay contours
can then be placed in juxtaposition with the usual type of production
possibility contours, or isoproduct maps.

Smith's valuable work, however, did not address itself to the corporate
financing problem in the explicit form in which we wish to consider it. We
shall accordingly differ from his interpretation and exclude from the current
or flow cost of fixed input the interest charge on capital outlay, or component

[36] Smith, *Investment and Production*, p. 63.
[37] *Ibid.*, pp. 67, 109.
[38] *Ibid.*, p. 163.

(2) in the preceding paragraph. The unit input costs incorporated in outlay contours and in equilibria determinations will include, first, only items (1) and (3) of Smith's components, or the depreciation, maintenance, servicing, and obsolescence costs. But we shall include in addition an imputed interest cost on the capital investment associated not only with the provision of money capital to finance the installation of durable assets or factors, but with the provision also of the current input items. Money capital funds are required and used for all such purposes and should be costed accordingly.

The precise form of our differences from earlier work in this area will emerge in the following chapter, but for the present a two-point summary will suffice to enable us to proceed. First, we shall employ the production function of Equation (6-1) given earlier:

$$Q = f(X, Y, \ldots)$$

where, for convenience of analysis and without damage to generality and for purposes of facilitating a subsequent graphical summary, X will refer to a variable or low durability input, and Y will refer to a unit of durable, fixed input capacity. The Y factor, that is, does not refer to a unit of equipment. It refers to a unit of capacity, more closely akin to the earlier neoclassical notion of a unit of "services" of fixed inputs. It will be seen below that a significant suboptimization problem exists in the recognition that a "unit of capacity" may in fact be provided in more than one physical form, associated with actual durable equipment of different expected economic lives and capital outlay costs.

Second, the transformation from the production function to the cost function will be effected by taking the flow cost of units of X and Y as γ_1 and γ_2 respectively, and we shall specify in the manner indicated below the precise form of γ_2 and the economic life of the equipment with which it is associated. But to enable us to do this we must first construct what we shall refer to as the money capital requirement function implicit in the enterprise production-investment relation. We shall return to the analysis of this function later. For the present, we are now in a position to begin the assembly of the elements of the general optimization model of the firm.

7

Production, Capital, And Finance:

Elements Of The Optimization Model

In the preceding chapters we have attempted to establish a perspective of theoretical economics from which the enterprise optimization problem can be viewed. But still at this point the most we have done is to indicate the general nature of the analytical standpoint from which we intend to approach our problem, the analytical predilections we espouse, and some of the methodological implications of our attitudes. It has not been possible to this point to indicate in a full or analytically significant sense the content of the explanatory functions or behavior relations we shall incorporate in what follows. We are now, however, in a position to begin a detailed specification of the building blocks of the model we shall erect, and the task will occupy us for the whole of this chapter.

But in doing this, a final point of considerable methodological importance should be kept in mind. The model that emerges from the analysis is basically a long-run decision-making or structural-planning model. The business firm, we have argued, should attempt to maximize its owners' wealth position by integrating the outcomes of its production, investment, and financing problems. Our explanatory model, therefore, must be addressed primarily to the determination of those *structural* questions that confront the management at what we have called its sequential decision-making dates. At each such date, at the beginning of each planning period, decisions will have to be taken on the structural questions of output, factor use, investments in assets, and financing sources. The structure of the business deducible from these decision outcomes is then reflected in the structure of the firm's financial statements, the balance sheet and income statement as already inferred. Only after such a structural model is available can we consider the probable reactions of the firm to changes in the external economic environment and to changes in its decision parameters between its sequential-planning dates. It is in this way that the question can be raised as to what, given the structure of the firm's operational plans as already established, might be its reaction to, say, short-run shifts in its average revenue function and the implied character of its short-run marginal cost function. Thus intraplan period behavior phenomena can be observed. But logically, the planning model is prior to the model of short-run behavior variations.[1]

Factor Use and Capital Costs

Our objective in the investment-cost analysis is to make it possible to construct the firm's cost and profit functions, as envisaged to lie behind the outcomes recorded in the income statement in Table 2 of Chapter 3. It is necessary for this purpose to specify the interest and capital costs involved in the enterprise process, and the manner of their imputation to the different factor employments. The procedure to be described is adopted for two main reasons. First, the employment of money capital is reflected pervasively in all phases of enterprise operations; and second, it is desired not to tie, for analytical purposes, any one piece of money capital financing with one particular piece of real capital assets. Such a procedure as the latter is implicit, as already noted, in Vernon Smith's analysis. The task we have set requires the specification of enterprise demand and supply functions for money capital, and introduces the next crucial concepts at this stage of the analysis: (1) the firm's money capital requirement function, and (2) the available money capital constraint.

Integration of Financial Position Analysis

It will be significant to note, as we proceed, the ways in which the economic theory is to be integrated with the financial statement concepts

---

[1] Recall the argument in Chap. 3, in the context of footnote 5 of that chapter, regarding the logical priority of the structural- planning decision over the intraplan-period-operating decisions.

and with the asset and liability thought forms of the preceding chapters. The possibility of specifying the flow costs of units of factors X and Y as incorporated in the production function, for example, is part of the analysis underlying the outcomes summarized in the income statement of the firm. The specification of the money capital requirement function and of the associated supply function we are about to consider is part of the analysis behind the structure of the balance sheet, and the implications that that has for the structure and economic viability of the firm.

The construction of methodological bridges between the levels of argument in the preceding chapters and the present chapter is, as observed at the beginning, one of the principal objectives of this book. From another perspective we are concerned to open channels of communication between practitioners who have in the past confined their interest all too exclusively to one or the other of these two levels. Foremostly, of course, our concern in achieving these objectives is that a more robust understanding might thereby be grasped of the interacting, interdependent, and mutually determinant forces which, taken together, determine the optimum enterprise planning, structure, and management.

With this in view, the analysis in the following sections must be regarded as a tentative step toward the larger task of specifying precisely the empirical forms of the functional relations we shall adduce. It is a step toward the pragmatic implementation of the economic-financial optimization rules we shall derive. There remain, beyond the level of this book, the extension and modification of the elements of the model to take account of varying industrial and corporate enterprise characteristics. But a start must be made.

The economic forces behind the income statement and the balance sheet of the firm reinforce four principal conclusions of the preceding chapters. First, the structural characteristics of the firm, and the stability or otherwise of the income expectations associated with it, determine in part the conditions on which ownership capital will be available. Taking account of the concomitant determinant, the nature of the owners' utility functions dependent on their risk aversion or risk predilection, the supply conditions of equity were subsumed under an equity capital supply function. This was interpreted from the equity owners' capitalization rate function, dependent on the amount and leverage characteristics of the total capital employed in the firm.

Second, and in a similar manner, the conditions of supply of debt capital were understood to depend upon, and were functionally defined in relation to, the stability of the net operating income, or the total income-generating ability of the firm. The cost of debt was related also to the degree of financial leverage in the enterprise structure.

Third, alternative formulations were given of traditional criteria for judging the economic worthwhileness of investing in fixed assets. These were related to the rates of return implicit in investment projects or to the capitalized economic values they could be expected to generate.

Fourth, we considered the way in which the forces determining the necessary investment in current assets could be taken together to define a net working capital requirement function, considering the need for cash, accounts receivables, and inventories respectively.

But all of the analysis leading to these results was clearly recognized at the time as providing a series of first approximation, partial equilibrium, or partial optimization approaches to total enterprise equilibria. We are now at the point, therefore, where the following sections will vindicate our conclusions regarding the earlier analysis, at the same time as full use is made of the definitional groundwork and necessary basic relations it has provided. We begin with the concept of the money capital requirement function of the firm.

The Money Capital Requirement Function

The money capital requirement function effectively entered the literature in Lange's essay on "The Place of Interest in the Theory of Production" in 1936, in his one-period circulating capital analysis. The notion was taken up most recently by Gabor and Pearce and Vernon Smith as already referred to, but since their specification and usage are different from what we shall adopt, we shall not discuss their work further on this particular point. The size of the firm's total money capital requirements will depend upon its total employment of units of factor X and units of fixed input capacity Y. The total capital funds employed will be reflected on the assets side of the balance sheet, and the structural relations between the various assets will be related to the structure of factor employments it is necessary to finance.

Let us suppose for the present that it is possible to specify a set of money capital requirement coefficients $\alpha, \beta, \ldots$ relative to the employment of a unit of factor $X, Y, \ldots$ respectively. The employment of a unit of factor capacity Y requires the investment in fixed assets of β dollars of money capital, and so on. It is supposed, in other words, that the provision of a unit of factor capacity requires an investment in an asset which then provides the factor services throughout its economic life. If, of course, the factor services were completely variable and did not require any investment in fixed assets, as would be the case, for example, with man-hours of labor input, the money capital requirement coefficient in such a case would be zero, and the periodic flow costs we previously referred to as gamma terms will be the pure cash outlays necessary to acquire the factor services. On the basis of these definitions it is then possible to specify a partial money capital requirement function as

$$K_1 = \alpha X + \beta Y \tag{7-1}$$

We shall see in a moment the ways in which the α and β money capital requirement coefficients of the respective factors, as well as the periodic flow costs of those factors, γ_1 and γ_2, may be specified more precisely. Immediately, however, three significant statements can be made about the capital requirement function described in Equation (7-1).

First, in so far as the money capital requirements are dependent, in the manner indicated, on the usages of factor X and factor Y, the actual total requirement cannot be known until it is first determined how large the total production output of the firm is envisaged to be, and with what combination of factors X and Y that output should be produced. But this optimum output and the optimum combination of factors must surely depend, in turn, on the necessary investments, or the money capital requirement coefficients associated with the respective factors. Moreover, it must depend also on the implicit cost of the money capital that is to be imputed to it in its various operational uses. Clearly, complex interdependencies in the analysis thus begin to emerge.

Second, the function specified in Equation (7-1) was referred to as only a partial description of the money capital requirements, for it took no account of what we have called the net working capital requirements. These latter may vary with changes in the level of output, and therefore with changes in the level of employment of the firm's productive factors. The underlying analysis of this matter in Chapter 5 is summarized in Table 7 and in Equation (5-14). Net working capital requirements were there specified as

$$W = f\left(\sum_i p_i Q_i \right) \tag{7-2}$$

where the index indicates a summation over all product outputs. It will be convenient and sufficient for our present purposes to incorporate the results of the earlier analysis into our present model by specifying a net working capital requirement function as

$$W = g(Q) \tag{7-3}$$

We shall keep in mind that by virtue of the dependence of Q upon the factor inputs X and Y as described in the production function, W is in turn related to the level of factor employments in the firm.

A more complete statement of the firm's money capital requirement function may accordingly be made in the form

$$K_2 = g[f(X,Y)] + \alpha X + \beta Y \tag{7-4}$$

Equation (7-4) combines the production function and Equations (7-1) and (7-3). The nature of the differentiability characteristics of this function will be clear to the reader. For example,

$$\frac{\partial K_2}{\partial X} = \frac{dg}{dQ} \cdot \frac{\partial Q}{\partial X} + \alpha \tag{7-5}$$

The third observation to be made on the basis of Equation (7-1) and of the more fully developed form of the capital requirement function is important for the basic methodological standpoint of our work. This is the fact that in this way, and in accordance with the procedures we shall develop from this foundation, the asset investment activity of the firm is being tied in directly with its decisions regarding the optimum usages of factors of production. This, in other words, is the logical precipitate of the priority, in decision making concerned with enterprise economic optima, of the structural-planning model.

More acutely, we now see that by tying in the asset investment decision with the factor usage decision via the factors' money capital requirement coefficients, and thus pointing to the mutual determination of asset structures, factor use, and capital employment, we are departing sharply from what we referred to in Chapter 5 as the traditional project approach to enterprise asset investments. To put the issue the other way around, we do not, as was envisaged in laying the definitional groundwork in Chapter 5, build toward an optimum enterprise structure by piecing together projects or sets of asset investments. Rather, we begin from the other end and determine the optimum structure of asset investments from considerations of optimum production and factor employments. Our approach is directed, as will be seen more fully, toward the realization of that overall or total enterprise structure which will optimize the economic position of the owners of the firm. In the case of the corporation this will imply the maximization of the market value of the shares of common stock ownership. It will accordingly become necessary not only to integrate the investment decision with the production decision as has just been noted, but to show also the interdependence of outcomes on both these levels with the simultaneous optimum decisions on the level of the financing problem.

Specification of β and γ Coefficients

However, in order to complete the interrelation envisaged at this level, we need to specify more precisely the factors' money capital requirement coefficients and, associated with them, the periodic costs to be attributed to the respective factors of production. It will be recalled that the factors in the production function necessitating asset investments whose durability extended over more than one operational time period were deemed to be measured in units of factor capacity, and that the direct costs per unit of capacity per time period, γ_i, were deemed to include both the periodic amortization cost and the maintenance and servicing cost. The interest charges on capital outlays were not tied directly to productive factors, but all factors, of varying degrees of durability, were understood to bear an imputed capital cost. This will later be seen to be imputed at a rate equal to the marginal productivity of money capital. The size of the imputation, it can reasonably be anticipated, will be dependent in each case on the estimated capital intensity coefficient of the factor in the money capital requirement function. To give precision to the concepts of the γ_i direct factor costs and the related coefficients in the capital requirement function, it will suffice for purposes of generality to consider the quantification of γ_2, the direct flow cost of factor Y, and β, its money capital requirement coefficient.

The logical puzzle involved at this point recognizes that we need to choose, as part of the total capital investment outlay of the firm, a physical asset of a size and technical characteristics adequate to provide the number of units of Y-capacity usage required per operational period, as determined by the solution outcome of the system. This solution, however, and therefore the investment requirements, cannot be determined until a value is known for γ_2 and β. But γ_2, the direct cost of a unit of capacity, cannot be known until we know the size, technical characteristics, and estimated economic life of the assets involved. Thus γ_2 is dependent on the capital outlay cost of the assets installed to provide the Y-capacity units, or in other words is dependent on β. But β is in turn dependent on the number of Y units required per period, for in the general case the capital outlay cost per unit of capacity will not increase proportionately with the capacity provided. Consider the cost function per cubic foot in warehouse construction, for example. It may be meaningful, as an approach to our problem on the conceptual level, to replace γ_2 and β in the model's objective function by the relations $\gamma_2(Y)$ and $\beta(Y)$ respectively. In other words γ_2 and β may both be regarded as functionally dependent on Y. Let us examine the possibilities of this approach.

Consider now the suboptimization problem of choosing the β and γ_2 coefficients in such a way as to minimize the effective periodic cost of providing one unit of capacity.[2] Let us suppose first of all that for planning purposes it is desired to install a physical asset capable of providing a

[2] This problem takes up the question of optimum equipment lives and replacement theory. An extensive and important literature exists on this subject and may be consulted via the bibliographies in Vernon Smith's *Investment and Production. A Study in the Theory of the Capital-using Enterprise*, Harvard University Press, Cambridge, Mass., 1961. In particular, difficult conceptual problems arise when it is recognized that it may be logically necessary to consider not simply the apparent life of a particular asset, but

stipulated number of Y-capacity units per period. To begin with we envisage a machine (or a building or whatever asset is involved) technologically capable of providing the required capacity. With reference to this machine we employ the following notation:

L = economic life

M = initial capital outlay cost

S = periodic maintenance and servicing cost

D = periodic amortization installment or contribution to a sinking fund necessary to provide for the replacement of the machine at the end of its economic life

r = rate of interest assumed for sinking fund computations

We shall suppose for purposes of planning that the sinking fund accumulated for asset replacement is not invested in the enterprise against which the amortization installments are being charged. The interest rate, r, assumed for sinking fund purposes will then conceivably be an approximation to the firm's so-called lending rate, and it may or may not be very closely related either to the *ad hoc* interest rate in any loan raised concomitantly with the acquisition of the particular asset, or to some notion of the average or overall cost of capital to the firm. Since it is possible to assume that maintenance expenditures and replacement are two different ways of providing for the productive presence of the machine in the business, the same sinking fund r will be used in what follows in the consideration of maintenance and servicing costs. Then γ_2 will be the sum of the optimum per unit values of D and S: $\gamma_2 = (D + S)/Y$.

The periodic maintenance and servicing cost can be expected to increase during the life of the asset and may be conceived, for purposes of example, to be equal to A dollars in the first period and grow at a rate of b percent per period. In any future period the relevant cost will therefore be Ae^{bt} dollars. The total monetary outlay connected with maintaining the productive presence of the asset is then made up of two parts: (1) the succession of periodic costs equal to Ae^{bt}, and (2) the provision of M dollars for replacement purposes at the end of the life of the asset, abstracting for the present from possible changes in price levels.[3] The total present value of

the optimum replacement chain of such assets, extending, conceivably, into the infinite future. Additionally, consideration might be given to taking fuller account of probable technological improvements in the future and their possible effects on the optimum structure of such an equipment chain. Our more modest objective, consistent with the general nature of our theoretical model, is to probe the question in sufficient depth to expose the nature of the principal causal relations involved. Our procedure will not, therefore, follow precisely any part of the literature referred to.

[3] The following argument assumes, for purposes of simplicity, that the scrap value of the asset is zero at the end of its economic life.

all such contemplated outlays can be stated as follows:

$$W = \int_0^L A e^{bt} e^{-rt} \, dt + M e^{-rL}$$
$$= A \int_0^L e^{(b-r)t} \, dt + M e^{-rL} \tag{7-6}$$

Differentiating this function partially with respect to L and applying the rule that the derivative of the integral with respect to its upper limit is the integrand valued at that limit, it can be shown that

$$\frac{\partial W}{\partial L} = A e^{(b-r)L} - rM e^{-rL}$$

and the optimum life of the machine becomes

$$L = \frac{1}{b} \ln \left(\frac{rM}{A} \right) \tag{7-7}$$

If b were zero and the annual servicing cost were therefore constant, this would imply an infinite durability, and the γ_2 we seek would equal A. But in actual fact, of course, the situation confronting the planner would involve the prospect of increasing annual costs as the proposed life of the asset is extended, offset by lower amortization charges for a given capital outlay. The optimum life L in Equation (7-7) minimizes the present value of the sum of all such charges.

But the quantity we are searching for, in order to be able to specify the γ_2 unit cost associated with the capacity requirement postulated in the planning study, is a constant periodic charge whose present value is equal to that of the overall series of charges incorporated in the preceding analysis. We want the constant periodic equivalent D and S charges to give $\gamma_2 = (D + S)/Y$.

We shall first consider D, the periodic amortization charge. It is required that the amortization sinking fund amount to M at the end of L periods, or that

$$M = \int_0^L D e^{rt} \, dt \tag{7-8}$$

Integrating Equation (7-8) yields

$$M = D \left(\frac{e^{rt}}{r} \right)_0^L$$

or

$$M = D \left(\frac{e^{rL}}{r} - \frac{1}{r} \right)$$

whence it follows that

$$D = \frac{rM}{e^{rL} - 1} \tag{7-9}$$

thus specifying the necessary periodic amortization sinking fund contribution.

Similarly, we can consider the constant periodic maintenance and servicing cost S associated with the asset investment, again making use of the optimum economic life L, for which, it is envisaged, the asset will be maintained. In this case we shall seek the constant annual S component of a stream of payments that has the same capitalized value as the actual stream of maintenance and servicing costs incurred by the investment. The following equation may therefore be established:

$$\int_0^L S e^{-rt} \, dt = \int_0^L A e^{bt} e^{-rt} \, dt \tag{7-10}$$

Integrating both sides of the equation yields

$$S\left(-\frac{e^{-rt}}{r}\right)_0^L = A\left(\frac{e^{(b-r)t}}{b-r}\right)_0^L$$

whence it follows that

$$\frac{S}{r}\left(1 - e^{-rL}\right) = \frac{A}{b-r}\left(e^{(b-r)L} - 1\right)$$

and

$$S = \frac{rA}{b-r}\left(\frac{e^{(b-r)L} - 1}{1 - e^{-rL}}\right)$$

or

$$S = \frac{rA}{b-r}\left(\frac{e^{bL} - e^{rL}}{e^{rL} - 1}\right) \tag{7-11}$$

Equation (7-11) indicates the constant annual equivalent maintenance and servicing charge we set out to specify. It may be noted in this connection that an interesting case arises when b, the annual rate of increase in the maintenance cost, equals r, the relevant sinking fund rate of interest used in the analysis. In this case it follows from Equation (7-10) that

$$\int_0^L S e^{-rt} \, dt = \int_0^L A \, dt$$

whence

$$\frac{S}{r}\left(1 - e^{-rL}\right) = AL$$

and

$$S = \frac{rALe^{rL}}{e^{rL} - 1} \tag{7-12}$$

In any event it follows that given the constant annual equivalents D and S respectively, the γ_2 we are seeking may then be derived from Equations (7-9) and (7-11), written in the following form:

$$\gamma_2 = \frac{D + S}{Y} \qquad (7\text{-}13)$$

The result of Equation (7-13) is then available for incorporation in the enterprise cost and profit calculations. Thus we have specified the annual or periodic flow cost per unit of capacity of factor Y. Or looking at the problem again from the viewpoint of the structural planning of the enterprise, we have derived a best estimate of γ_2 relevant to a postulated level of factor Y-capacity requirements. Such a planning procedure, having regard to available technological data, could conceivably be repeated for varying possible levels of Y-capacity requirements, and for each such level of factor Y utilization a suboptimized functional relation between γ_2 and Y could be established. In the enterprise cost and profit functions, therefore,

$$\gamma_2 = \gamma_2(Y) \qquad (7\text{-}14)$$

But all this, of course, has merely established a method of analysis or attack on our problem. We need no longer stay with the initial assumption that there exists a single unique way of providing a stipulated number of units of factor Y capacity per period. It may, on the contrary, be possible to provide the requisite capacity by investing in any of several different asset structures, each having its own technological characteristics. Different types or models of equipment may exist having, among other things, different prospective durabilities, initial capital outlay costs, maintenance and service charge characteristics, and thus different optimum economic lives.

In the light of these possibilities, a schedule of economic characteristics of different alternatives may be drawn up, where L_i, M_i, A_i, b_i, and, by the procedure established, D_i, S_i, and γ_i represent the relevant data for the ith such alternative. It follows that for any given or desired level of Y-capacity requirements, the optimum real capital investment to be called for would be that promising the minimum γ_i as thus ascertained, and it would be this magnitude which should be incorporated in the planning stage in the functional relation $\gamma_i(Y)$, as specified in Equation (7-14).

It will also be clear that the procedure which thus establishes the choice of asset investment to provide the Y-capacity units will thereby provide the optimum initial capital outlay associated with that factor utilization, or M_i in the foregoing analysis. Given then the necessary asset investment for each intensity of factor utilization, the desired money capital requirement coefficient for that factor is specified, and in the general case,

$$\beta = \frac{M_i}{Y} \tag{7-15}$$

Given the dependence of M_i, the money capital outlay, on the level of factor usage required, the general specification follows that

$$\beta = \beta(Y) \tag{7-16}$$

and the factor's money capital requirement coefficient is again functionally dependent on the level of factor usage envisaged.

With this analysis in hand we may return to the enterprise money capital requirement function as described in Equation (7-4). The corresponding general form may be written in the following manner, continuing to assume for the present a single-product firm:

$$K = g[f(X,Y)] + \alpha(X)X + \beta(Y)Y \tag{7-17}$$

The derivatives of the function for variations in factor usages, analogous to Equation (7-5), may be correspondingly specified.

The Money Capital Availability Constraint

It is possible now to consider, against the background of the firm's total money capital requirement function, the supply of money capital available, the terms, costs, and conditions on which the availability may be increased, and the manner in which the relevant total supplies of money capital may constitute a constraint against which the firm's entire optimization decision has to be made. At this point we confront, in one of its sharpest forms, the meaning of our earlier conclusion that enterprise optimum decision making is, in the general case, constrained decision making. Fortunately a lengthy consideration of the supply conditions of money capital is not required at this point, since we can again call to mind the discussion of the enterprise structure and decision nexus contained in Chapters 2 and 3.

The conditions on which equity capital is available to the firm turn on the nature of the stability conditions associated with the firm's operations, the owners' or potential owners' risk aversion or risk predilection, and the degree of financial leverage in the total capital structure. Following our earlier discussion of these matters, the equity capital supply conditions were summarized in terms of the equity owners' capitalization rate function in Equation (4-29), reproduced here in its general form

$$\rho = \rho(\theta,M,L) \tag{7-18}$$

In this equation θ refers to the coefficient of variation of the net operating income stream, M represents the total capital employed in the firm, and L refers to the financial leverage, or debt-equity ratio. In our earlier discussion and in the analysis to follow, the equity capital at work in the firm, measured at its book value, is referred to by the symbol K and the debt capital by the symbol D. The earlier analysis also contained a full discussion of the differentiability characteristics of the equity capital cost function, notably its responsiveness to changes in the amount of debt capital at work in the firm, one of the most important of the enterprise decision variables. It was observed by definition that $M = K + D$.

Similarly, an analysis was made of the conditions of supply of debt capital to the firm, and the relevant debt cost function was summarized in general form in Equation (4-32). It is here reproduced in its general form as

$$r = r(V_o, L) \qquad (7\text{-}19)$$

In this expression V_o refers to the coefficient of variation of the net operating income stream of the firm (the total earnings on a before-tax basis available to pay the interest on the debt), and L again refers to the degree of financial leverage in the total capital structure. The differentiability characteristics of the debt cost function were also discussed in the earlier analysis. Again we shall be most concerned with the way in which the average rate of interest on the firm's indebtedness, r, may vary with the level of the debt capital employed in the firm. In the general case, therefore, and recalling the full discussion and the specified forms of the money capital cost functions, the following simplified statement of the principal relationships is in order. Both the equity capitalization rate ρ and the average rate of interest on the debt r can be expected in the general case to be monotonically increasing functions of the level of debt:

$$\rho = \rho(D) \qquad (7\text{-}20)$$

$$\frac{d\rho}{dD} \geq 0 \qquad (7\text{-}21)$$

$$\frac{d^2\rho}{dD^2} \geq 0 \qquad (7\text{-}22)$$

$$r = r(D) \qquad (7\text{-}23)$$

$$\frac{dr}{dD} \geq 0 \qquad (7\text{-}24)$$

$$\frac{d^2r}{dD^2} \geq 0 \qquad (7\text{-}25)$$

It might be noted that in actual fact the debt cost function might not be of the continuous differentiable form here assumed for purposes of analysis. Indeed, considerations of the possible monopsonistic position of the borrowing enterprise may well mean that it is confronted with what Hart has called a "stepped market."[4] But these considerations do not affect the logic involved in our present discussion, and the form we have hypothesized can usefully be employed.

The task of analysis at this stage of our work can be seen in clear focus by bringing together the supply conditions of money capital on the one hand and the firm's requirements of money capital on the other. In our initial approximation to the enterprise optimization model in the following chapter we shall examine the case in which the firm, as of a specified decision-making date, possesses a given amount of equity capital we shall designate as $\overline{K}$. On the basis of its possession of these funds, it will be possible for the firm to "trade on the equity" and acquire a certain amount of additional capital by way of borrowing, given, as already indicated, the conditions on which such loan funds are available. It follows, therefore, that the supply and demand sides of the firm's money capital problem can now be pieced together and the important concept of the enterprise money capital availability constraint defined. Taking the money capital requirement function as in Equation (7-17), and simplifying to the form in which it will be used in the following initial approximations, it follows that the money capital availability constraint may be specified in the following manner:

$$g(Q) + \alpha X + \beta Y \leq \overline{K} + D \qquad (7\text{-}26)$$

When, moreover, the cost conditions associated with money capital availability are also taken into account in the firm's cost, profit, and valuation functions, the relevant specifications of ρ and r in Equations (7-18) and (7-19) or in (7-20) and (7-23) may be employed. It follows from the previous analysis that in the tasks ahead it will be necessary to show clearly the ways in which the money capital availability constraint of inequality (7-26) influences the determination not only of the firm's equilibrium or optimum money capital usage, but also the structure of its asset investments and factor combinations. In particular it will be discovered that the conditions of availability of money capital influence not only the capital widening, but also the capital deepening undertaken by the firm. In this last point lies one of the more important, if subtle, conclusions of the enterprise optimization theory which has evaded the traditional formulation of the problem.

---

[4] Albert G. Hart, *Anticipations, Uncertainty, and Dynamic Planning*, The University of Chicago Press, Chicago, 1940, p. 44. See also Eli Schwartz, "Theory of Capital Structure of the Firm," *Journal of Finance*, vol. 14, March, 1959.

Elements of the Optimization Model

For the present, however, it will be sufficient to conclude this chapter by bringing together the several functional relations that our analysis thus far has posited and examined, recognizing them now as the building blocks of the optimization model in the following chapter.

First, the firm's profit function may be specified as in Equation (1-1) or as in Equation (3-1), here reproduced in simplified form as

$$\pi = p(Q)Q - \gamma_1 X - \gamma_2 Y - r(D)D \qquad (7\text{-}27)$$

The assumption of a single-product activity is retained, though in due course it will be relaxed, and the unit selling price of output is understood as a function of the quantity produced and sold, $p = p(Q)$. Conditions of imperfect competition in the output market are envisaged as the analytical norm. The interest on the debt is specified in Equation (7-27) as functionally dependent on the amount of debt capital employed in the firm.

Second, the valuation function may be specified as in Equation (2-6), here summarized as

$$V = \frac{\pi}{\rho(D)} \qquad (7\text{-}28)$$

In this expression V represents the economic value of the ownership of the firm, and ρ, the rate at which the residual equity earnings π are capitalized, is also understood as functionally dependent on the amount of debt capital employed in the firm. The fuller analysis of the form of the relevant debt and equity capital cost functions and the manner in which the amount of debt capital employed, or the debt-equity ratio, is relevant to the outcome need not be repeated in this summary statement.

Third, the profit or value functions in Equations (7-27) and (7-28) may now be maximized, subject to the money capital availability constraint of inequality (7-26), to determine the interdependent optimum solution outcomes on the levels we set out to consider, namely, production, capital investment, and finance.

This summary of the optimization problem points to the general mathematical techniques of constrained maximization. In the forms in which the argument will appear in the following chapter the nature of the mathematical programming problem will emerge. For the main part it will be convenient to rely on the differential calculus technique of Lagrange multipliers and to recognize the relation between our own procedure and the well known Kuhn-Tucker theorems which generalize the marginalism of classical economics.[5]

---

[5] While no extensive anticipation of the mathematics is necessary at this point, the reader might bear in mind the *locus classicus* of the argument in H. W. Kuhn and A. W.

In our construction of the enterprise optimization model we shall proceed, via successive approximations designed to take account of the neoclassical contributions on which reliance is being placed, to exhibit precisely the points and nature of the departures with which we are most concerned. To this task we turn immediately in the following chapter.

Tucker, "Nonlinear Programming," *Proceedings of the Second Berkeley Symposium on Mathematical Statistics and Probability*, U. Neyman (ed.), University of California Press, Berkeley, Calif., 1951. A clear exposition of the Kuhn-Tucker optimality conditions is contained in the appendix to Smith, *op. cit.*, and a further discussion is contained in Robert Dorfman, Paul A. Samuelson, and Robert M. Solow, *Linear Programming and Economic Analysis*, McGraw-Hill Book Company, New York, 1958, pp. 199–201.

8

The General Optimization Model:

Initial Approximation To Constrained Solutions

We have observed at some length in the preceding chapters that the enterprise optimization model is to be grounded in the marginalist thought forms of neoclassical equilibrium analysis on the one hand and in more recent constructs of production-capital theorizing and the theory of finance on the other. It will be useful now to consider the essence of the neoclassical model and examine some typical situations and conclusions of the received theory of the firm. It will then be possible to suggest such reconstructions of the theory as are required for the purposes we have indicated.

A Profit Maximization Model

Consider first a simple model of profit maximization under conditions of capital saturation. We shall suppose initially that no debt capital is employed in conjunction with the equity capital supplied by the owners of the firm. In this case the enterprise objective is that of maximizing the profit function

$$\pi = p(Q)f(X,Y) - \gamma_1 X - \gamma_2 Y \tag{8-1}$$

using the notation established in our earlier analysis. The first term on the right-hand side of Equation (8-1) describes the total revenue of the firm, or the total quantity of output produced and sold multiplied by the selling price per unit. The output of the firm is here expressed in terms of the production function $f(X,Y)$, and the selling price is recognized as functionally dependent on the quantity sold. The latter assumption simply acknowledges the normative significance of imperfect competition in the output market. The remaining terms on the right-hand side of Equation (8-1) represent the direct costs of factors X and Y respectively.

The familiar optimization conditions, confining the argument at this stage to the necessary or first-order conditions, are obtained by differentiating Equation (8-1) partially with respect to X and Y and setting the resulting expressions equal to zero:

$$\frac{\partial \pi}{\partial X} = \left(p + Q\frac{dp}{dQ}\right)f_x - \gamma_1 = 0 \qquad (8\text{-}2)$$

$$\frac{\partial \pi}{\partial Y} = \left(p + Q\frac{dp}{dQ}\right)f_y - \gamma_2 = 0 \qquad (8\text{-}3)$$

From Equations (8-2) and (8-3) it follows that

$$\frac{f_x}{f_y} = \frac{\gamma_1}{\gamma_2} \qquad (8\text{-}4)$$

The quantity in parentheses in Equations (8-2) and (8-3) will appear in a similar form in subsequent expressions also, and will be recognized as the marginal revenue of output. The value of this marginal revenue term will depend on the form of the firm's selling price function, or what is often referred to as its average revenue function or demand curve. At the level of theoretical abstraction at which we are presently working, no point is to be served by specifying such a function in anything other than the general form in which we have expressed it. Consistent with the received theory on the subject, we might bear in mind a general negatively inclined unit revenue function, or the general assumption of $dp/dQ < 0$. Or again, referring to the firm's total revenue by the symbol R, we may specify the general form of the revenue function by noting the twofold assumption of $dR/dQ > 0$ and $d^2R/dQ^2 < 0$. Total revenue is assumed to increase as the quantity of output sold increases, but the negative sign on the second derivative indicates that it increases at a decreasing rate. The terms f_x and f_y in Equations (8-2) and (8-3) will also reappear frequently in subsequent expressions; they represent the partial derivatives of the production function with respect to factors X and Y respectively. These terms may be referred to alternatively as the marginal physical products of the respective factor inputs.

The simple model now before us yields the usual textbook conclusions. Rearranging Equations (8-2) and (8-3) by transferring the gamma terms to the right-hand side of the final equality sign yields the following optimization condition. The optimum employments of factors will be such that the marginal revenue product of each of the factors will be equal to its unit input price, assuming for the present that the firm is purchasing its inputs in perfectly competitive markets and that the unit factor cost is therefore not dependent on the amounts of factors acquired. We have already noted in an earlier discussion the ways in which the gamma cost prices may be functionally dependent on the quantities of factors purchased. But for purposes of the present argument we may set that particular complexity aside. Effecting the suggested rearrangement of Equations (8-2) and (8-3) and dividing (8-2) by (8-3) yields an equally familiar optimization condition. At the optimum factor input combination the ratio of the marginal physical products of the factors will be equal to the ratio of their unit prices. The result is shown in Equation (8-4).

But these results are based on the extremely unrealistic assumption that the firm, in making its optimum production and factor use decisions, does not face any shortage of money capital. As Lange pointed out with remarkable clarity in his early paper, "the equations of the traditional theory of production are based on the tacit assumption that there is always available the money capital necessary to enable all firms to choose the best method of production."[1] This, Lange further observes, "is a theory of production in a state of perfect *saturation* with capital," and against this he goes on to develop "a theory of production subject to a shortage of capital."[2] From this latter analysis Lange then constructs his theory of the rate of interest. While our own theoretical objectives, and therefore our mode of analysis, are different from those of Lange, a close parallel exists between his work and the following argument in those instances where common ground is covered.

The Geometry of the Model

It will be useful to have before us also, for comparison with the more complex cases to follow, a partial geometrical treatment of the simple traditional model. We begin with the production function and present in Figure 6 a sectional view of the three-dimensional relationship involved. Given a production function of the general form $Q = f(X,Y)$ as already explained, it is of interest to consider the technological possibilities

[1] Oskar Lange, "The Place of Interest in the Theory of Production," *Review of Economic Studies*, vol. 3, pp. 159–192, June, 1936; see p. 177.
[2] *Ibid.*, p. 190; italics in original.

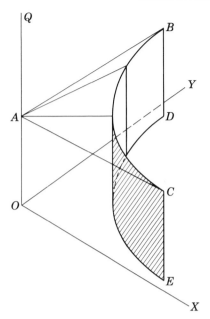

Figure 6.   A sectional view of the production function

of substitution between the factors X and Y. To the extent that the factors are substitutable, or to the extent that we can specify the nature of the elasticity of substitution between them,[3] it will be possible, from the technological viewpoint, to produce a desired output Q with any of several different combinations of factor inputs. If we assume, for mathematical convenience and for expository purposes, that the production function is continuously differentiable in both factor X and factor Y, it would be possible to show, in a diagram such as Figure 6, a "product hill" depicting the increase in output Q, measured vertically along the product axis, as we increased the inputs of factors of production. The latter are measured along the axes X and Y in what may be called the factor input plane.

Let us focus now on this factor input plane and consider the relations between a desired level of output OA in the figure and the different possible factor combinations with which it might be produced. In whatever way these possible factor combinations are described, at least we can make the following statement in relation to them. Measuring in the vertical direction

---

[3] For a clear mathematical discussion of the elasticity of substitution see R. G. D. Allen, *Mathematical Analysis for Economists*, Macmillan & Co., London, 1938, pp. 341f. The notion of the elasticity of substitution in the production function has lately become prominent in theoretical economics, and a valuable survey appears in A. A. Walters, "Production and Cost Functions: An Econometric Survey," *Econometrica*, vol. 31. pp. 1–66, January–April, 1963. See also the references cited in footnote 27 of Chap. 6.

the size of the maximum output they are each capable of yielding, the "product hill" will, by definition, be the same vertical distance above each such factor combination. If, for example, the factor combination represented by point D in the factor input plane were technologically capable of producing, as a maximum attainable output, the same output as the factor combination represented by point E and if the equal-product output thus envisaged were in fact OA as we have posited, then the magnitudes of OA, DB, and EC in the figure must all be equal. Conceiving, then, the possibility of such equiproduct outputs and factor combinations, it will be possible to describe a curve such as BC in the output dimension which represents the locus of points describing the constant output OA. If now we take a vertical slice through the product hill along all such equiproduct points, we may describe the section $BCED$ in the figure, a vertical section resting in the factor input plane.

What, now, determines the characteristics of this $BCED$ section, notably its convexity to the output axis OQ? The answer depends again on the elasticity of substitution existing between the factors in the production function, and the analytical significance of the relations may be explored more fully with the aid of Figure 7. Here we are concentrating on the X-Y factor input plane, each member of the family of curves in the figure representing the image in that plane of the locus of equal-product outputs in the third dimension of Figure 6. Each such curve in Figure 7 will therefore be called an isoproduct curve. It will be taken as the locus of all those combinations of factors technologically capable of producing, as their maximum output, a given output level. For example, isoproduct curve II in the figure might correspond to the curve DE in the input plane of Figure 6, which in turn is the image of the third dimensional locus BC.

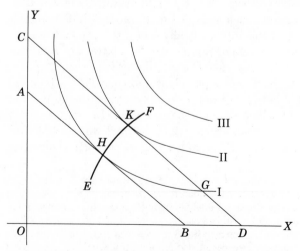

Figure 7.   The production function factor input plane

It will be clear from the properties of the posited production function, or, if preferred, from the nature of the product hill referred to in discussing Figure 6, that isoproduct curves I, II, and III in Figure 7 represent successively larger levels of product output. For the same reasons, the product contours and the curves in Figure 7 will not intersect, each curve describing the maximum possible output attainable with the varying combinations of factors envisaged. We can now concentrate on the general form of the isoproduct curves and consider the significance for optimum decision making in the firm of whatever convexity, or curvature, the curves may possess.[4]

If we assume now, as in the model described by Equations (8-1) through (8-4), that the firm is producing in conditions of money capital saturation, it may nevertheless decide to operate at any given time with a factor cost budget of a certain specified size. We may then be interested in the following twofold question: First, what is the actual size of that budget; and second, how does the relation between the unit factor costs determine the possible factor combinations the firm could acquire within that budget limit? It may be the case, for example, that at a cost budget size of M dollars and at constant unit factor costs of γ_1 and γ_2 for factors X and Y as previously, a total amount of factor X represented by $OB = M/\gamma_1$ could be acquired. Alternatively, if only factor Y were purchased, an amount represented by $OA = M/\gamma_2$ could be acquired. It then follows by elementary algebra that the line AB is the locus of all factor cost combinations, the purchase of which would exactly exhaust the budget of size M dollars. A similar locus described by the line CD may be taken to refer to a factor cost budget of a larger total size.

---

[4] It should be pointed out that it is not intended or necessary to set out in complete array all the analytical properties of this neoclassical model. We are concerned only with what is necessary to build the methodological bridges to our own subsequent analysis. The material omitted here is explored in depth in Sidney Weintraub, *Price Theory*, Pitman Publishing Corporation, New York, 1956, and in James M. Henderson and Richard E. Quandt, *Microeconomic Theory: A Mathematical Approach*, McGraw-Hill Book Company, New York, 1958.

It should be noted also that throughout our analysis we shall discuss at length the necessary or first-order optimization conditions. In a more extensive development of our subject, particularly when we are dealing with constrained objective functions, it would be desirable to consider explicitly also the sufficient or second-order conditions, and to examine the solution conditions on the signs of the relevant bordered Hessian determinants. For our present purposes we shall assume that the forms of the underlying functions in the model (the negatively inclined unit selling price function, the diminishing marginal productivities in the production function, the increasing marginal money capital costs) suffice to lead to true maximum solutions. But the extension of the analysis that we here pass over is important for a complete treatment and should be borne in mind. The reader may consult the relevant mathematics in the Henderson and Quandt volume referred to above, especially chap. 3 and pp. 273–274.

The question may now be asked as to what is the optimum factor combination with which to produce a given output level, say that represented by isoproduct curve I. To take only the cases described in the figure, the specified output quantity may be produced by using completely the money resources of either of the factor cost budgets referred to above. In one case, the factor combination represented by the point G may be employed, since the relevant factor combination exhausts the CD cost budget and also satisfies the production function conditions by virtue of its lying on isoproduct curve I. It is clear, however, that the same output could also be produced by the factor combination represented by point H in the figure, and that this is superior or preferred to the previously suggested factor combination at G, by virtue of its lying on the lower total-cost budget line AB. In the same way it follows that the optimum factor usage with which to produce any desired output quantity will be the least-cost combination chosen from the set of technologically feasible factor combinations. The factor combination at point K on isoproduct curve II is another such description of optimum factor employment.

We shall use in the present chapter more complex analogues of the relations adduced from this simple production analysis. For this reason it will be useful to clarify and emphasize two basic properties of the model: first, the significance of the curve, such as EF in Figure 7, representing the locus of optimum factor usages, or points of least-cost factor combinations; and second, the logical or mathematical properties of the optimum solution points such as H and K in the figure.

The curve EF in Figure 7, or the locus of optimum factor employments, has frequently been referred to as the expansion path, indicating either the rate of increase in the cost budget absorbed for given increases in the scale of operations or the attainable increases in output levels consistent with given increases in operating budgets. The family of budget lines such as AB and CD will be parallel if unit factor costs remain unchanged as successively larger quantities of both factors are purchased. The curve EF is the image in the factor input plane of the locus, along the edge of the product hill, of the points of intersection of the factor input cost or budget planes (of which, in turn, the lines AB and CD are images) and of the output dimension of the production function. Thus the form or the slope of the EF curve will be determined partly by the behavior of the family of input cost or budget planes and partly by the form of the production function. It is the latter that determines the steepness of the product hill, or the potentialities of returns to scale in the production function as the inputs of both factors of production are increased.

For our present purposes, emphasis is laid on a single feature from among these characteristics of the EF curve. This is the fact that the so-called expansion path as here represented is the one that would be attained if, at whatever output level it were desired to operate, the assumption of capital saturation continued to be satisfied. In such a case there would presumably be no reason why the firm should not decide to operate at any budget level which, for one reason or another, it thought to be desirable. This, in fact, is the general nature of the assumptions and the argument in the general classical and usual textbook model.[5] If, however, the assumption of capital saturation does not continue to be satisfied along the expansion path, the entire picture and underlying analysis are seriously changed. While the reasons involved are quite simple in themselves, they are radical in their import from the point of view of the traditional model. The principal issue will be seen to turn on the notion of the marginal cost of money capital and its imputation to the different factors employed in the firm.

So long as the traditional model is confined to the analysis of a short-run single-operating-period situation in which the factors are all understood as variable factors whose durability does not extend beyond the operating period, the model may escape the strictures we are now adducing. But if this is so, the price it pays is heavy. Its relevance for any enterprise optimum structure analysis is completely evacuated. Abandoned completely, thereby, is any hope of integrating the production and capital investment analysis into a mutually determinate optimum decision outcome. If the variable factor combination problem is the only point of analysis to which the relations of Figure 7 can be addressed, then we are not really talking about a meaningful enterprise production function at all. We are back in what we referred to as the virtual agnosticism in production function analysis which the Lutz model espoused. In such an event nothing in an adequate sense is being said about the optimum employment of capital in the firm.[6]

The Model and the Employment of Capital Factors

But if, more realistically, the arguments in the production function, X and Y in the present discussion, refer to all factors employed, conceivably variable factors on the one hand and the services of durable capital assets on the other, then we must recognize the unit costs of all factors as including not only the direct cost of purchasing and maintaining the factors, but also an imputed cost of the money capital funds, the investment of which is necessitated by the factor employment. In the preceding chapter we unraveled the meaning of attributing a constant annual per unit cost to factor services provided by durable assets. We considered there the

[5] Copious instances may be found in the textbook literature already referred to.
[6] See the fuller discussion in Chap. 6 above.

logic of the quantification of the γ_2 and β coefficients referable to factor Y in our initial production function. But this γ_2 is still in the nature of a direct per unit factor cost. The moment we recognize that factor employment necessitates the investment of money capital, the effective marginal cost of a given factor is not simply the direct cost, such as γ_2 in the case in hand. The effective marginal cost is then the amount made up of this direct cost on the one hand plus the imputed marginal cost of money capital on the other. It is then the sum of these two components which is the relevant determinant in the enterprise optimization decisions. But the details of the imputation argument must be deferred for the present.

We are now in a position to notice clearly, however, that so long as we hold to the traditional assumption of capital saturation, money capital is not a scarce resource, its marginal cost is therefore zero, and no imputation of capital costs to the various factors need be, or indeed can be, made. In that event the slope of the budget line, AB or CD in Figure 7, is simply the ratio of the direct factor costs γ_1/γ_2 as in the foregoing case. When it is thus disclosed that the traditional capital assumption takes away from money capital its character as a scarce resource, and thereby reduces its marginal cost to zero, the weakness of the analytical construct is patent. If, on the other hand, we do regard money capital as scarce, and as importing a marginal cost into the optimization model, the principal implication of this for the present argument can then be stated quite clearly: The extent or degree to which each factor will be required to carry a capital cost imputation will depend on that factor's money capital intensity, or what we referred to previously as the factor's money capital requirement coefficient. But again the details of the imputation argument must be deferred for the present.

Capital Costs and the Expansion Path

More important at this stage is the understanding of the relevance of the foregoing argument for the point of analysis at which we began, namely, the characteristics of the expansion path EF in Figure 7. Having exposed the implications at this point of the traditional argument, only two things further need be said. First, the ratio of effective factor costs will no longer be γ_1/γ_2, as in the figure and as shown also in Equation (8-4), but will change to include also the imputed capital costs. This means that the slope of the budget lines AB and CD in the figure will change, and the expansion path will be pulled away from its indicated course, either downward toward the X factor axis or upward toward the Y factor axis. The direction and extent of such a movement will depend on how the different capital intensities of the factors determine the degree of capital costs they bear, and thereby determine the contour of the cost ratio curve.

Second, we may emphasize now what will emerge as one of the most important results of the argument for the entire enterprise optimization decision. This is the fact that since the conditions of money capital availability (or what we shall call the severity of the money capital availability constraint) are now seen to determine the optimum combination of factor inputs, the terms on which money capital may be acquired determine in part the entire productive process and asset structure of the firm. We put this point at an earlier level by saying that the conditions of money capital availability determine not only the extent of capital widening in the firm, but also the extent of capital deepening. It does this via its impact on the effective factor costs and the structures of optimum factor combinations these induce. This sorting out of the causes and implications of capital deepening and capital widening is an insight not disclosed by the traditional model. It has not yet been taken properly into account in the burgeoning finance literature nor in the nascent attempts to derive a financial theory of the firm. But more on this follows.

An Alternative View of the Optimization Condition

The final respect in which it is desired to emphasize the logical properties of the traditional model has to do with the form of the isoproduct curves, and behind them the form of the production function and the specification of the tangency optimization points such as H and K in Figure 7.

Consider first the production function in the form in which we have posited it:

$$Q = f(X,Y) \qquad (8\text{-}5)$$

The mathematical properties of the isoproduct curve are now demonstrable from the total differential of Equation (8-5). This takes the form

$$dQ = f_x \, dX + f_y \, dY \qquad (8\text{-}6)$$

where f_x and f_y refer respectively to the partial derivatives of the production function with respect to factors X and Y. The very same quantity was previously interpreted in the system of Equations (8-1) through (8-4) as the marginal physical productivities of the respective factors. If now we focus attention on the possible variations in factor combinations that will keep us on a given isoproduct curve, or that refer, that is, to a constant given output level, then for such variations in X and Y, Equation (8-6) may be set equal to zero. Proceeding in this manner and rearranging the resulting expression it follows that

$$\frac{dY}{dX} = -\frac{f_x}{f_y} \qquad (8\text{-}7)$$

But dY/dX is recognized as the first derivative of the isoproduct curve, and the result is thereby formalized that the slope of the isoproduct curve is equal to the negative of the ratio of the partial derivatives of the production function with respect to its respective arguments. The mathematical content of the argument will be recognized as very similar to that spelled out at some length in Chapter 2 in considering the relations between the individual's utility function, his indifference relations between risk and return, and the implied form of the equity income capitalization rate function. If we were to proceed in the same manner as previously, we could establish both the negative slope of the isoproduct curves, as in Equation (8-7), and their curvature, depending in this case on the demonstrable positivity of the second derivative, or d^2Y/dX^2. To do this we should take the total derivative of Equation (8-7). The mathematics need not detain us, since the general argument has already been well established in the earlier context. It will be clear intuitively, and may be demonstrated by appropriate differentiation, that the elasticity of substitution between the factors in the production function is inversely proportional to the degree of curvature in the isoproduct curve.[7]

Continuing with the relations in Figure 7, however, we may consider the set of factor combinations consistent with the exhaustion of a factor cost budget of size M dollars, and constituting therefore the locus AB as previously argued. The different possible factor combinations in view are implicit in the budget relation

$$M = \gamma_1 X + \gamma_2 Y \qquad (8\text{-}8)$$

where γ_1 and γ_2 are, as previously, the posited unit costs of factors X and Y. Applying the same mathematical procedures as were employed in similar situations in earlier contexts, it will be clear that for factor substitutions within the assumption of the given budget M, the total differential of Equation (8-8) may be set equal to zero, and the following relations may be deduced:

$$dM = \gamma_1\, dX + \gamma_2\, dY = 0 \qquad (8\text{-}9)$$

It follows from Equation (8-9) that

$$\frac{dY}{dX} = -\frac{\gamma_1}{\gamma_2} \qquad (8\text{-}10)$$

The slope of the budget line is thus shown by Equation (8-10) to be equal to the negative of the ratio of the unit factor costs.

If now we bring together the results of Equations (8-7) and (8-10), the proposition is established that at the optimum factor combination,

$$\frac{f_x}{f_y} = \frac{\gamma_1}{\gamma_2} \qquad (8\text{-}11)$$

---

[7] See Allen, *loc. cit.*, for the relevant mathematical demonstration.

and again it is seen that the ratio of the marginal physical productivities of the factors will be equal to the ratio of their marginal costs. The conclusion is precisely the same as that obtained in a different manner in Equation (8-4) in our initial statement of the traditional model. This accordingly completes the exposition of the main points of the basic model, so far as the understanding of it is necessary for our further development of the total enterprise optimization model. We turn immediately in the following section to a more advanced approximation to our objective.

The Money Capital Constraint

The primary defect of the basic model of the firm, we have argued at length, is its failure to take account of the form, and significance for the enterprise structure, of the money capital availability constraint against which the optimization decisions have to be made. In this section, therefore, we shall consider a profit maximization model incorporating at least an elementary formulation of some of the building blocks we prepared in the preceding chapters.

We shall imagine for the moment that the firm is employing only equity or ownership capital, that a given amount of this capital, designated as $\bar{K}$, is available, but that no borrowed funds or debt capital is introduced into the firm. In the second place, we shall assume a money capital requirement function that incorporates simply the direct money capital requirements, depending on the quantities of the factors employed and their money capital requirement coefficients. It is not necessary at this point to introduce the net working capital requirement function of the preceding chapter. The sacrifice of realism that we shall be making at this stage of approximation will enable us to bring out more sharply some of the new analytical relations we wish to adduce. Putting together, then, the equity capital availability and the money capital requirement functions, we have the initial form of the money capital availability constraint inequality

$$\alpha X + \beta Y \leq \bar{K} \tag{8-12}$$

The profit function we are concerned to optimize is still that specified in Equation (8-1). But now we cannot set out to optimize or maximize it directly, as in the preceding case. Rather, we are now concerned with what is known as constrained maximization, or maximization subject to a specified constraint, or to an inequality side condition. Let us concentrate on the constraint condition for a moment. Taking the form as shown in inequality (8-12), we can say that whatever combination of factors is decided upon by the firm, it must be such that the money capital investment in assets necessitated by the factor usage, represented by the left-hand side of the inequality, does not exceed the total amount of money capital available. The inequality is therefore expressed in a less-than-or-equal-to form. If the actual factor usage exactly exhausted the money capital available (if, in other words, the constraint were actually binding or operative), the following capital usage equation would result:

$$\overline{K} - \alpha X - \beta Y = 0 \qquad (8\text{-}13)$$

If, of course, the equality sign in Equation (8-13) were, at the solution decision outcome, replaced by a greater-than sign, this would mean that the firm was using a combination of factors X and Y that left a residue of available money capital unutilized, and that the constraint was therefore not operative. But in such an event there is no shortage of money capital, and we are right back in the classical case of capital saturation. Money capital is then not a scarce resource, it therefore has no marginal cost, and there is then no meaningful capital cost to be imputed to the factors of production.

The Constrained Optimization Model

What we are concerned with in fact, however, is the task of discovering the combination of factors X and Y that will provide the firm with the maximum profit output at the same time that it satisfies the condition in Equation (8-13). A method of tackling the task mathematically is that of setting out to maximize an amended profit function such that the attainable profit as shown in Equation (8-1) will thereby also be maximized. The amended maximand function with which we shall work is made up of the original profit function plus the constraint condition as represented by the left-hand side of Equation (8-13). On each occasion on which a function of this new general form is written in the remainder of this book we shall designate it by the symbol φ and refer to it either as a "Lagrange function" or a "constrained objective function." In the present instance we are concerned with the following expression:

$$\varphi = p(Q)f(X,Y) - \gamma_1 X - \gamma_2 Y + \mu(\overline{K} - \alpha X - \beta Y) \qquad (8\text{-}14)$$

The interpretation of the variables in Equation (8-14) will be clear from what has gone before, and only a comment is required on the mathematical meaning of the addition of the constraint condition to the basic profit function. Placing the constraint condition in parentheses, we associate with it a variable μ, which can be referred to as the coefficient of the constraint condition, or the coefficient of the constraint variable. In this case, of course, the so-called constraint variable is the available equity capital represented by $\overline{K}$. For the present it need only be said that μ can be looked upon as a pure number, the solution value of which will be determined by the general solution of the Lagrange function. Subsequently it will be seen also that the solution value of μ has a very important economic interpretation, and this will emerge in the argument that follows. Alternatively, and in purely mathematical terms, μ may be referred to as the Lagrange multiplier in the Lagrange function. This too will be examined further in what follows.

Before we set the constrained optimization model of Equation (8-14) in motion, let us notice one final thing in connection with the solution values of the X and Y factor inputs we expect to derive. Clearly, the values of X and Y that will maximize the φ function of Equation (8-14) will also, and in the very process, be maximizing the π function of Equation (8-1) under the conditions specified. This is necessarily the case, because at the solution values of X and Y the value of the expression in the final parentheses of Equation (8-14) becomes equal to zero, and the expression for φ is then identical with the earlier expression for π. In other words we now set out to maximize the φ expression, noting that the values of the variables that maximize φ will, at the same time maximize the attainable value of π. The latter, of course, is our real and ultimate objective.

Let us proceed then to discover the values of the X and Y factor inputs that will maximize the value of the φ function in Equation (8-14). To do this we first of all take the partial derivatives of the function with respect to X, Y, and μ and set the resulting expressions equal to zero to satisfy the general first-order optimization conditions:

$$\frac{\partial \varphi}{\partial X} = \left(p + Q\frac{dp}{dQ}\right)f_x - \gamma_1 - \mu\alpha = 0 \qquad (8\text{-}15)$$

$$\frac{\partial \varphi}{\partial Y} = \left(p + Q\frac{dp}{dQ}\right)f_y - \gamma_2 - \mu\beta = 0 \qquad (8\text{-}16)$$

$$\frac{\partial \varphi}{\partial \mu} = \bar{K} - \alpha X - \beta Y \qquad\qquad = 0 \qquad (8\text{-}17)$$

In this way we have derived three equations in the three unknowns X, Y, and μ. On the basis of our knowledge of the forms and parameters of the underlying functions (the production function, factor input costs, and money capital requirement coefficients), we may solve for the three unknowns. It is not necessary to spell out the algebraic solution at this point.

If, now, Equations (8-15) and (8-16) are rearranged by transferring the negative terms to the right-hand side of the final equality signs, and Equation (8-15) is then divided by Equation (8-16), the following relationship is obtained:

$$\frac{f_x}{f_y} = \frac{\gamma_1 + \mu\alpha}{\gamma_2 + \mu\beta} \qquad (8\text{-}18)$$

At this point it will be instructive to compare Equation (8-18) with Equation (8-4) in the first model we considered. The conclusion emerges that under the conditions of capital shortage, or what the finance literature has called capital rationing, the classical textbook optimization solution of equating the ratio of marginal products to the ratio of direct marginal factor costs no longer holds. In this case also, as may be seen from the suggested rearrangement of Equations (8-15) and (8-16), the equilibrium conditions no longer equate the marginal revenue products and the unit factor costs. [Compare the system of Equations (8-1) through (8-4)].

Rather, in the present capital availability constraint case, the equilibrium conditions may be restated as follows. First, the marginal revenue product of a factor input will equal the effective marginal cost of the factor. Taking Equation (8-15), for example, and reading the magnitude of the marginal revenue product as before, what we have just referred to as the effective marginal cost of factor X is made up of two components. These represent the direct unit cost γ_1 and an additional term $\mu\alpha$, which will turn out in a moment to be the imputed capital cost the factor is called upon to carry. This latter component is simply the factor's money capital requirement coefficient α multiplied by the coefficient of the capital constraint variable μ. It will turn out that μ may be interpreted as the marginal efficiency of money capital, and the imputed capital cost of factor X is therefore the number of dollars of money capital investment in assets required for each unit of factor X employed, multiplied by the marginal efficiency per dollar of money capital. But more will follow in a moment by way of vindication of this conclusion. Meantime, the second equilibrium condition in the present case is that the ratio of marginal physical products, as seen in Equation (8-18), is equal to the ratio of what we have just described as the effective marginal factor costs.

Marginal Efficiency of Money Capital

When we have solved the simultaneous equation system (8-15) through (8-17), we have derived the solution values of the factor inputs on the one hand and the Lagrange variable μ on the other. Let us consider the economic interpretation of this latter variable. For this purpose we recall firstly that insofar as the available money capital is fully employed and the relevant constraint is therefore operative and μ takes on a positive value, the constraint relation may be understood to assume the following form, consistent with the solution conditions:

$$\overline{K} = \alpha X + \beta Y \qquad (8\text{-}19)$$

Consider now the total differential of this equity capital constraint condition:

$$dK = \alpha \, dX + \beta \, dY \qquad (8\text{-}20)$$

For the present we may leave this differential equation in the form shown and consider also the firm's unconstrained profit function, shown as the first three terms of Equation (8-14) or as Equation (8-1). We take now the total differential of this unconstrained profit function and derive the following expression:

$$d\pi = \left[\left(p + Q\frac{dp}{dQ} \right) f_x - \gamma_1 \right] dX + \left[\left(p + Q\frac{dp}{dQ} \right) f_y - \gamma_2 \right] dY$$

$$(8\text{-}21)$$

It will be recognized that the first bracketed term in Equation (8-21) appears in the solution condition shown in Equation (8-15), and in the equilibrium situation it is seen from that equation to take on a value equal to $\mu\alpha$. Similarly, the second bracketed term in Equation (8-21) is seen from Equation (8-16) to take on the value $\mu\beta$. If, therefore, we substitute Equations (8-15) and (8-16) into Equation (8-21), the following condition holds at the solution values of the model:

$$d\pi = \mu(\alpha \, dX + \beta \, dY) \qquad (8\text{-}22)$$

Our final transformation to achieve our present objective is to divide Equation (8-22) by Equation (8-20), whence it follows that

$$\frac{d\pi}{dK} = \mu \qquad (8\text{-}23)$$

This, of course, is the definition of μ we have been seeking. It is seen to be equal to the derivative of the firm's profit function with respect to money capital. In economic terms it is measuring the amount by which the firm's profit could be increased by an increase at the margin of a unit of money capital. It measures, therefore, the marginal efficiency, or the marginal profit productivity, of money capital. Thus it turns out that money capital costs are to be imputed to productive factors at a rate equal to the marginal productivity of money capital. This, of course, it might be noted, is a particular demonstration of an important general theorem from the mathematical economics of constrained maximization. A more general argument in the context of a more complex model will be given in the next chapter. For every operative constraint in such a constrained objective function, the coefficient of the constraint variable will similarly turn out to be equal to the derivative of the objective function (or the maximand or the variable it is desired to maximize) with respect to the constraint variable. It may in every such case, therefore, be similarly interpreted as a marginal productivity measurement. Further instances of the argument will be observed in the final section of this chapter.

Effective Cost and Product Contours, and Factor Substitution

Finally, our understanding may be assisted at this point if the following single anticipation of our fuller analysis is noted. The left-hand side of Equation (8-18) can be recognized as the slope of the isoproduct contour determined at equilibrium by the form of the production function, and the right-hand side of the equation, the ratio of the effective marginal factor costs, can be recognized as the slope of the isooutlay contour. In equilibrium, the outlay contour will be tangential to the product contour. In the general case, then, in the presence of a money capital constraint, the optimum factor combination will differ from that of the capital saturation case, as may be seen by comparing Equations (8-4) and (8-18). In the special case of capital saturation, Equation (8-18) reduces to Equation (8-4), since μ equals zero. The constraint in that case being ineffective, or capital being in more than adequate supply, the Lagrange multiplier cannot take on a positive value. There is no economic meaning in a positive imputed marginal cost price of a resource in surplus supply. The concept of the Lagrange multiplier is here recognizable as the analogue of the dual shadow price in a corresponding Kuhn-Tucker generalized model.[8] It can readily be shown in the Kuhn-Tucker–Lagrange generalization that a price can be imputed only to a resource that is sufficiently scarce to constrain the equilibrium solution value of the variables in the objective function. Only scarce goods are in effect economic goods. But in the world as it is, the artificial textbook case of capital saturation does not hold, given opportunities of alternative employments, and Equation (8-18) with its imputed capital costs is therefore a meaningful first step toward the more general explanatory model. It is still possible, of course, that in the presence of a capital constraint the optimum ratio of factor inputs implicit in Equation (8-18) may be unchanged from that in the unconstrained case, Equation (8-4). But this would be so only where the ratio of the factors' money capital requirement coefficients α/β equaled the ratio of direct factor unit costs γ_1/γ_2. There is no reason why this particular case should be encountered.

Following this argument further, a question of considerable interest is prompted by the observation that the relative marginal factor cost line, analogous to the lines AB and CD in Figure 7, will, in the general case, take on a different slope in the capital constraint case from that in the earlier capital saturation case. This means, as already noted, that the capital constraint induces a change in the optimum factor combinations. The question now is whether any theorem can be adduced to explain the direction in which the substitution of one factor for another can be expected

[8] See footnote 5 of Chap. 7 for references to the literature on the Kuhn-Tucker theorem.

to occur. Intuitively the outcome would seem to depend on the relative capital intensities of the respective factors and on the nature of the imputed capital costs that as a consequence they are required to bear.

To consider this question let us concentrate first on the equilibrium value of the ratio of the marginal productivities of the factors f_x/f_y as shown, for example, in Equations (8-4) and (8-18). It follows that the ratio will be lower in the capital constraint case than it will be in the capital saturation case if the following expression, also derived from Equations (8-4) and (8-18), holds:

$$\frac{\gamma_1 + \mu\alpha}{\gamma_2 + \mu\beta} < \frac{\gamma_1}{\gamma_2} \qquad (8\text{-}24)$$

It can be shown by algebraic transposition and rearrangement that inequality (8-24) will in fact be satisfied so long as the condition holds that

$$\frac{\beta}{\gamma_2} > \frac{\alpha}{\gamma_1} \qquad (8\text{-}25)$$

Alternatively, the left-hand side of inequality (8-24) may be differentiated with respect to μ, whence it can be shown that the negativity condition that must be satisfied to ensure that the ratio diminishes as μ increases is once again the condition specified in inequality (8-25).

But what, it may now be asked, would be involved in the statement that the ratio just discussed, f_x/f_y, is lower in the capital constraint case than in the capital saturation case? The ratio, it is clear, reading from the isoproduct curve as shown in Figure 7, is the measure of the marginal rate of substitution between the factors at the point of equilibrium factor combination. But if this marginal rate of substitution is lower, it is implied that at the equilibrium-factor combination the slope of the isoproduct curve is lower, and either of the following statements can then be made: First, at the solution point, a lesser sacrifice of factor Y than would otherwise be the case can now be made for an incremental increase in factor X if it is desired to remain on a given isoproduct curve; or second, a larger increment in factor X would be required to compensate for a unit loss of factor Y if it is desired to remain on a given isoproduct curve or at a given output level.

Piecing together the foregoing observations and considering the cost and productivity relations in Figure 7, we can make the following summary statements regarding the optimum factor usage. First, given an operative capital availability constraint, or given, that is, a positive marginal efficiency of capital measured by the variable μ, the slope of the isoproduct curve at the equilibrium factor combination will be lower than would otherwise be the case. Second, the greater the severity of the capital constraint, or the larger the marginal efficiency of capital or the solution value of μ, the lower will be the equilibrium slope of the isoproduct curve, or the marginal rate of substitution of factor X for factor Y. Third, these conditions are shown to hold so long as β/γ_2 is greater than α/γ_1. But these last two ratios measure the relationship between a factor's money capital requirement coefficient and its direct unit cost. If they are now taken as measures of the money capital intensities of the factors, the entire foregoing argument on this point can be summed up as follows. The existence of an operative money capital availability constraint leads to a *relative* economizing on the more capital intensive factor of production. In the case in hand, and with reference to Figure 7, this means that the lines describing the ratios of effective marginal costs are shallower to the X axis at equilibrium than would otherwise be the case.

But the foregoing conclusion that the existence of a money capital constraint will induce a relative economizing on the more capital intensive factor of production is all that can be said. It must not be imagined that the conclusion also permits a statement to be made about the way in which the actual combination of factors will change as the availability of capital changes. For if the severity of the capital constraint should change, this will cause the actual attainable level of output to change also, and the equilibrium solution values will then be described on a different isoproduct curve than would otherwise have been the case. And nothing a priori can be said about the direction of the movement from one isoproduct curve to another. No a priori statement can be made, that is, about the slope of the expansion path such as EF in Figure 7, in the presence of a changing capital availability constraint, compared with expansion under a continual capital saturation assumption. For, as we noted in an earlier discussion, the way in which movement along the expansion path will occur depends also on the form of the production function, or on the relations between the members of the family of isoproduct curves. Or in still another perspective it depends on the characteristics of returns to scale implicit in the production function and the technological relations it describes.

But the point of profound importance for the enterprise optimization model we are constructing, and for the insights it will disclose, should nevertheless emerge sharply from the foregoing argument. It can here be stated in one sentence: The question of the optimum structure of the productive process, and therefore the optimum structure of the enterprise, is not independent of the conditions of availability of investable money capital. This is all that need be said to expose once and for all the shallowness of proceeding to solve the problem of investing, and the financing of investments in the firm, without considering also the impact and effects on the entire enterprise structure. For what seems to be an optimum investment project considered simply and by itself may actually turn out to be inferior to some alternative way of using the additional money capital becoming available, if the effects on the total enterprise structure are consistently examined. But this is to say that the time has to come to be more in earnest about finding ways to build meaningful models of the structure of the enterprise, and to caution the nascent enthusiasm for piecemeal approaches to the investment or financial theory of the firm.

We note finally, in connection with this introductory model, that from the solution to the equation system (8-15) through (8-17) the following relationship may be derived:

$$\mu = \frac{1}{\alpha}\left[\left(p + Q\frac{dp}{dQ}\right)f_x - \gamma_1\right] = \frac{1}{\beta}\left[\left(p + Q\frac{dp}{dQ}\right)f_y - \gamma_2\right] \quad (8\text{-}26)$$

It is here being stated that at the optimum factor combination the ratio of surplus marginal revenue products [that is, the quantities in the brackets in Equation (8-26), or the marginal revenue product minus direct factor costs] will equal the ratio of the factors' money capital requirement coefficients. Or in other words, the marginal efficiency of money capital equals the ratio of the factor's surplus product to its money capital requirement coefficient. This, of course, is a derivation consistent with the equimarginal optimizing principles of the neoclassical theory. It says that the net marginal revenue productivity of money capital should, in an optimized equilibrium situation, be equal in all lines of expenditure. The notion of surplus net revenue products will engage us further below.

9

The General Optimization Model:

A Second Approximation

We move now to analogous but more complex situations in which fuller account will be taken of the various determinant functions elaborated in the preceding chapters. We shall continue to deal at this stage with a profit maximization model, but two principal changes now have to be made. First, the total money capital available to the firm need no longer be restricted to the amount of equity capital provided by the owners, but on the basis of the equity capital existing in the firm, the borrowing of debt capital may also be envisaged. Second, a fuller specification of the enterprise money capital requirement function can be made, incorporating the additional element of the net working capital requirements. We shall examine the question of borrowing and debt capital first.

The Use of Debt Capital

In Chapter 4, in the course of a fairly full discussion of the structural characteristics of the firm and of its operating, investment, and financing decision nexus, an examination was made of the forces determining the costs to the firm of varying amounts of debt and equity capital. At that point logical specifications were made of the empirically likely forms of these cost functions, or of the money capital supply functions confronting the firm. Then subsequently, in the context of a capital requirement and usage analysis, appropriate summarized forms of the relations were submitted in Equations (7-18) through (7-25). For our present purposes, and without sacrifice of logical generality, it will be sufficient to work with the last-mentioned or reduced forms of the money capital cost equations. In our immediate context we shall be introducing the level of debt capital into the model as a decision variable, and it will therefore have to be recognized that the average and marginal rates of interest paid on the debt will be functionally related (probably via the more complex relations previously adduced) to the amount of debt capital employed.

The precise manner in which this phenomenon will be introduced will be to imagine for the present that the amount of equity capital in the firm is given and fixed, and that on the basis of the equity cushion or borrowing ability thus provided the firm's indebtedness is increased to some equilibrium or optimization level. This assumption is probably not a serious deviation from actual practice in many corporations, though account will have to be taken later also of the possibility of changing the underlying amount of equity capital in the firm. Increases in equity may occur by means of new issues of common stock or, more importantly in actual fact, by means of the retention and reinvestment of current earnings not distributed as dividends to the owners.

Our money capital availability can therefore now be described as

$$M = \overline{K} + D \qquad (9\text{-}1)$$

where the terms on the right-hand side refer to equity and debt capital respectively. At the same time, the average rate of interest on the firm's total debt capital is understood to depend on the amount of debt capital employed, and may be written as $r = r(D)$, giving a total interest cost to the firm in any operating period of $r(D)D$. The total periodic interest cost is equal to the average rate of interest on the debt multiplied by the total amount of debt outstanding.

At the same time that debt capital and interest costs are introduced into the firm, an amended specification of the residual equity owners' profit function is also required, and this may be written in the following form:

$$\pi = p(Q)f(X,Y) - \gamma_1 X - \gamma_2 Y - r(D)D \qquad (9\text{-}2)$$

The familiar general character of the profit function is retained, and the terms contained in it will be self-explanatory on the basis of preceding discussions.

In Chapter 7 a discussion of the extended form of the money capital requirements function was given, and this was further summarized in

Equation (7-26). We may now reproduce it in the same form. Combining the money capital requirement function with the capital availability conditions, we have the fuller form of the money capital availability constraint which will be incorporated in the extended models:

$$g(Q) + \alpha X + \beta Y \leq \overline{K} + D \qquad (9\text{-}3)$$

The content of inequality (9-3) will be self-explanatory from the earlier discussions of its components.

Our task now is to consider the constrained optimization model whose constrained objective function, or, as before, Lagrange function, may be written in the following form:

$$\varphi = p(Q)f(X,Y) - \gamma_1 X - \gamma_2 Y - r(D)D$$
$$+ \mu[\overline{K} + D - g(Q) - \alpha X - \beta Y] \qquad (9\text{-}4)$$

In the models examined prior to this point we have concentrated on emphasizing the interdependence between the firm's production decision and its capital investment decision. This was done by exhibiting the manner in which the investment of money capital in assets is to be tied in with the different possible usages of the respective factors of production. The implied integration of capital theory and production theory at the level of the firm was properly seen as a significant advance beyond the usual stance of the traditional theory of the firm. Now in the model described in Equation (9-4), however, a further and most significant advance is being made. For here the amount of debt capital at work in the firm is also being introduced as a decision variable. But it is introduced in such a way as to make clear the manner in which its optimum usage influences also the optimum solutions to the prior problems of asset investments, factor employments, and the productive structure of the firm.

Even before we examine the potentialities of the model now before us, the analytical significance of the foregoing remarks should be clearly noted. What is being accomplished in this way is the vindication of the summary propositions presented in the introductory section of Chapter 1. On the operational level, we are witnessing the mutual determination of the firm's production, capital investment, and financing policies. On the analytical level we are establishing an integration of the economic theories of production, capital, and finance. But more conclusions pertinent to these methodological levels will be able to be made after considering more robust models of the firm.

The task now is the specification of the optimization conditions and the determination of the solution values of the decision variables in the model described in Equation (9-4). The decision variables are X, Y, and D, and we also have once again the coefficient of the money capital constraint variable μ. As before, the constrained objective function must be differentiated partially with respect to each of these four variables, thus providing the requisite set of simultaneous equations for the derivation of the solution values of the variables. The partial derivatives with respect to the three decision variables are written as follows:

$$\frac{\partial \varphi}{\partial X} = \left(p + Q\frac{dp}{dQ}\right)f_x - \gamma_1 - \mu[g'(Q)f_x + \alpha] = 0 \qquad (9\text{-}5)$$

$$\frac{\partial \varphi}{\partial Y} = \left(p + Q\frac{dp}{dQ}\right)f_y - \gamma_2 - \mu[g'(Q)f_y + \beta] = 0 \qquad (9\text{-}6)$$

$$\frac{\partial \varphi}{\partial D} = -\left(r + D\frac{\partial r}{\partial D}\right) + \mu \qquad\qquad\qquad = 0 \qquad (9\text{-}7)$$

The notation in the equation system (9-5) through (9-7) will again be familiar, with the following exceptions. In the first two of these equations, $g'(Q)$ is understood as the derivative of the net working capital requirement function with respect to the change in output. It follows from the familiar chain rule of the differential calculus that in order to find the partial derivative of the $g(Q)$ function with respect to factor X, the function must first be differentiated with respect to its own independent variable Q, and the result multiplied by the partial derivative of the function describing Q, $[Q = f(X,Y)]$, with respect to X. All this is simply taking account, in the necessary mathematical form, of the fact that if the employment of factor X is increased, the output will be increased, and thereby the net working capital requirements will be increased. The term in parentheses in Equation (9-7) represents the increase in the total interest payments of the firm, consequent upon introducing an additional unit of debt. The term is precisely the value of $d[r(D)D]/dD$.

It will assist the interpretation of the solution conditions implicit in Equations (9-5) through (9-7) if the first two equations are rearranged. From Equation (9-5) it follows that

$$[m - \mu g'(Q)]f_x = \gamma_1 + \mu\alpha \qquad (9\text{-}8)$$

where m refers to the marginal revenue of the product sold. The bracketed term is accordingly an expression for the surplus net marginal revenue, after taking account of the increased working capital costs that would result from an increase in output. If a similar rearrangement of Equation (9-6) is effected and the result is then divided into Equation (9-8), the same equilibrium factor employment condition will be obtained as in the preceding case:

$$\frac{f_x}{f_y} = \frac{\gamma_1 + \mu\alpha}{\gamma_2 + \mu\beta} \qquad (9\text{-}9)$$

The implications of this relation have already been discussed. No change is made in this model to the logic of the imputation of capital costs to the respective factors of production. But it should be clear that while the form of these optimization relationships necessarily remains as before, the values of the variables at the solution points will be different. The introduction of the additional money capital requirement element (the net working capital requirements) will necessarily shift the equilibrium outcome to a different output level, or to a different isoproduct curve, from that previously in view.

Of considerable interest is the result obtained in Equation (9-7). This states that at the solution point, the introduction of debt capital into the firm will have been carried to the level at which the marginal interest cost on the debt is equal to the marginal productivity of the debt capital in the firm. This latter is precisely the same thing, of course, as the marginal productivity of money capital, the resource which, in the present context, is constraining the level and structure of the firm's operations. But in the interpretation of this result an important caution is in order. The statement just made regarding the equality at equilibrium of the marginal cost and the marginal productivity of money capital is a logical proposition identical in form to the equilibrium conditions of the neoclassical economic model. But beyond the question of logical form we must also, in the context of our present model, be interested in the absolute solution values assumed by the variables contained in the relation. At this point it needs to be remembered that the marginal productivity of money capital, and the marginal cost of debt that is equated to it, will be determined by the interrelations between the interdependent functions determining the optimum structure of the firm. It is not necessary to repeat all the preceding arguments on these very important points. But it is necessary, perhaps, to remind ourselves that the use to which money capital should optimally be put, the structure of the firm that accordingly exists, the actual amount of debt capital it is profitable to raise, and therefore the marginal cost and marginal productivity of it, and therefore again the absolute magnitudes in the relation specified in the solution condition in Equation (9-7) — all these things will conceivably be different in a mutually determinate, optimum structural model from what they might become in a nonintegrated one-project-at-a-time investment and financing approach.

The Value Optimization Model

With the foregoing analysis in hand, the final step can now be taken in setting out the general enterprise optimization model. The problem that we set at the beginning of our work and spelled out again in our discussion of the enterprise decision nexus in Chapter 3 was that of optimizing consistently the economic position of the owners of the firm. In the context of the corporate form of enterprise, this has been interpreted as the maximization of the market value of the shares of common stock ownership.[1] It is necessary, therefore, to work ultimately not in terms of the profit maximization models we have been examining thus far, but in terms of an ownership valuation model. In such a model the economic value of the firm is understood as the capitalized value of the income stream being generated for the owners.

Using the symbols π, ρ, and V for the variables profit, capitalization rate, and value, the model we are now concerned with must be of the general kind

$$V = \frac{\pi}{\rho} \tag{9-10}$$

It was in order to move toward this kind of conclusion that we erected the basic optimization problem in the form we did in Chapter 1. Then, on the basis of the assumption of general risk aversion in the owner's utility function, we generated an expression for the equity capitalization rate as a function of the degree of risk or uncertainty in the profit expectations. Finally, on the basis of an analysis of the financial structure of the firm, the capitalization rate function was transformed into a function in the coefficient of variation of the total earning ability of the firm and the degree of financial leverage in its capital structure. For purposes of incorporating the principal causations into our present exposition, we have suggested that a reduced form of the function might be employed. As in the case of the debt cost function above, the equity capitalization rate was seen to depend on the amount of debt capital at work in the firm, given, as indicated, the amount of equity capital provided by the owners. Now in our fuller specification of the optimization model we shall again be taking the amount of debt capital as a decision variable and be interested in the manner in which, concomitant with the change in debt, the equity capitalization rate, and thus the value of the ownership, can also be expected to change. It is not necessary to repeat at this point the nature of the complex relations through which the relevant forces may work out their effects.

In the same manner as in the earlier cases, the model may be described in terms of a constrained objective function:

$$\varphi = \frac{1}{\rho(D)}[p(Q)f(X,Y) - \gamma_1 X - \gamma_2 Y - r(D)D]$$

$$+ \mu[\overline{K} + D - g(Q) - \alpha X - \beta Y] \tag{9-11}$$

---

[1] Abstracting from the day-to-day fluctuations in security market values, we are here interested in some general average of market value levels over some meaningful time period, say a month or a quarter, which need not be specified precisely for purposes of the theoretical abstraction with which we are dealing.

Again the set of simultaneous equations necessary to solve for the equilibrium values of the decision variables X, Y, and D and for the coefficient
of the constraint variable μ is obtained by taking the partial derivatives
of Equation (9-11) with respect to these four variables. We need work
here only with the derivatives with respect to the three decision variables
in order to bring out the significant differences from the preceding models.
We shall consider the arguments of the production function first.

$$\frac{\partial \varphi}{\partial X} = \frac{1}{\rho}\left[\left(p + Q\frac{dp}{dQ}\right)f_x - \gamma_1\right] - \mu[g'(Q)f_x + \alpha] = 0 \qquad (9\text{-}12)$$

$$\frac{\partial \varphi}{\partial Y} = \frac{1}{\rho}\left[\left(p + Q\frac{dp}{dQ}\right)f_y - \gamma_2\right] - \mu[g'(Q)f_y + \beta] = 0 \qquad (9\text{-}13)$$

If, now, we transpose and rearrange Equations (9-12) and (9-13) and
then divide Equation (9-12) by Equation (9-13), the following optimization
condition is obtained:

$$\frac{f_x}{f_y} = \frac{\gamma_1 + \rho\mu\alpha}{\gamma_2 + \rho\mu\beta} \qquad (9\text{-}14)$$

The condition is analogous to those previously explored, but perhaps
interpretation may be assisted if it is put in the form

$$\frac{f_x}{f_y} = \frac{\gamma_1/\rho + \mu\alpha}{\gamma_2/\rho + \mu\beta} \qquad (9\text{-}15)$$

Here the constraint coefficient μ is not to be interpreted as the marginal
profit productivity of the constraint variable, money capital, as previously.
Since we are now dealing with a valuation rather than a profit maximization
model, the constraint coefficient will represent, in a corresponding way, the
marginal *value* productivity of money capital. In Equation (9-15), therefore, the numerator of the right-hand side represents the capitalized value
of the direct factor cost γ_1/ρ, plus the marginal value productivity of
money capital times the factor's money capital requirement coefficient $\mu\alpha$.
This last term is the valuation of the capital cost to be imputed to the
factor of production, and the nature of the equilibrium condition may
from this point be interpreted analogously to the foregoing instances.

Rather more interest attaches to the equilibrium conditions that
emerge from the partial differentiation of the objective function in Equation (9-11) with respect to the remaining decision variable, the amount
of debt capital employed in the firm. For this purpose we remember that
the first bracketed term in Equation (9-11) is the profit function of the
firm, and this may be incorporated into the optimization conditions as
follows:

$$\frac{\partial \varphi}{\partial D} = -\frac{\pi}{[\rho(D)]^2} \cdot \frac{\partial \rho}{\partial D} - \frac{1}{\rho(D)}\left(r + D\frac{\partial r}{\partial D}\right) + \mu = 0 \qquad (9\text{-}16)$$

We recall also that μ represents the marginal value productivity of money capital, and on the basis of Equation (9-16) it may be examined more closely in the following terms:[2]

$$\mu = \frac{1}{\rho}\left(r + D\frac{\partial r}{\partial D}\right) + \frac{\pi}{\rho^2}\cdot\frac{\partial \rho}{\partial D} \qquad (9\text{-}17)$$

We have already seen that in the present case the pressure on what was previously the equity capital constraint is alleviated by the availability of debt capital, but that the use of debt not only changes the cost of borrowing but also the rate at which the residual equity earnings are capitalized. In the outcome it is now seen from Equation (9-17) that the marginal value product of money capital μ must exceed the capitalized value of the marginal interest cost by an amount, indicated by the second term of the equation, sufficient to take account of the induced increase in the equity capitalization rate and the consequent depressing effect on the capitalized value of the income. This last term in Equation (9-17) will be greater, the greater the indicated derivative of the $\rho(D)$ function, or the greater the rate of increase in the equity capitalization rate for a given increase in debt capital.

The relationship expressed in Equation (9-17), however, is subject to further interpretation. If we are given a certain equity capital base in the firm, $\bar{K}$ as here assumed, and a given debt cost function $r(D)$, in terms of which debt may be added to the total capital employed, then the greater the derivative $\partial\rho/\partial D$, the greater will have to be the equilibrium or solution value of μ, or the marginal efficiency of money capital. But the question is: What is involved in saying that, for given forms of the debt cost and equity cost functions $r(D)$ and $\rho(D)$, the solution value of the marginal efficiency of money capital will remain at a higher level than might otherwise be the case? This is implying that, because of the more sharply rising capital costs, not as large a total amount of money capital as might have been used in the firm will now be employed. If, in accordance with the usual postulates of the neoclassical theory, we assume that the marginal productivity of capital function is downward sloping or, concentrating on the valuation function, that the rate of increase in value for additional capital investment is diminishing, then the situation now in view means that the rate of increase in capital costs will restrict the size and rate of expansion of the firm. It will thereby limit its total employment of capital and influence also its combination of the different factors of production.

These conclusions, moreover, can be stated in a rather different way, with perhaps more intuitive appeal. In Equation (9-17) we may substitute

---

[2] A further interpretation of these equilibrium conditions will be made in Chap. 10 in the context of the discussion of the *optimum optimorum* structure of the firm.

the expression $V = \pi/\rho$, multiply and divide the final term by D, and rearrange to give an expression for μ as follows:

$$\mu = \frac{r}{\rho}\left(1 + \frac{D}{r}\cdot\frac{\partial r}{\partial D}\right) + \frac{V}{D}\left(\frac{D}{\rho}\cdot\frac{\partial \rho}{\partial D}\right) \tag{9-18}$$

The second term in the first parentheses will now be recognized as the elasticity of the interest cost function with respect to an increase in debt capital, and the term in the final parentheses will similarly be recognized as the elasticity of the equity cost function with respect to the same change in debt. Writing these elasticity measures as E_r and $E\rho$ respectively, the level to which the marginal efficiency of money capital is bounded by the capital cost functions may now be restated as

$$\mu = \frac{r}{\rho}(1 + E_r) + \frac{V}{D}\cdot E\rho \tag{9-19}$$

Thus it is being said that the marginal efficiency of money capital will have to be higher, or the extent to which capital investment in the firm can be increased will be lower, as any of the following three magnitudes are higher: first, the ratio of debt cost to equity cost, r/ρ; second, the elasticity of the interest cost function; and third, the elasticity of the equity cost function with respect to the change in debt.

Finally, the variable μ, the marginal value product of the new money capital being introduced into the firm, may be replaced by its equivalent, $\partial V/\partial D$, and Equation (9-19) rearranged in the following manner:

$$\frac{D}{V}\cdot\frac{\partial V}{\partial D} = \frac{rD}{\rho V}(1 + E_r) + E\rho \tag{9-20}$$

It follows from Equation (9-20), reading the left-hand side of the equation as the elasticity of the valuation function with respect to the change in debt and the first factor on the right-hand side as its equivalent rD/π, that

$$E_v = \frac{rD}{\pi}(1 + E_r) + E\rho \tag{9-21}$$

This equation is stating that the elasticity of the value function is positively related to the ratio of debt interest to residual equity income and to the elasticities of the capital cost functions as previously described. But if the elasticity of, or the potential increase in, the value function is thus higher at the equilibrium solution point than might otherwise be the case, this is saying again in different terms that the amount of capital investment is being constrained below what it might otherwise have been, and that the marginal efficiency of money capital is thus being maintained at a higher level.

This analysis of the constraining characteristics of the money capital availability function, which is now seen to depend on the supply or cost conditions in the money capital market, has been employed at some length in order to clarify its relevance to the firm's optimization decisions. In our earlier analysis in Chapter 4 of the problem of achieving an optimum capital or financing structure for a given level of total money capital employed in the firm, it was seen that a set of optimization conditions very similar to those in the foregoing paragraphs could be specified. The slight difference in formulation in the present case stems from the fact that we are not now looking on the employment of debt capital as constituting a substitution for equity capital in a constant level of total capital employment. We are envisaging instead an increase in total capital employed as the amount of debt capital is increased. But the nature of the economic forces lying behind the separate models is the same.

The crucial determinants, within the context of the forms of the capital cost functions, have to do with the extent of the desired risk aversion on the part of the suppliers of capital funds and the success the managers of the firm can achieve in their attempts at monopsonistic discrimination against the supply side of the money capital market.[3] The more successful the managers can be in this respect, the lower will be the elasticity of the debt cost function, the larger the amount of debt capital that may profitably be employed, the larger the total capital employment in the firm, the lower the equilibrium value of the marginal efficiency of money capital, and the higher the debt-equity ratio in the financing structure in the optimum situation.

Summary: The Significance of the Optimization Model

In the last two chapters we have discussed the principal features of the enterprise optimization model we set out to construct. The argument has been developed against the background of the traditional model in neoclassical economic theory. In the following chapters we shall draw attention to some of the more interesting extensions of the model and suggest some lines for further analytical developments. It will be useful here, as a background to that task, to summarize briefly the main characteristics of the model and indicate the ways in which it meets the demands of our original theoretical perspective. In this we called for a clearer understanding and solution of the firm's production, capital investment, and financing decision problems. To the extent that light has been thrown on these three problem areas, it will be realized that progress has been made in integrating, on the level of economic analysis, the theory of production, the theory of capital, and the theory of finance.

[3] See the fuller discussion in Chap. 4 of the possibilities of monopsonistic discrimination in the money capital market.

For summary purposes we can refer to the model in its fullest form as described in Equation (9-11). Here we have an integration of seven of the crucial determinant functions in the firm's optimization decision nexus: (1) the product selling price or revenue function $p(Q)$; (2) the production function $f(X,Y)$; (3) the factor cost functions $\gamma_1(X)$ and $\gamma_2(Y)$; (4) the money capital requirement coefficient functions $\alpha(X)$, $\beta(Y)$, and $g(Q)$; (5) the total money capital availability constraint function, or the final bracketed expression in the equation; (6) the debt cost function $r(D)$; and (7) the equity cost or equity capitalization rate function $\rho(D)$. In an ordinary language sense, the forms these different functions assume will operate as constraints on the freedom of optimum decision making enjoyed by the firm. The solution outcomes of the optimum planning model will be what they are because the forms of the functions are what they are. But perhaps it is preferable to reserve the word "constraint" to the mathematical usage we have given it so far and speak of the relations just summarized as determinant functions.

As for the scope of the solution outcome of this planning model, the following can be said. The objective function in Equation (9-11) sets out the overall maximization objective as the value of the firm or the capitalized value of the residual equity income. Then the solution conditions are seen to be such as to provide equilibrium or optimization values of X, Y, D, μ, p, Q, r, and ρ. It is not necessary to spell out at this point the algebra of the procedure necessary to derive the solution values on the basis of the solution conditions in Equations (9-12), (9-13), and (9-16), the capital availability constraint, and the underlying forms of the determinant functions. But we can usefully note what the solution values mean.

First, the solution has provided the optimum combination of input factors and the optimum level of production, thus offering a solution to what we referred to in the beginning as the production problem.

Second, the structure of factor use thus determined will, in conjunction with the form of the money capital requirement function, determine the total level of investment in assets, at the same time that it determines the structure of real capital employment on the one hand and the structure of the assets side of the balance sheet on the other. This, therefore, offers a solution to what we described in the beginning as the investment problem. It might be noted, moreover, that in the comparative static planning model we are dealing with, this solution leads precisely to the optimum level and structure of capital employment, and does not, in the form in which we have derived it, provide an explicit theory of investment. The latter requires not only an equilibrium theory of optimum capital stock, but also a theory of the optimum time rate of change in that stock. Such a capital-change theory follows fairly directly from a capital requirement theory, but some difficulties arise in the treatment of sunk investment in capital assets in the context of dynamic change, and these will be discussed further in the following chapter.

Third, the solution outcome of the model also determines the optimum level of debt capital financing, given the endogenously determined capital requirements, the supply conditions in the capital market, and the size of the available equity cushion in the business. And this offers a solution to what we referred to as the financing problem, or the optimum combination of money capital sources on the one hand and the structure of the liabilities side of the balance sheet on the other.

Thus the model determines, on a level of theoretical generality, the simultaneous solution outcomes of the production problem, the investment problem, and the financing problem, the objective with which we began our investigations.

10

The
Optimum
Optimorum:

The
Ownership
Investment
In
The
Firm

In the preceding chapter we set out the essential structure of the enterprise optimization model, or what we envisaged initially as a sequential decision-making, optimum structural-planning model. The motivation behind our work was that of piecing together the various causal relations that determined the enterprise optima, so that decisions could be made sequentially, or at successive planning dates, in such a way as to optimize consistently the economic position of the owners of the firm. It is clear that the model brings together and exhibits in their interdependent relations a large number of determinant forces. But we have not at this stage exhausted all that needs to be said about changes that may occur in the forms of the underlying functions in the model.

In the remaining analysis, therefore, we shall confront explicitly the different possible forms in which decision possibilities present themselves at what we have called the sequential-planning dates. In particular, we must confront the possibility that the optimum-planning decision for the firm may include a partial or total disinvestment in certain activities or projects or divisions, and we can wonder how the logic of the planning model can be adapted to such contingencies. Moreover, we have still left totally untouched the question of how the model relates to the intraperiodic problem of adapting the firm to short-run changes in basic determinant relations such, for example, as shifts in the demand curve or changes in factor costs.

The Supply of Ownership Capital

First, however, we draw attention to a feature that bears in a more fundamental way than has yet been recognized on a crucial aspect of the model. This has to do with the specification of the money capital availability constraint, and in particular with the amount of equity capital the owners may choose to supply to the firm. In the argument to this point, we have taken account of the way in which debt capital may be raised on the assumption that a given amount of ownership capital was already in the firm, and we have worked out the ways in which the optimum enterprise structure may be achieved on various levels as a result. But what, in the last analysis, determines the actual amount of equity capital with which we have to work? What determines the extent of the owners' investment or the commitment whose economic value we are endeavoring to maximize? And what determines when further investment should logically be made by the owners, or when a partial liquidation of their investment is called for? Granted, in other words, that a maximum value position may be specified on the basis of a *given* equity investment, is it possible to define the *maximum maximorum* position that may be attained with the *optimum* equity base?

The Maximum Maximorum

Our approach to this problem can best be made by considering from a different perspective the interpretation of the coefficient of the constraint variable in the model. We may refer to the equation system (9-11) through (9-15) which contains the fullest statement of the model to this point. As in the earlier instances, in the description of the simpler sets of relationships, the μ variable in these equations can again be understood as the measure of the marginal efficiency of money capital. If the money capital availability constraint is operative and μ is therefore positive, the money capital is then the variable whose magnitude is constraining the decision outcomes of the firm. In the particular instance before us, it is recalled, we are dealing with a valuation model, and μ is therefore to be interpreted as the marginal *value* productivity of money capital, not as the marginal *profit* productivity as in earlier formulations of the model.

Now consider the supply of money capital to the firm. This is made up of the given amount of equity capital plus the amount of debt that has been borrowed. Under what conditions, we may ask, will the measure of the marginal value productivity of money capital be giving the signal that additional capital might profitably be brought into the firm? Clearly, it appears, when the solution value of μ is greater than unity. For in such a case the incremental amount of economic value which the introduction of an extra dollar of capital would bring about is actually greater than one dollar. Recalling our basic discussion of investment values, the net increment in the value of the firm — interpreting this consistently as the economic value of the ownership — will be increased as a result.

But if the value of μ is greater than unity and the signal is thereby given for the introduction of more money capital, the question then arises as to how the incremental capital should in fact be provided. Should the firm introduce more debt capital or more equity capital, or perhaps some of both kinds? The answer and the reasons for it will doubtlessly have been intuited from the preceding discussions. But the matter is of considerable importance for the understanding of the total enterprise optimization argument, and it can therefore be summarized as follows.

In the situation now envisaged, a further introduction of debt capital would not be economically meaningful. For the fact is that the model has already generated a set of optimized solution values, and it must be concluded, among other things, that the amount of debt has been carried to its optimum level consistent with the forms of all the determinant functions. In particular, the debt then in the firm will be consistent with the form of the interest cost function determining its supply conditions. Any further introduction of debt capital would therefore reduce the value of the firm below its optimum value, or diminish the solution value of the maximand described by the objective function in the model, for example Equation (9-11). It is well to recall that the reduced forms of the debt cost and equity cost functions in the model of Equation (9-11) have already been described as serving as proxies for the more complex functions elaborated earlier in the argument. In particular, the significant variable in the capital cost functions was seen to be the degree of financial leverage, or the debt-equity ratio, the firm's capital structure. On the assumption, as incorporated in the models to this point, that no change was envisaged in the equity capital, or the denominator of the financial leverage ratio, the thing required for the generation of solution conditions of the model was an understanding of the way in which a change in the debt capital caused changes in the capital cost functions. Quite apart, therefore, from the precise forms of these cost functions, and quite apart from the detailed ways in which the techniques of the differential calculus have to be put to work, the thing we required for the solution process of the model was the partial derivative of the capital cost functions with respect to the amount of debt, and it was for this reason that the reduced forms already referred to were introduced into the model's objective function.

If, therefore, the signal for the introduction of more money capital is given by the solution value of μ, and if the optimum amount of debt capital for the given equity base is already in the firm, the thing required is quite simply the introduction of more equity capital. If more such ownership capital is introduced, this will change the set of solution values of the model and make possible the introduction of more debt capital on the larger equity base. If we assume, moreover, the general pervasiveness of the laws of diminishing marginal returns, the action we have just envisaged will result also in depressing the solution value of μ below its previously observed level. If additional money capital is introduced into the firm, its marginal value productivity can be expected to diminish. It follows, therefore, that the signal we are looking for, to indicate when the optimum amount of ownership capital is employed in the firm, is given by changes in the solution value of μ. When μ has been reduced to the value of unity, the owners of the firm have attained what from their point of view we referred to as the *maximum maximorum* position.

It might be asked in this connection whether the owners of the firm should not take into account, in addition to the prospects for generating larger net economic values by investing further in the firm, the prospects that exist also in investments in other lines of activity outside the firm, specifically in projects having a comparable degree of risk. It might be asked, in other words, whether sole reliance can be placed, in the manner suggested, on the μ variable in the model of the firm. The answer, of course, is that this is all that needs to be attended to. For the question of the nature of available alternative investments, particularly again the available rates of return in other investments of a comparable degree of risk, is already taken into account in the form of the equity capitalization rate function incorporated in the model. The effect this has in determining the value outcome of the solution process is to envisage a change in the owners' required rate of return, and thus in the capitalization rate, as the capital structure and the degree of risk in the firm change as the system moves to its optimization solution values. The detailed significance of this observation is examined from a different perspective in the discussion in the context of Equations (9-16) and (9-17).

The preceding analysis can be given concreteness by considering further the equation system (9-11) through (9-14) and in particular the solution conditions specified in Equations (9-12) and (9-13). These equations can be rearranged in the following respective forms:

$$\frac{1}{\rho}\left[\left(p + Q\frac{dp}{dQ}\right)f_x - \gamma_1\right] = \mu[g'(Q)f_x + \alpha] \qquad (10\text{-}1)$$

$$\frac{1}{\rho}\left[\left(p + Q\frac{dp}{dQ}\right)f_y - \gamma_2\right] = \mu[g'(Q)f_y + \beta] \qquad (10\text{-}2)$$

The notation in Equations (10-1) and (10-2) is the same as that employed in Chapter 9. Equation (10-1) may now be further interpreted as follows. The first term in the bracketed expression on the left-hand side of the equation is the marginal revenue product of factor X, and the remaining term in brackets is the direct unit cost of factor X. Thus the bracketed term as a whole can be conceived of as the surplus marginal revenue product of factor X, analogous to the corresponding concept discussed in the context of Equation (8-26). Taking now the bracketed expression on the right-hand side of Equation (10-1), the first term is, as before, the incremental net working capital requirement induced by the marginal employment of factor X, and the second term is the familiar money capital requirement coefficient of the factor. The bracketed expression as a whole, therefore, can be regarded as a measure of the marginal money capital requirements of factor X.

With this interpretation in hand we may write

$$\mu = \frac{M_x/\rho}{C_x} \qquad (10\text{-}3)$$

where M_x and C_x are respectively the surplus marginal revenue product and the marginal money capital requirement of factor X. It follows similarly that

$$\mu = \frac{M_y/\rho}{C_y} \qquad (10\text{-}4)$$

where M_y and C_y have analogous interpretations. In both Equations (10-3) and (10-4) the numerator is the capitalized value of the surplus marginal revenue product and may be referred to as the marginal value contribution of the factor. This marginal value contribution will thus be the optimum solution value of the surplus marginal revenue product capitalized at the simultaneous solution value of the equity capitalization rate.

If we bring together Equations (10-3) and (10-4) we can conclude, analogously again with Equation (8-26), that at the optimized equilibrium structure of the firm the combination of factors employed will be such that the ratios of the marginal value contribution to the marginal money capital requirement for the respective factors are equal. This is simply saying that the marginal value contribution per dollar of marginal money capital investment is equal for all factors employed. And this is stating in other terms an implication of the familiar proposition of neoclassical equilibrium theory that the marginal value productivity of money capital investment should be equal in all lines of expenditure.

This analysis, moreover, while it is helpful in this way in throwing further light on the planning model's optimization conditions, is also of use in our original problem in deciding upon the signals that might alert the owners of the firm to the economic worthwhileness of making additional equity investment. We decided previously that further such investment would be desirable or economically meaningful when the solution value of μ was greater than unity. It is now seen, reading from Equation (10-3) or (10-4), that this will be the case when the marginal value contribution of any given factor is greater than its marginal money capital requirement.

The Optimum Reexamined

With the foregoing analysis in view, we are now able to note a final interpretation of the variable μ, the marginal productivity of money capital. We can do this in such a way as to throw further light on the analysis in Chapter 4 of the partial optimization financing mix, and on the conclusions we reached on the solution value of μ in the general optimization model in Chapter 9.

Consider first the solution value of μ as shown in Equations (9-16) and (9-17), there implicit in the partial derivative of the constrained objective function with respect to the amount of debt capital employed in the firm:

$$\mu = \frac{1}{\rho}\left(r + D\frac{\partial r}{\partial D}\right) + \frac{\pi}{\rho^2}\cdot\frac{\partial \rho}{\partial D} \tag{10-5}$$

The expression can be written in the following form:

$$\mu = \frac{1}{\rho}\left(r + D\frac{\partial r}{\partial D} + V\frac{\partial \rho}{\partial D}\right) \tag{10-6}$$

It will be recognized that the first two terms in parentheses on the right-hand side of Equation (10-6) constitute what we referred to earlier as the marginal direct cost of borrowing, or $d[r(D)D]/dD$. Now that we are dealing with a value optimization model we have also to take account of the way in which the increased risk in the equity owners' position induced by the increased use of debt will cause an increase in the equity capitalization rate or the owners' required rate of return. The final term in parentheses in Equation (10-6) has therefore come into the picture to take account of precisely this effect. It is clear, then, that taking the expression in parentheses in Equation (10-6) as a whole, this may be referred to as the full marginal cost of borrowing, as distinct from the marginal direct cost of borrowing we have previously noted, or we may refer to it in short simply as the marginal cost of debt. It will be recognized similarly that the solution value of ρ as shown also in Equation (10-6) can be regarded for purposes of definition as the marginal cost of equity.

The equation system now before us, therefore, and the solution conditions of the optimization model from which the argument is derived, imply the following relationships. So long as the model's solution value of μ is greater than unity, as was previously argued may well be the case, the marginal cost of debt, the expression in parentheses in Equation (10-6), must be greater than the marginal cost of equity, ρ in the equation, or the owners' required rate of return for the risks involved. It is in precisely the fact that this marginal cost of equity is less than the marginal cost of debt that there lies the inducement and motivation to introduce more equity capital into the firm, and to continue the movement toward the *optimum optimorum* we previously envisaged. Alternatively, the same issue can be put in other words by noting the following relations. First, because equity capital is in short supply, such as to constrain the solution outcomes, its marginal productivity is high. A high marginal cost of debt capital is therefore acceptable so long as it is accompanied by the high marginal productivity. In that case payment of high debt costs by the firm is desirable in the interests of improving the owners' economic values, even after allowing for the fact that their required rate of return will tend to increase. Second, to say now that the marginal productivity of equity capital is greater than the owners' capitalization rate at the margin, is simply to say that the rate of return available at the margin for the risks involved is larger than the owners' required rate of return for this given degree of risk. Thus the motivation is present to exploit the marginal opportunities, should additional ownership capital be able to be provided for this purpose. It follows that when the amount of equity in the firm has been increased sufficiently to drive the solution value of μ down to unity, such inducements for further investment will have been exhausted, both sides of Equation (10-6) will be equal to unity, and the marginal cost of debt and the marginal cost of equity will then be equal. The marginal capital costs are equal at the *optimum optimorum* outcome.

At this point, however, an apparent difficulty enters the analysis. This relates to our earlier conclusion regarding the optimum financing mix in the partial optimization argument of Chapter 4. It was concluded there that if an attempt is made to discover the optimum combination of financing sources with which to finance a specified level of total money capital employed in the firm, debt capital should be substituted for equity capital until the condition specified in Equation (4-62) is satisfied. The relevant expression is reproduced here as Equation (10-7):

$$\rho = r + B\frac{dr}{dB} + V\frac{d\rho}{dB} \qquad (10\text{-}7)$$

where B and V refer to the market values of the firm's debt capital and equity capital respectively. The left- and right-hand sides of Equation (10-7) may be seen to define respectively the marginal cost of equity and the marginal cost of debt. It would appear, then, on the basis of Equation (10-7), that when an optimum debt-equity ratio is attained the marginal costs of debt and equity will be equal. If such a conclusion is imported back into Equation (10-6) it would seem that the right-hand side of the equation must then be equal to unity. It would follow on the basis of Equation (10-6), then, that when the amount of debt capital has been carried to its optimum level for any given level of equity capital, the solution value of μ must be identically equal to unity, contrary to the results of our earlier general optimization analysis.

The resolution of this paradox in the following manner will throw valuable light on the underlying forces in the general optimization conditions. First, consider again the initial interpretation of μ as that has been used consistently in our constrained optimization analysis. Recognizing that the constrained objective function, as in Equation (9-11) for example, is made up of a maximand function and a constraint condition, the coefficient of the constraint condition μ has been interpreted as the derivative of the maximand function with respect to the constraint variable. In the general case, μ is therefore equal to dV/dK, or the marginal value product of equity capital, the latter again referred to here as K. In Equation (9-16), on the other hand, μ appears as equal to the absolute value of the partial derivative of the maximand function with respect to debt, or $\partial V/\partial D$. Thus we have two legitimate aspects from which to consider the solution value of μ, as dV/dK or as $\partial V/\partial D$. Use was made of the latter aspect in Equation (9-20).

It must now be remembered, however, that consistently, in the general optimization analysis, the amount of equity capital, referred to in the preceding paragraph as K, has been measured at what can be called the book value on the balance sheet, or simply as the actual number of dollars of equity capital committed to the firm. Granted that the general optimization objective is the maximization of the economic value of a given equity investment, we are effectively concerned with the maximization of the economic value of each dollar of equity investment at work in the firm. It is the function of the forces in the securities market, we have seen, to establish as the market value of the equity ownership precisely what we have been referring to here as the economic value of the ownership, or the capitalized value of the equity owners' expected income stream. A conceptual distinction can be drawn, therefore, between the dollar amount of equity capital committed to the firm and the market valuation of that investment, in our analysis K and V respectively. It is for this reason that we could speak throughout of the relation between the two and consider whether dV/dK was or was not greater than unity. In other words the most fundamental interpretation of μ is the recognition of it as the marginal value productivity of a dollar of equity capital investment, or as the market or economic value achievable by an additional dollar of equity capital investment.

Let us return now to Equation (10-6). It will be clear from the foregoing that the expression in parentheses on the right-hand side of the equation can be interpreted as the addition to the total earnings stream of the firm, such that when this is capitalized at the rate ρ it provides the marginal value product μ of the incremental money capital introduced in the form of debt. In relation to the marginal dollar of money capital, the earnings in the expression in parentheses represent the marginal rate of return on the investment. But, it can now be asked, how much of the new value produced, μ, is added to the economic or market value of the existing ownership capital? The answer, it is clear, is none at all. For part of the earning ability of the marginal debt capital is absorbed to pay the marginal direct interest cost of borrowing, the first two terms in parentheses, and the remainder, the final term in parentheses, is the required additional earnings that must accrue to the equity owners simply to offset the increase in the equity capitalization rate and thereby leave the economic value of the ownership unchanged or prevent any dilution of it. But if we can recognize that the expression in parentheses in Equation (10-6) describes the earning ability of an incremental dollar of money capital, what change would occur if that marginal unit of money capital were introduced in the form of equity rather than debt? The underlying earning ability would be the same, but in this case the entire additional income would accrue to the equity owners, and their economic values would be increased as a result. In fact their economic values would be increased more than proportionately, because the presence of increased equity in the firm, consistent with the posited form of our capital cost functions, would tend to reduce the interest cost of debt and the capitalization rate of the equity.

It emerges, therefore, that so long as the additional income opportunities are such, in the manner just argued, that the value of the equity ownership can be increased by more than one dollar by introducing an additional dollar of equity capital, such an additional investment is economically desirable. As such additional investments are made, the incremental income opportunities will diminish, at the same time that the marginal capital costs are changing in recognition of the implied variation in the financial leverage ratio and in the degree of the owners' risk. If the process is continued, the marginal productivity of equity capital, μ in Equation (10-6), will be driven down to unity, and the marginal cost of debt and the marginal cost of equity, also read as before from the equation, will be equal. What we are here calling the marginal cost of equity will, however, be greater than the marginal direct cost of borrowing. In fact it can now be seen that at the establishment of this optimization level the full capital equilibrium condition involves an equality between the three-fold quantities of (1) the marginal cost of debt, (2) the marginal cost of equity, and (3) the marginal rate of return, measured at the net operating income level, on invested money capital.

Of prime importance, however, is the fact that this analysis enables us to see the partial optimization analysis of Chapter 4 in a perspective that could not otherwise have emerged. We can refer again to Equation (4-62), shown also as Equation (10-7). If it is desired to argue, in the manner indicated there, that the firm can move toward an optimum debt-equity ratio by substituting debt for equity until the marginal costs of debt and equity are equal, such a target relationship will in fact provide an optimum situation for the owners only if the marginal rate of return on investment is also equal to these marginal capital costs. If the rate of return available at the margin is greater than the marginal capital costs, the economic interests of the owners will be served by continuing to raise debt capital and invest up to the indicated limit, and then, conceivably, invest still more equity capital. All this is saying, in other words, that these complete conditions will hold only at what we have now seen to be the *optimum optimorum* structure and capitalization of the firm. Methodologically it is thereby being said that the partial optimization financial analysis, set out as a first approximation in Chapter 4, fails to achieve a meaningful statement of equilibrium conditions unless it is interrelated with the partial optimization investment analysis in Chapter 5. But as soon as it is seen that an interdependence exists in this way between the investment and the financing problems of the firm, it is seen also that the same kind of interdependence spills over into the production problem area, or to the matter of the optimum structure of the productive process in the firm. Here again, derived and exhibited in a different way, is the vindication of our consistent preoccupation. It is not necessary to adduce our previous arguments in detail to show again at this point that consistent economic optima in the firm require an integration, on both the empirical and theoretical levels, of the production, investment, and financing problems.

The resolution of the optimization argument in this way thus estab-lishes a close connection between the investment and financing sides of the firm's capital budget decision. The attempt to equate the full marginal cost of debt and the required rate of return on the equity is meaningful only when the rate of return on investment at the margin is also equal to these marginal capital costs. In the more traditional language of capital budgeting analysis, this condition is stating that investment should have been carried to the capital budget cutoff point. The thing of final importance to us now, however, is that the foregoing analysis allows us to clarify a further issue on the partial optimization analysis of Chapter 4. As we did not at that stage possess the full optimization constructs we have now developed, it was necessary to defer final consideration of the issue to this stage.

In Equations (4-50) and (4-61), the propositions were adduced that optimum capital structures, or combinations of money capital sources, would be employed in the firm when the following relations were satisfied: In the first case $i/r = (1 + E_D)/(1 + E_K)$, and in the second case $\rho/r = (1 + E_r)/(1 + E_\rho)$. In the first of these cases, it is recalled, i represents the attainable rate of return on the equity capital committed to the firm. In the second case ρ represents the owners' required rate of return on that equity. In both cases the relations just described, and the solution value of the variables at which the conditions would be established, depended on the responsiveness of the money capital costs to the variations in the debt-equity ratio in the firm's financing mix.

It can now be recalled that the respective conditions specified in the preceding paragraph both involve a relationship between the underlying forces of the kind summarized in Equation (10-7). More particularly, the first of the two relations in the preceding paragraph was derived from the assumption, explained in the context of Chapter 4, that as debt was substituted for equity the expression $dD = -dK$ obtained, where D represented a unit of debt capital and K referred again to the actual equity capital committed to the firm. The second of the two relations was adduced on the assumption that in a similar way $dB = -dV$, where B and V referred to the market values of debt and equity respectively. Granted this, we focus now on the last of these statements and ask under what conditions we can in fact state that $dB = -dV$, or that the absolute value of dV/dB is equal to unity. Clearly, it will immediately be seen from the optimization arguments of this chapter, this condition is satisfied precisely when the marginal productivity of money capital, or the solution value of μ, is also equal to unity. In fact, we are simply dealing with two different ways of saying the same thing. The proposition, moreover, which is central to our optimization argument is that the alternative ways of specifying the meaning of the marginal productivity of money capital imply that when dV/dB is equal to unity, dV/dK is also equal to unity. And when such is the case the dK in the derivation of Equation (4-50) has taken on the same value as the dV in the derivation of Equation (4-61). For at that point, as is central to our preceding arguments, the economic value of the marginal unit of equity capital in the firm is precisely equal to that marginal unit.

From this it follows that the conditions specified in Equations (4-50) and (4-61) must both in fact describe the same optimized debt-equity ratio in the firm, at whatever point both conditions can be shown to hold.

And it can now be seen that they each will hold only at the point at which investment in the firm has been pushed to the margin of profitability, or where the marginal value productivity of equity capital is unity. The conclusion follows that again, as in a previous context, the partial optimization equilibrium conditions have lurking behind them more significant assumptions than are clearly visible at the outset. In short, we have seen again that the partial optimization conditions hold rigorously only at what our general model has specified as the *optimum optimorum* structure of the firm.

This analysis completes the argument necessary at this point on the optimization planning solution of the firm. It will be useful in the interests of clarity, however, to make the following point. It has been seen in the course of the analysis that at the optimum solution outcome the marginal productivity of equity capital will be equal to the marginal cost of equity, or the owners' capitalization rate. In the terms of the general model, $d\pi/dK = \rho$. This is clearly an equilibrium condition at the margin, and should not give rise to the impression that the variables i and ρ in Equations (4-50) and (4-61) must also be equal at the optimum solution point. The former refers to the rate of profit actually being earned on the total equity investment in the firm, and the latter refers to the required rate of return at the margin of equity investment. It is implicit in the entire optimization analysis that at the solution point, i will be greater than ρ. In other words $i = \pi/K$ and $\rho = \pi/V$. In the nature of the case V will be greater than K, it being the economic value of the K investment. If these facts are imported back into Equations (4-50) and (4-61), the reasons for the consistency of the propositions will be recognized from the different functional forms implicit in the E_K and E_ρ elasticity measures in the equations. Both of these were elaborated in the relevant contexts of Chapter 4.

Finally it may be said that if, at the mutually determined solution values of the decision variables in the model, the value of μ should be less than unity, too high a level of ownership investment will have been posited. This may involve a partial liquidation of an existing firm in the manner of the structural replanning decision which will be considered in the following chapter.

The Tax Effect

The foregoing analysis provides us with a statement of what it is that essentially determines the economic position of the owners of the firm. It must be noted, however, that throughout our work, apart from an introductory reference in Chapter 1, we have avoided completely any reference to the firm's income tax liability. In this manner an economy of exposition has resulted, but it must now be emphasized that the incidence of the corporate income tax does in fact play an important role in the choice of optimum policies. The nature of the causal and interconnected relationships discussed in the preceding chapters is unaltered by the tax effect, but the estimate and quantification of optimum outcomes might well be changed when the incidence of the tax is accounted for. It will suffice for present purposes to draw attention to three features of the relevant analysis that need to be borne in mind in the present context.

First, the economic value of the owners' investment — which, we have argued, should consistently be brought to an optimum or maximum level subject to the constraints we have specified — should be understood as the capitalized value of the income stream earned for the owners after the payment of corporate tax. The expenses deductible for income tax purposes are precisely the kind we have specified in the maximand functions incorporated in the constrained objective functions of the models we have examined. The firm may deduct for tax purposes all factor costs incurred during an operating period, including an allowance for the depreciation or amortization of fixed assets whose economic lives extend over more than one such period. It may deduct also the interest paid to the providers of debt capital, thus incorporating all the expense items included in our previous objective functions.

It would seem, then, subject to some modifications of detail we shall refer to below, that the maximand component of our constrained objective function can be converted to an after-tax basis by multiplying by $(1 - t)$, where t refers to the corporate tax rate as a percentage of the taxable income or the income tax base. In the most fully developed model, where a valuation rather than a profit maximand is involved, such a procedure would then give us the capitalized value of after-tax income, or the true residual economic values with which proposed commitments of equity capital to the firm may be compared.

The second point, implicit in what has just been noted in connection with our maximand, is that because the interest payments on debt capital are deductible for income tax purposes, an additional incentive might thereby be provided for the employment of debt, tending to raise what might be considered the optimum debt-equity ratio in the firm's financing mix. This indeed may well be the case. But we should remember also that insofar as the amount of debt capital in the firm is for this reason increased, its effects should be traced, in the manner already argued, on the expected stability or the coefficient of variation of the residual equity income stream, and thereby on the equity owners' capitalization rate or required rate of return. Against the lowered effective or after-tax cost of debt, we have at work also the implicit upward pressure on the cost of equity capital, and both these effects must be taken into account in determining the optimum capital structure.

The way in which the income tax status of debt financing exerts its effects may be seen by reference to the equation system (9-4) through (9-7). The maximand in that context is a profit function and in Equation (9-7) the optimization condition is stated that the marginal interest cost of borrowing, $(r + D\partial r/\partial D)$, must be equal to the marginal productivity of money capital μ. If, now, the maximand function were multiplied by $(1 - t)$ to take account of the tax effect in the manner proposed, the optimization condition could be amended to state that the marginal productivity of money capital should equal the after-tax marginal interest cost of borrowing, or the term referred to above multiplied by $(1 - t)$. But this reduction in the equilibrium level of the marginal interest cost implies that the solution value of μ is also lower. Because of the income tax effect, therefore, a larger amount of money capital can profitably be introduced into the firm than would otherwise be the case.

While this analysis and conclusion are essentially correct, they need, as we have said, to be amended to take account also of the effects the increased debt financing exerts on the equity capitalization rate. For this purpose we can refer to Equation (10-6) and the discussion in that context of the *optimum optimorum* solution value of μ. In the case now envisaged, when full taxation effects are considered, μ will refer to the capitalized after-tax value of equity earnings at the margin, and the envisaged solution value must still be unity. But in the manner already referred to, the right-hand side of Equation (10-6) must be multiplied by $(1 - t)$, indicating that when the mutually consistent solution values of the variables have been determined, the following optimization condition will hold: The equity capitalization rate at the margin, or what we referred to in the earlier context as the marginal cost of equity, must be equal to the after-tax full marginal cost of debt.

The taxation arguments adduced thus far, it is recalled, are based on the supposition that the tax effect is accounted for by applying a tax adjustment multiplier of $(1 - t)$ to the maximand in our model's objective function. While such a procedure is logically quite meaningful and correct in indicating the nature of the causation involved in the problem, there are at least three reasons why in actual fact the working out of the total effects may be rather more complex. We shall mention these at this point, but shall not reopen our discussion at all points to take account of the issues raised. We shall note simply that on the theoretical level an important task remains to be done in incorporating the taxation question completely into the detailed and operational parts of the analysis; and on a theoretico-pragmatic level there is a large scope for joint analysis by corporate and fiscal economists.

First, the corporate tax factor referred to in the foregoing as t is not in fact a constant, owing to the very moderate progression in corporate tax rates. Detailed specifications of the kind involved need not detain us for purposes of the arguments of this book. Second, account may need to be taken in fact of special *ad hoc* taxation provisions, such as the institution from time to time of investment allowances and similar tax credits designed to stimulate business fixed asset expenditures. Such allowances would clearly need to be incorporated in the analysis described in Chapter 7, in connection with the specification of the periodic flow costs and the money capital requirement coefficients to be associated with the provision of different levels of factor capacities.

This, however, leads us to recognize the final, and acutely difficult, problem we need to note at this point in connection with the tax effects. The issue can best be summarized in the following terms. The firm, we have said, is permitted to deduct from gross revenue for income tax purposes all factor costs and depreciation allowances incurred in producing income in the year for which the tax is being paid. But it is conceivable that the depreciation of fixed assets charged for tax purposes, probably in accordance with an official government depreciation schedule, may differ from the effective depreciation provision that is being costed to the asset facilities in accordance with the optimization sinking fund analysis referred to in Chapter 7 above. Moreover, it is recalled that our same analysis derived, as the periodic flow costs of the factor services provided by durable assets, constant annual equivalents of varying streams of maintenance and servicing expenditures. In the computation of the actual annual tax liability of the firm, on the other hand, the factor costs deductible for tax purposes may include not the constant annual economic equivalent as we have argued, but the actual expenditures incurred in the period in question. Should such be the case, detailed allowances would need to be made, in the computation of the economic costs we have worked with in our models, for the differential effects of the tax factors involved.

The matters of the kind that we have referred to in the preceding paragraphs raise operational issues on a level of particularization different from that on which we have chosen to work in the principal theses of this book. To state this fact, however, is not to minimize the importance of the issues involved. It is to point instead to the potential analytical richness of the fields that are opened for investigation in the total task of the optimization of the firm's economic position.

Sources of Equity Capital

Let it be granted that the criterion is established for the economic worthwhileness of additional ownership investment in the firm. A question now arises concerning the form in which the additional equity capital should be provided. There are two possible sources. First, the managers of the firm may retain part of the residual income stream rather than distribute the entire earnings as dividends to the owners; and second, new shares of common stock may be sold either to the existing owners or to new shareholders.

Insofar as the assumption was maintained throughout the preceding arguments that the amount of equity capital in the firm was given, it was implicitly assumed that the earnings generated by the owners' investment would in fact be distributed to them in the form of dividends. For as soon as a particular earnings retention and reinvestment policy is assumed, the assumption of a given amount of ownership capital is no longer in force, and induced changes in borrowing ability, usage of debt, and the other interactions in the decision model come into play. What, then, is to be said of the firm's dividend policy decision? The answer to this question conveniently goes to the methodological foundation of the planning model we have proposed. Let us examine again briefly that methodological groundwork.

The thing we have been concerned to do in this book is to erect what can now be called in more detail a comparative static, or steady state, sequential decision-making, structural-planning model. There is no need to repeat at this point all the structural features and decision problem areas with which we have dealt and which we have endeavored to integrate into a determinate decision model. It is envisaged, however, that in an operating firm the decision makers who manage the firm on behalf of the owners will set a planning period, of greater or less calendar length, such that at the beginning of each planning period, at what we referred to as the sequential-planning dates, decisions will have to be made regarding the optimum structure of the firm. Now at each such decision date the production and market potentialities will be those implicit in the technological characteristics of the production function on the one hand and the nature of the market demand and the firm's revenue function on the other. In the same way, and without repeating the full specification of the determinant functions already examined, the total planning data will also include the characteristics of factor costs, asset lives, and capital supplies, all presenting their specific forms and elasticities and all potentially interacting in the decision nexus. For our present purpose our concern is not with the detail of such planning or decision data. It is rather with the fact that on the basis of the data available to them and on the basis of the forms of the relevant determinant relations, whether they are observed, postulated, or estimated, the managers of the firm must make a decision as to what the optimum structure of the enterprise should be.

Nothing in the nature of the relations that bear on the optimization problem, nothing in the logic of the model that allows these relations to interact in the decision outcomes, and nothing in the nature of the world or the economic milieu in which the decisions are made — nothing in any of these levels or aspects requires that an enterprise optimum structure decided upon at a given planning date must necessarily remain an optimum structure for all planning periods in the future. All that is being said is that the optimum structure and the optimum plan the firm should adopt at any planning date are what they are because the underlying data and relations are what they are. If the underlying data and relations are different at the next planning date, the optimum structural decisions will be different at that date. The operational problems which at that date will then confront the managers will be those of changing the structure and productivities of the firm from what they were prior to the planning date now in view to what, on the basis of the new decisions, they should become.

But the point to be settled at present relates to the firm's decision as to dividend distribution to the owners, as against the retention and reinvestment of earnings as previously suggested. If now the structural-planning period can be made to coincide in calendar length with the dividend period, then the question of the preferability of paying dividends or reinvesting may logically be settled, at least on the level of economic criteria, by choosing that dividend policy which, *ceteris paribus*, permits the best move toward the owners' *maximum maximorum* position. If, for any reason, it is desired to adopt a dividend or a retentions policy different from that having the characteristics just inferred, at least it can be recognized what economic cost is involved in adopting what, from the standpoint of the decision model, must be seen as a suboptimum decision in this respect.

Clearly, in the problems we are now discussing, the possibility is envisaged that at each planning date the decision makers in the firm will have to generate possible solution values to the decision variables in the planning model under any number of different assumptions regarding the availability of money capital for investment in the firm. While it is not our purpose here to discuss a detailed solution algorithm for the model, nevertheless it can be seen that repetitive runs through the relevant mathematical program will be required, in order that alternative plans may be generated and the optimum plan chosen.

It may be the case that what from the planning viewpoint may be a suboptimum dividend or reinvestment policy may have to be adopted or be advised, out of consideration of possible security market reaction to differing policies. In such a case any of varying assumptions relevant to such a decision problem may be incorporated in alternative runs through the solution algorithm. Or if it is thought that different possible policies may have different effects on security market sentiment, and via this on the effective form or rate of change in the equity capitalization rate function, this too may be incorporated in alternative assumptions on the basis of which alternative decision values, and therefore plans, may be generated. Or again, it may be thought by the managers and decision makers that attempts by them to improve security market and investor information may affect the reactions and attitudes and estimates of money capital suppliers, and thus may influence the effective capital supply functions on the basis of which decisions should be made.

A familiar respect in which the optimum decision outcomes recommended by the planning model might not in fact be followed deserves explicit mention. This has to do with the instances in which the firm or its owners or managers have set some maximum limit to the financial leverage, or debt-equity ratio, above which they are not prepared to go in their use of debt capital. Such a condition may then be incorporated into the model as an additional constraint, though it will be realized that under different assumptions regarding the amounts of equity capital that may be supplied to the firm, any such side condition on a maximum acceptable leverage ratio will also imply different possible amounts of debt financing.

This analysis of the question of dividend payments, and the solution of the dividend problem within the context of the structural-planning model, raises the question of the logical difference between the comparative static model we have constructed and possible alternative models such as might incorporate a certain periodic growth rate assumption.[1] Further comment will be made on this matter below, but in the present context it will be useful to make the following point. The question needs to be asked as to how, in this respect, the business firm's optimization problem and the general solution of it may best be faced. If it is imagined that at a given point in time a business firm can and does formulate a time vector of investment, dividend, income, and financing plans extending over long time horizons, then conceivably the building of growth models with locked-in assumptions as to growth rates, earnings opportunities, and financing maneuvers is what, on the level of analysis, is really required. But if, on the other hand, it is thought that a firm is more likely in fact to set a definite horizon in its planning postulates and in the time vector of changes it is prepared to envisage at any moment in time, conceivably the sequential-structural planning of the firm will be best understood, on the analytical level, in terms of comparative static, sequential, decision-making models. It is the latter course that we have adopted.

[1] An indication of the kind of model building referred to and references to the relevant literature are contained in Douglas Vickers, "Profitability and Reinvestment Rates: A Note on the Gordon Paradox," *Journal of Business*, vol. 39, pp. 366–370, July, 1966.

New Equity Issues

Quite apart from the question as to how the dividend policy can best be fitted into the firm's planning procedures and quite apart from the matter of the formulation of different plans to take account of different possible situations, there remains the possibility that if the coefficient of the money capital availability constraint is signaling the desirability of additional equity capital, this may be obtained by a new issue of equity shares. Immediately, therefore, there arise two related questions that need to be looked at briefly. These have to do with the price at which new equity shares should be issued to the public, taking account of the possibility that some or all of them may be acquired by purchasers who are not at present shareholders of the firm, and the possibility that if shares of stock are sold to new shareholders at too low a price the economic value of the existing shareholders' position may be worsened or diluted as a result.

This latter possibility follows from the fact that after the new issue has taken place and the new capital has been incorporated into the firm, the new shares and the previously existing shares of common stock will then constitute one total homogeneous ownership. Henceforth all shares of common stock, all representing a given proportionate share in the income stream and capital value of the firm, will be perfect substitutes for one another, and all such shares will therefore command a common economic or market value. There can be said to have been a dilution of the economic position of the existing owners of a firm if the terms of issue of new shares of common stock to outside investors are such that the market value of the shares of stock after the new issue is lower than it would have been if the new financing and investment had not taken place.

If, of course, all the new shares of common stock are being acquired by the existing owners in proportion to their present shareholdings, then the question of dilution does not arise in the form we have just considered. In such a case the price at which the new shares are being issued is a matter of secondary importance, simply because the question of the number of new shares that come into existence for a given total capital issue is of secondary importance. If all new shares are being acquired proportionately by the existing shareholders, the only thing determined by the issue price, and therefore the number of shares issued, is the proportionate share of the total economic value of the ownership which will be represented subsequently by each of the homogeneous shares of stock in the firm. But if the previous owners continue to share in the total ownership in precisely the same proportions as previously, then provided the basic criterion of economic worthwhileness is satisfied, the shareholders' economic positions will not be worsened by the decision as to the issue price of the new shares. The basic economic criterion, from the point of view of the owners contemplating new investment in the firm, is, as examined at length already, simply that the marginal value contribution of the new investment should be greater than the amount of new capital it is proposed to invest. This is again the familiar condition on the solution value of μ in the general optimization model.

To give concreteness to the preceding case, consider a firm whose size and structure are such that the total value of the ownership is represented by the amount V_1 and the number of shares of common stock outstanding is M. Imagine now that a number, N, of new shares of common stock are to be sold to investors who are not currently owners of the firm, and that after the new financing and investment have taken place the total value of the ownership of the firm rises to V_2. Then at the margin of desirability the following per share value relationship must hold:

$$\frac{V_2}{M + N} = \frac{V_1}{M} \tag{10-8}$$

It follows that

$$N = M\left(\frac{V_2}{V_1} - 1\right) \tag{10-9}$$

indicates the maximum number of new shares of stock that may be issued without diluting the value of the previously existing shares below the value they enjoyed before the new financing.

Given the total amount of new capital that must be introduced to realize the envisaged plan and raise the value of the ownership to V_2 as contemplated, the relation between the new investment required and the number of new shares N also determines the issue price (abstracting from issue costs) at which the new shares should be issued. It should be noted, however, that the issue price thus determined is a minimum price, for it is the lowest price that will just make it possible for the value of the previous shares to be maintained. If such minimum conditions should therefore hold, it means that all the surplus value contribution being generated by the new investment, and by the consequent change in the structure of the firm and its activities, actually accrues to the new owners. If it were desired that any such net marginal value contribution be shared between the old and the new owners, the issue price of the new shares would need to be higher, and a smaller number of new shares would then be issued for any given total new investment.

11

Issues In Structural Planning

The problems we shall consider in this chapter are significant for enterprise planning because of their implications for the structural flexibility of the firm. Specifically, we shall be interested in the first place in the rate at which the total economic value of the firm may be expected to change as variations are made in the planned capacity of the firm. Formally, and in the language of the mathematical methodology we have adopted, we shall now be interested in possible enterprise plans where the objective function in our model is constrained not only by a money capital availability constraint as before, but also by an output capacity constraint. In the same way that it was possible previously to interpret the coefficient of the money capital constraint variable μ as the marginal efficiency or marginal productivity of money capital, it will now be possible, by an analogous construction, to speak of the marginal productivity of output. Moreover, it will be possible to offer an economic interpretation of the interaction between these respective marginal productivities; and the derivative of one with respect to the other, or the positive or negative direction of change of one for a given change in the other, will be seen to bear on the motivation and outcome of the structural-planning decision.

For concreteness again we shall specify the objective function of the reinterpreted model as follows:

$$\varphi = \frac{1}{\rho(D)}[p(Q)f(X,Y) - \gamma_1 X - \gamma_2 Y - r(D)D]$$
$$+ \lambda[\bar{Q} - f(X,Y)] + \mu[\bar{K} + D - g(Q) - \alpha X - \beta Y] \quad (11\text{-}1)$$

In Equation (11-1) all notation has the same meaning as previously, except for the new expression in the second bracket. The first term in this bracket,

190

$\overline{Q}$, represents the given or postulated level of output to which, in a given planning study, the level of operations and the structural planning are assumed to be constrained. The second term in the bracket is the familiar production function of the firm. The bracketed term as a whole, therefore, has the same kind of interpretation as the other constraint functions with which we have dealt. At an equilibrium decision at which this output constraint is operative or binding on the valuation function, the value of the expression within the bracket will be equal to zero, and the value of λ, the coefficient of the constraint variable, will indicate the marginal productivity of the output constraint.

Marginal Productivities of Multiple Constraints

Before the complete economic interpretation of this model is attempted, it will be useful to digress and consider more deeply the interpretation of the marginal productivities we have already referred to. For this purpose, let us revert to the basic form of the optimization model as shown, for example, in Equation (9-11). The model may now be described in the following reduced form:

$$F(X,Y,\mu) = h(X,Y) + \mu[M - g(X,Y)] \qquad (11\text{-}2)$$

Here the objective function of Equation (9-11) is interpreted by the left-hand side of Equation (11-2) as a function of the factor inputs X and Y and of the Lagrange variable μ. For the present we abstract, for purposes of clarity, from the possibility of employing debt capital in the firm, and the profit function of the basic model is interpreted in the first term on the right-hand side of Equation (11-2) as a function h, of unspecified form, of the factors X and Y. Similarly, the remaining term on the right-hand side of Equation (11-2) presents the money capital availability constraint, for a given money capital M, and a money capital requirements function g, again of unspecified form, written as a function of the factors X and Y. The kinship of Equation (11-2) with our earlier models is thus established, and we are here presenting in its most general form the essence of our problem, namely, the maximization of the h function subject to the constraint specified by the g function.

We recall that for optimized equilibrium outcomes the partial derivatives of Equation (11-2) with respect to the decision variables X and Y may be set equal to zero:

$$\frac{\partial F}{\partial X} = h_x - \mu g_x = 0 \qquad (11\text{-}3)$$

$$\frac{\partial F}{\partial Y} = h_y - \mu g_y = 0 \qquad (11\text{-}4)$$

In Equations (11-3) and (11-4) the symbols h_x and h_y refer respectively to the partial derivatives of the h function with respect to X and Y, and an analogous interpretation attaches to the subscripted variables g_x and g_y. In the remainder of this section this subscript notation will be employed without further comment to indicate the partial derivatives of corresponding maximand and constraint functions.

Leaving Equations (11-3) and (11-4) in their present forms, consider now the total differentials of the profit maximand and the constraint functions in Equation (11-2). These are shown in Equations (11-5) and (11-6) respectively.

$$dh = h_x\, dX + h_y\, dY \tag{11-5}$$

$$dg = g_x\, dX + g_y\, dY \tag{11-6}$$

Substituting Equations (11-3) and (11-4) into Equation (11-5) yields

$$dh = \mu g_x\, dX + \mu g_y\, dY \tag{11-7}$$

or

$$dh = \mu(g_x\, dX + g_y\, dY) \tag{11-8}$$

Finally, substitution of Equation (11-6) into Equation (11-8) yields

$$dh = \mu\, dg \tag{11-9}$$

This, of course, is the familiar expression we reached from a comparable argument in the context of Equations (8-19) through (8-23). For purposes of what follows, we now point out a further characteristic of Equation (11-9). This discloses that our basic model envisages the equilibrium value of the h function as itself sustaining a functional relation to the posited value of the g function, and we may write this summary implication as

$$h = h(g) \tag{11-10}$$

In differential notation, such as will be used in more complex forms in the following argument, we may write, from Equation (11-10),

$$dh = \frac{\partial h}{\partial g}\, dg \tag{11-11}$$

Comparing Equations (11-9) and (11-11) it appears that μ equals $\partial h/\partial g$, or that the coefficient of the constraint variable, μ, is the partial derivative of the maximand function with respect to the constraining variable. And logically this is of course the case. It is simply that in the kind of two-variable function with which we are dealing in Equation (11-9) there is no point in proceeding through the differential argument of Equation (11-11), and the interpretation of μ may be read more directly from the transposition of Equation (11-9). It emerges as the total derivative of h

with respect to g. In either form of the mathematical statement the economic interpretation of the case is in this instance the same, and μ emerges as the marginal productivity of money capital as already argued.

With this understanding of the mathematics in hand, let us put the concepts to work in a more complex case. In the same way that we established the logical equivalence between Equation (9-11) and Equation (11-2), Equation (11-1) may be reduced to the following equivalent form:

$$F(X,Y,\lambda,\mu) = h(X,Y) + \lambda[\bar{Q} - f(X,Y)] + \mu[\bar{M} - g(X,Y)] \qquad (11\text{-}12)$$

Proceeding as before, we set the partial derivatives of Equation (11-12) equal to zero:

$$\frac{\partial F}{\partial X} = h_x - \lambda f_x - \mu g_x = 0 \qquad (11\text{-}13)$$

$$\frac{\partial F}{\partial Y} = h_y - \lambda f_y - \mu g_y = 0 \qquad (11\text{-}14)$$

We now write the total differentials of the h, f, and g functions:

$$dh = h_x\, dX + h_y\, dY \qquad (11\text{-}15)$$

$$df = f_x\, dX + f_y\, dY \qquad (11\text{-}16)$$

$$dg = g_x\, dX + g_y\, dY \qquad (11\text{-}17)$$

Substituting Equations (11-13) and (11-14) into Equation (11-15) and collecting terms yields the following expression, analogous to Equation (11-9):

$$dh = \lambda\, df + \mu\, dg \qquad (11\text{-}18)$$

Recognizing now that via the nature of the constraint functions f and g we may envisage the relation $h = h(f,g)$, we may write the total differential of this equation as

$$dh = \frac{\partial h}{\partial f}\, df + \frac{\partial h}{\partial g}\, dg \qquad (11\text{-}19)$$

Comparing Equations (11-18) and (11-19), the following equivalences are immediately clear:

$$\lambda = \frac{\partial h}{\partial f} \qquad \mu = \frac{\partial h}{\partial g} \qquad (11\text{-}20)$$

Expression (11-20) is thus indicating that the λ and μ coefficients of the constraint functions are in fact equal to the partial derivatives of the maximand function with respect to the constraint variables. The λ is thus to be interpreted as the marginal productivity of additional output, and μ again becomes, as in the simpler case we examined previously, the marginal productivity of money capital. The only difference is that in this more complex constrained objective function the marginal productivities have now to be interpreted as partial rather than total derivatives.[1]

We desire now to make further use of the proposition in the foregoing that h can be interpreted in terms of its functional relation to f and g. That this should be so can be intuited from the fact that the maximand function h and the constraint functions f and g are all described in terms of the same input arguments X and Y. If, for example, the value to which the f function is being constrained is set at a certain level, a marginal relaxation of that constraint and the envisaging of a higher level of output will involve either a different proportionate combination of factors X and Y or perhaps an increase in both these inputs, but in either case the change in the factor usage must react through the determinant relations and induce a change in the equilibrium value of the maximand h function. Similarly, a marginal increase in available money capital, or a partial relaxation of the constraint at that point, will increase the volume of factor inputs that can be acquired by the firm, thus again inducing a change in the attainable profits, or in the optimized value of the h function.

We revert, then, to Equation (11-18) and by transposition write this in the following form:

$$\mu\, dg = dh - \lambda\, df \tag{11-21}$$

The following equivalence may then be established:

$$dg = \frac{1}{\mu}\, dh - \frac{\lambda}{\mu}\, df \tag{11-22}$$

With this form we are in possession of an expression from which useful new information may be extracted. Taking g as a function of h and f, as suggested by Equation (11-22), we write the total differential of this g function in a manner analogous to the preceding instances as

$$dg = \frac{\partial g}{\partial h}\, dh + \frac{\partial g}{\partial f}\, df \tag{11-23}$$

From Equations (11-22) and (11-23) the following equivalences can be noted:

$$\mu = \frac{\partial h}{\partial g} \quad \text{and} \quad -\frac{\lambda}{\mu} = \frac{\partial g}{\partial f} \tag{11-24}$$

The first statement in expression (11-24) is of course familiar, and it has simply provided again in a different manner the interpretation of μ as the marginal productivity of money capital. New interest attaches,

---

[1] For a generalization of the mathematical theory of constrained optimization see G. Hadley, *Nonlinear and Dynamic Programming*, Addison-Wesley Publishing Company, Inc., Reading, Mass., 1964, especially chap. 3 and 6.

however, to the second statement in expression (11-24), as we shall see immediately in what follows.

The question to which we can now turn is that of the relation between the marginal productivity of money capital on the one hand and the marginal productivity of output on the other. We are interested explicitly in understanding what economic interpretation may be attached to the manner in which μ in the foregoing formulation may vary for a given or induced change in λ. In mathematical terms, we are interested in the derivative of μ with respect to λ, or in $\partial\mu/\partial\lambda$. We may establish this fairly readily with the aid of the foregoing arguments.

First we notice the interdependence between the two constraint functions via their common arguments X and Y. Then this interconnection, which is already implicit in our arguments to this point, may be used to establish the differential calculus chain rule equivalent of the derivative we seek:

$$\frac{\partial\mu}{\partial\lambda} = \frac{\partial\mu}{\partial g}\cdot\frac{\partial g}{\partial f}\cdot\frac{\partial f}{\partial\lambda} \tag{11-25}$$

Consider now the first and third elements of the product term on the right-hand side of Equation (11-25). These two terms are asking the question as to how the marginal productivity measures μ and λ can be expected to change as their corresponding constraints are relaxed. Given the pervasiveness of the law or assumption of diminishing marginal productivity we can make the following statements with regard to μ and λ. As the availability of money capital is increased, the marginal productivity of money capital will diminish, and as successively higher levels of output are posited the marginal productivity of output will diminish. The partial derivatives $\partial\mu/\partial g$ and $\partial\lambda/\partial f$ will therefore be negative. Thus the first and third elements in the product term on the right-hand side of Equation (11-25) will be negative.

But what of the middle element of this expression, $\partial g/\partial f$? If we refer now to expression (11-24) we recognize this last-mentioned partial derivative as the negative of the ratio of the μ and λ terms. The sign of the derivative therefore depends on the sign of these marginal productivity measures. Now it is known, on the basis of the mathematical methodology we established initially and which underlies all our model building in this book, that μ and λ can take on only nonnegative values at optimum or infraoptimum values of the decision variables in the model. We established at the beginning, and need not discuss in detail at this point, the fact that so long as a given constraint was operative and binding, and was actually constraining the decision outcomes of the model, the associated Lagrange multiplier, or our present marginal productivity measure, must be positive. If the variable represented by the constraint function was in fact in surplus supply and was not therefore constraining the decision outcomes, the marginal productivity would be zero. We saw that no economic meaning was to be attached to a constraint variable in surplus supply, except to say that it was no longer scarce and was not therefore capable of economic valuation at the margin.

If, therefore, μ and λ are restricted to nonnegative values and if, as in the case we are about to examine, they can actually be expected to take on nonzero or positive values, the sign of $\partial g / \partial f$ in expression (11-24) will be negative. This, then, establishes that each of the elements in the product term on the right-hand side of Equation (11-25), and therefore the sign of the total expression, is negative. We are thereby told that as λ diminishes μ will tend to increase, and we are now ready to explore the implications of this proposition for the economic interpretation of the model we have specified in Equation (11-1).

The Capacity Decision

A model such as this is capable of asking and providing economically meaningful answers to more than one kind of question. Imagine, for example, that the decision makers in the firm have specified a maximum output level above which, for various reasons, they do not desire to produce and that this maximum permissible level is introduced as the $\overline{Q}$ variable in the λ function, the output constraint function, in Equation (11-1). Now this posited output volume may be less than, equal to, or greater than the global optimum volume that would be generated by the solution values of the basic model described in Equation (9-11). The posited output volume may be different, that is, from the optimum volume derived from the basic optimization model of the preceding chapters, in which the only constraining factor is the availability of money capital or, even more basically, the available amount of equity capital in the firm.

If the posited volume to which it is desired to constrain the decision outcomes is less than such a global optimum, the marginal value productivity of further output will be positive, λ will therefore be positive, and the firm will be functioning at what is economically a suboptimum size and structure. It will be operating, that is, at a lower level than is attainable on the basis of the available equity capital. Thus the statement that the firm will be operating at a suboptimum level is made with relation to the conceivable global optimum, and it is still true to say that so long as a posited output volume is constraining the firm's decisions in this way, the model of Equation (11-1) will actually derive the optimum values of all the decision variables for that level of output. This says that if the decision makers do in fact wish to constrain the firm to a certain maximum size, the model of Equation (11-1) will determine the optimum factor combination, the optimum asset investments, and the optimum combination of financing sources with which to maintain the productive process necessary to produce the posited output.

It may be of interest to the firm's decision makers to postulate varying possible values of the output constraint in Equation (11-1) and to observe the manner in which the structural characteristics of the firm may change as different output levels are planned for within the conceivable global optimum. More importantly, perhaps, note might be taken in such an analysis of the way in which the value of the objective function, the economic value of the ownership, might vary as the alternative plans move through the suboptimum output ranges toward the global optimum. An understanding may thereby be provided of the stability of the marginal value productivity of output in the region surrounding the optimum level.

Interest may also attach to the structural flexibility of the firm at planned output levels at or near the optimum and to the ease with which changes may at any desired time be made from one plan or structure of the firm to another. It may make perfectly good economic sense to adopt a suboptimum plan and structure in the present, if flexibility is thereby provided for future planning maneuvers. The thing the planning models will be providing in such a case is a measure of the economic cost of flexibility, indicated by the economic values sacrificed by adopting a suboptimum plan.

If now the size of the posited output in the various plans based on Equation (11-1) is increased until the optimum output consistent with the available capital constraint is in view, what will have happened to the λ variable in the equation? Clearly it will have been depressed to zero, and we can therefore offer an alternative formulation of the objectives of the enterprise-planning process. The concern of the decision makers, we may say, is to increase the envisaged output sufficiently to drive λ to zero, where output no longer has a positive marginal value productivity. When that point has been reached, the λ function in Equation (11-1) vanishes, and the model and its solution values become identical again with those in the basic formulation in Equation (9-11).

Now at this point we can usefully invoke the results of our earlier arguments regarding the behavior of μ, the marginal productivity of money capital, for posited or induced changes in λ. As λ is depressed toward zero as successively higher — but infraoptimum — output levels are envisaged, what is happening to μ? First of all we should point out that our initial concern was with the partial derivative of μ with respect to λ, and from the nature of the arguments to be based on such partial derivatives, this indicates that if no other change in the enterprise was envisaged, the decrease in λ would tend to induce an increase in μ.

Two interesting economic observations can now be seen to follow from this proposition. First, if a higher level of output was in fact produced without there having been an immediate increase in the available money capital, the higher output could have been attained only by such a change in the factor combination as continued to exhaust — but whose requirements did not exceed — the money capital available. But second, it was observed in Chapter 8 in the discussion following inequalities (8-24) and (8-25) that this relative scarcity of money capital would involve the substitution of the relatively less capital intensive factor of production for the relatively more capital intensive factor. This issue of the substitution between factors and the changing capital intensity of the planned productive process will be referred to again in connection with Figure 8 on page 201. But it can be said immediately that here we have emerging in a new form the proposition we insisted upon earlier in a different context: The optimum structure of factor usage in the firm, and therefore the optimum structure of the productive process and the optimum asset investment, is not independent of the availability of money capital.

Operationally it can be readily conceived why the marginal productivity of money capital should rise in the situation envisaged, or why, to use the mathematical expression, μ should tend to increase as the value of λ is being depressed by the posited increases in output. For as the output volume and the revenues generated by the firm increase, the operating income and the residual earnings on the invested capital may also be expected to increase. So long, therefore, as no change has yet been made in the total capital employed, the relative attractiveness of further money capital investment will have risen owing to the higher rate of earnings on the invested capital, and the marginal productivity of money capital has thus been pushed to a higher level. In this way, then, the posited increase in output will not only have made an increase in money capital desirable, but it will actually have brought about a motivation or inducement to increase the capital investment, by reason of its having raised the indicated measure of the marginal efficiency of money capital.

It will be useful at this point to sum up the logic of the preceding argument in such a way as to exhibit the symmetry of the conclusions that emerge from it. If the profit or value function of the firm is constrained by two operative constraint functions, a partial relaxation of one constraint will increase the marginal productivity of a relaxation of the other constraint. In our present context, for example, if the money capital and the output constraints in Equation (11-1) were both operative and μ and λ were therefore both positive, an increase in available money capital would tend to lower μ, would raise λ, and would tend to induce an increase in output. As the output was increased, the value of λ would fall again to a new equilibrium or constrained optimization level. Similarly, if the output constraint were relaxed, the value of λ would fall, the value of μ would increase, and an inducement would emerge to increase the amount of money capital in the firm. As the money capital employed was increased, the value of μ would fall again to a new equilibrium level.

We have not, of course, in the foregoing analysis, generated the full set of optimization conditions implicit in Equation (11-1) which summarized the model we have been considering. The solution conditions may be developed in the same manner as in the earlier models of the same kind discussed in the preceding chapters. One point, however, might usefully be emphasized before we proceed. If we continue to assume, as in most instances in the preceding models, that the amount of equity or ownership capital in the firm is fixed, then the way in which the money capital supply is to be increased following the rise in its marginal efficiency is by the introduction of further debt capital.[2] But we have seen that at the equilibrium solution values of the decision variables in the model, a precisely definable relation will exist between the marginal efficiency of money capital on the one hand and the marginal interest cost of borrowing on the other. A full discussion of the equilibrium relationship was given in the context of Equations (9-16) through (9-21).

If, in the case envisaged in Equation (11-1), a constrained optimization position is established with the solution values of λ and μ positive for the reasons previously examined, then the relationship just envisaged between μ and the marginal cost of borrowing must also hold at the solution point. It is necessary that this should be so, for otherwise the solution values of the decision variables generated by the model could not properly be said to be optimized values, or in this case, of course, constrained optimization values. Thus we can say, in a different interpretation of the working of the model, that when the relaxation of the output constraint has increased the marginal efficiency of money capital, the introduction of additional debt capital will reestablish the same formal relationship as previously existed between μ and the marginal cost of borrowing. But the level of borrowing costs or the rate of interest at which the relationship exists may quite well be different from the previous equilibrium level. If, as we have argued at length in earlier contexts, the debt cost function is positively related to the amount of debt or to the degree of financial leverage in the firm, the marginal cost of borrowing will be rising, and when the new capital is introduced, the equilibrium relationship we now have in view will be reestablished at a higher level.

Thus the induced effects, the stimulus of constraint relaxations, the reaction of marginal productivity changes, further induced constraint varia-

[2] We discussed in the preceding chapter, and need not reopen at this point, the possibility that the ownership capital in the firm might also be increased, depending on whether the solution value of μ has or has not been depressed to unity.

tions, and the emergence of new equilibrium positions, formally similar but structurally and quantitatively unique — these developments can be visualized as proceeding until either (1) the decision makers are holding the constraint variables at some desired levels, and are satisfied with the suboptimum solution values of the decision variables; (2) the decision variables have been brought to their optimum values consistent with the amount of ownership capital in the firm; or (3) the ownership capital has also been increased sufficiently to depress the value of μ to unity, and the firm has accordingly attained, consistent with the forms of the underlying determinant functions, what we previously referred to as the owners' *maximum maximorum* position.

In summary, the principal conclusion to emerge from the analysis, apart from an understanding of the *modus operandi* of the enterprise-planning-and-decision system, is that the nature of the constraints against which the firm is operating does determine the optimum structure of the enterprise, its investment, and its productive process. It is the kind of interdependent causation we have witnessed in operation in the foregoing that we have had in mind consistently when speaking of the firm's trilogy of planning problems: the production problem, the investment problem, and the financing problem. And it is this same interdependence that is reflected on the analytical level in our consistent argument for the logical integration of the theory of production, the theory of capital, and the theory of finance.

A Partial Geometry of the Model

A robust and integrated theory of the kind we have explored cannot easily be reflected in simple two-dimensional geometry. But perhaps some further clarification might be obtained from the partial representation shown in Figure 8. The magnitudes shown in the figure must at best be impressionistic, and the following comments will emphasize only the principal relations involved. We shall not refer to all the points in our previous exposition at which the relations we adduce were discussed in detail. The main conclusions will by now be quite familiar.

We begin with the assumption of a model constrained by both a specified level of output and a specified amount of available money capital. These constraints are represented respectively by the isoproduct curve $\overline{Q}_o$ and the capital availability constraint $\overline{M}_o$ in the figure. The concept of the isoproduct curve does not require further clarification at this stage. The capital constraint function $\overline{M}_o$ may be regarded as the image in the factor input plane of the boundary of the money capital constraint plane. The form of this boundary will no doubt be nonlinear, depending on the complex form of the total money capital requirement function. The $\overline{M}_o$

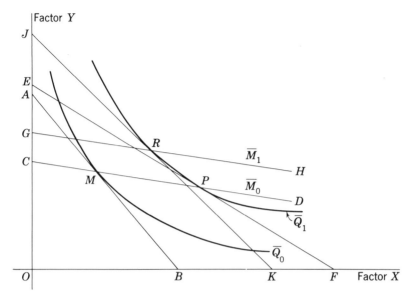

Figure 8.   Enterprise production optimization

function is drawn as a linear and negatively inclined function in the figure, however, principally to emphasize the implications of the assumption, maintained throughout our models, that factor Y may be considered the more capital intensive factor.

If, now, the model is constrained by both the output and the capital constraints, consider initially the equilibrium point M. The fact that this point lies on both the $\overline{Q}_o$ and the $\overline{M}_o$ functions indicates that both constraints are satisfied. The slope of the isoproduct curve at point M equals the ratio of the marginal physical products of the factors X and Y, as determined by the form of the production function. This also equals the slope of AB, the ratio of the effective marginal costs of the factors, after taking into account the imputed capital costs. These latter, it has been seen, depend on the solution magnitude of μ, the marginal efficiency of money capital or the rate at which the capital costs are imputed to the factors. Thus the factor combination represented by point M is the optimum factor combination with which, under the conditions posited, to produce the output level stipulated.

We can imagine now that the output constraint is relaxed from $\overline{Q}_o$ to $\overline{Q}_1$. If no increase occurs immediately in the available money capital, the operative factor combination on the higher isoproduct curve must lie on the same capital constraint boundary, $\overline{M}_o$. The point P describes such a factor combination. But we know that at this point also the factor combination must be such that the ratio of marginal physical products again equals the ratio of effective marginal factor costs. This condition will be satisfied if the latter ratio has changed from that represented by the slope of AB to that described by the lesser slope of EF. But it was seen at an early stage of our analysis that the ratio of effective marginal factor costs, after taking account of imputed capital costs, would in fact change in this direction only if the marginal efficiency of money capital increased. We have seen also in a foregoing argument that this can be expected to occur if the output constraint is relaxed without an immediate relaxation of the money capital constraint, and point P therefore satisfies the qualitative implications of the analysis.

Conceivably, however, the firm would not plan to produce output $\overline{Q}_1$ with the factor combination represented by P, at the higher marginal efficiency of money capital implicit in slope EF. The value of the maximand function can be increased further by taking advantage of the higher marginal efficiency of money capital to introduce more debt capital and to move the boundary of the capital constraint plane from, say, CD to GH or from $\overline{M}_o$ to $\overline{M}_1$. If this is done, the new optimum factor combination is that represented by point R. The reasons for this will be clear from the foregoing. At this point, both constraints are satisfied, and the ratio of marginal products equals the ratio of effective marginal factor costs.

The last point, however, calls for brief comment. In this instance the value of the relevant ratio is measured by the slope JK. As seen from Figure 8 this slope is less than that in the original factor-cost ratio as measured by AB but greater than that as measured by EF. But this implies that the capital imputation cost, or μ, in the ratio at R is greater than at M but less than at the intermediate point P. These features again are a precise confirmation of the qualititative nature of the relationships in the planning and optimization models we have considered at length.

Intraperiodic Plan Variations

The foregoing analysis has focused principally on three different aspects of enterprise planning: first, the problems of achieving the optimum enterprise structure for various levels of output; second, the possibilities of achieving a maximum value position for any given availability of money capital resources; and third, the further possibility of achieving a *maximum maximorum* position from the point of view of the owners of the firm. It should be perfectly clear, however, that this leaves quite untouched the important question of the reaction of the firm to intraperiodic changes in the level or form of the underlying determinant functions in the model.

Suppose, for example, that at a given planning date of the firm an optimum enterprise structure is decided upon and brought into existence (abstracting for the moment from the necessary implementation time) on the basis of the determinant functions and the decision data then available — on the basis, that is, of the technological production possibilities expressed in the production function, the direct factor costs, the market sales and revenue possibilities, the supply conditions in the money capital market, and the risk predilections and investment or dividend preferences of the owners of the firm. It can be conceived that when such an enterprise structure is attained, the firm will produce and function at the level and in the manner indicated until a change in the determinants warrants a further change in the structure and stance of the firm. Conceivably, the firm may conduct fairly continuous studies of economic developments, demand and cost determinants and production possibilities, and may be ready at frequent intervals to react to indications of the need for structural change. Or alternatively, the firm may adopt, as we suggested at an earlier point, a policy of reconsidering the structural questions at what we called sequential-planning dates. The interplanning date period that exists in such a case will conceivably have some flexibility, however, and the calendar of decision dates can be changed as conditions or developments warrant. The degree of change and the extent or thoroughness of plan revisions between normal planning dates might be expected to depend on the seriousness or permanence of the change in the structural determinants, or on the deviations of the developments in the economic milieu from the expectations on which the existing plan was based.

Whatever procedures the managers of the firm may adopt in these respects, our present objective of setting out a robust theory of the firm requires that we acknowledge some final features of the decision problems and the decision makers' reactions. Apart from some special problems and their analytical implications which we shall refer to in the following chapter, our concern is with three major issues: first, the intraplanning period, or interplanning date, operational variations of the firm; second, the degree of thoroughness or structural radicalism that may be feasibly incorporated in plan revisions; and third, the time lags that must occur in fact between plan decisions and their implementation.

The first of these issues is contiguous, if not coincident, with the general content of the neoclassical, neo-Marshallian theory of the firm. Fortunately, therefore, we need only note at this point the similarities between our present problem and the general neoclassical problem, and not discuss the theoretical analysis in detail. The usual province of the theory of production and the theory of factor usage is concerned with the optimum employment of variable factors and the optimum level of output for a given total employment of fixed factors or a given size or scale of operations. We discussed this theoretical preoccupation more fully in Chapter 6, where we examined some necessary background ideas in the theories of production and capital, and the matter need not be reopened at this stage. We can point out, however, that our own preoccupation has caused us to adopt a rather different order of development of the underlying theory of the firm. It was necessary to argue, in an appropriate context and at the methodological foundation of our work, that the theory of the comparative static structural optimization of the firm was logically prior to the theory of short-run operating behavior.

The details and direction of the logical development of our argument need not be considered again at this point. It is sufficient to note that our order of development of the components of the theory has been the inverse of that generally adopted in the traditional textbook exposition of the subject. The best instances of the latter consider first the theory of production levels and variable factor usage within an assumed size and scale of operations, the law of diminishing marginal productivity or law of varying factor proportions, the firm's demand curve for inputs and supply curve of outputs, and their related technical implications. Then at a later stage the question of the optimum scale of operations is confronted, and the laws of returns to scale, the theory of economies or diseconomies of scale, and the long-run cost curves of the firm are adduced. But by the time this final stage is reached, the order of logical development in such an analytical scheme has inhibited completely any possibility of a significant integration of the theory of production and the theory of capital. In many, as opposed to the best, of the theories of the firm derived from the neoclassical theorems, no clear interpretation is attempted of the arguments in the production function, and though the presence of capital as a factor of production is acknowledged, the exposition proceeds without an awareness of the complications that differing factor durabilities really introduce into the optimization problem.

This has been said in order to make perfectly clear the fact that the interrelationships in the models we have elaborated do not describe the temporary and short-run changes in conditions once the optimum plan to which they point has been implemented. If we give to the short run its usual Marshallian economic interpretation, we can say, in the same way as in the familiar neoclassical analysis, that in the interplanning date period, changes in marginal revenue earning opportunities can be expected to be exploited depending on the usual short-run marginal cost–marginal revenue relationship. Taking the firm's profit function as embedded in our basic optimization model, for example, and assuming in a given interplanning date period that the available capacity of factor Y is unalterable, the question of whether the short-run level of the firm's output should be changed will depend on the marginal revenue productivity and the marginal cost of factor X. This, of course, is derivable by appropriate differentiation of the firm's new profit function, and as the exercise is repeated in many places in the literature it need not be discussed at length here.

In the same way, once we are in possession of a functioning enterprise of a size and structure determined by the solution values of the decision variables in the optimization model, we can again use familiar theoretical constructs to derive the firm's short-run demand curve for variable factor inputs, its short-run marginal cost, or output supply function, and its short-run revenue-generating or profit possibilities.

If we piece together the various elements of the short-run management and operating problems, we can throw some further light on one of the fundamental issues we confronted at the beginning of our work. It was recognized at that time that the economic value of the ownership of the firm, which we were setting out consistently to maximize, depended not only on the normal level of profits the enterprise plan could be expected to generate, but also on the appropriate capitalization rate at which those expected earnings should be capitalized. This capitalization rate, in turn, was seen to depend on the degree of instability in the expected income stream, or on the degree of uncertainty as to what the actual earnings for the owners of the firm would be. The precise uncertainty at issue was related to the degree of certainty with which the expectation could be held that the actual profit of the firm would in fact be the value, from within the range of possible values, that coincided with the normal expected value. Precisely, the measure of the degree of uncertainty, or the riskiness of the owners' investment in the firm, was taken to be the variance of the probability distribution of possible income values. It will be recalled that the matter of risk thus adduced was discussed more deeply in terms of the coefficient of variation of the expected operating income stream of the firm and of the further potentially destabilizing effects of the degree of financial leverage in the firm, or the ratio of debt capital to ownership capital in the firm's financing structure. The implications of these magnitudes were then brought together to express the manner in which, for an assumed variability of the actual gross-revenue-generating ability of the firm, the owners' capitalization rate depended on the amount of capital employed and the manner in which that total capital was provided.

When once an enterprise plan is decided upon, or indeed for any particular plan that might be posited, the decision makers can recompute on the basis of that plan the degree of risk that would be involved in the implementation of it. The plan, it is recalled on the basis of the equations in the model, will have specified the contemplated level of output, the factor combination, the fixed and variable production costs, and the fixed financial costs. The decision makers will now be in a position to consider not only the contemplated level of output, but also the probability distribution of the sales volume around that output level. Now, moreover, given also the cost structure of the contemplated plan and its implied production process, they can take note also of the relative degree of fixity or flexibility of the cost components within it. If, therefore, the decision makers were to take any number of simulated observations of sales or output volumes from the probability distribution of possible output volumes around the level expected and specified by the model, they would then be able to prepare pro forma income statements for each of the simulated output observations. In this way it would be possible to build up from these pro forma income statements a probability distribution of the net incomes that might be confronted by the firm if the plan being contemplated were in fact adopted.

Finally, the variance and the coefficient of variation of this distribution of revenues could be computed, and the measure of risk thus derived could be checked for consistency with the initial assumptions of risk, on the basis of which the solution values of the planning model were generated. The precise point at which the assumption of risk was introduced into the model was exhibited in developed form in Equations (4-22) through (4-26). If, of course, the simulated riskiness of a contemplated enterprise plan is out of line with the initial risk postulates in the optimization model, a reconsideration of the planning data and postulates is called for. For if an enterprise structure is contemplated, having a higher implicit degree of risk (coefficient of variation of expected earning ability) than that originally postulated, then in due course, when the higher-risk characteristics of the firm have been communicated to the owners, they can logically be expected to increase their required rate of return as a reaction to, or in compensation for, the increased degree of risk. But this is saying, of course, that the owners' capitalization rate will be levered upward, and this will imply a lower total valuation for any expected level of the income stream.[3]

Periodic Plan Revisions

In various ways, therefore, the managers of the firm can consider the short-run operating implications of whatever enterprise plan might be suggested by the optimization model. These considerations lead, however, to the second of the issues to which it was desired to draw attention in

[3] It is not thought necessary to discuss at this point the statistical properties of the simulation techniques by which the implicit degree of risk in a contemplated enterprise plan can be estimated. A good discussion of the techniques, though with application to a different problem, can be found in James E. Walter, *The Investment Process*, Harvard University Press, Cambridge, Mass., 1962, chap. 11. See also William Beranek, *Analysis for Financial Decisions*, Richard D. Irwin, Inc., Homewood, Ill., 1963, chap. 12; Alexander A. Robichek and Stewart C. Myers, *Optimal Financing Decisions*, Prentice-Hall, Inc., Englewood Cliffs, N.J., 1965, pp. 140–158; and Anthony J. Curley, *A Stochastic Simulation of the Personal Investment Decision*, unpublished Ph.D. dissertation, University of Pennsylvania, 1967.

this chapter. This refers to the extent to which, or the degree of radical thoroughness with which, plan revisions or changes in the structure of the firm may be made at a given planning date. We have already observed that the solution values of the decision variables in the model, and therefore the structural plan envisaged, must depend on the forms of the input functions, on the exogenous data and the parameters and postulates relevant to the planning decision, and on the endogenous, interdependent working of the relationships within the model. If the input to the planning problem is different, the answers that determine the planning decision must be different.

Consider now what might be done at a given planning date if it were desired to reconsider the structure of the firm in the most thoroughgoing manner possible. We can imagine that an entirely new plan might be constructed *de novo*. The technological form of the production function with which the firm has to work could be derived from the usual engineering and technical sources, and the possibilities of factor substitutabilities and potential combinations could be specified accordingly. There is no reason why the form of the production function confronting the firm should remain unchanged from one plan date to the next. Indeed, given the pace of technological progress, more or less drastic changes in production possibilities may in fact be expected. Or again, new products may be envisaged and incorporated precisely into the models we have constructed, specifying their anticipated revenue functions and the related production and cost functions.

More difficult is the specification of the money capital availability that should logically be incorporated into the optimization model if, as suggested above, it is desired to plan *de novo* in the presence of an inherited enterprise structure. Reflection on the basic model will make it clear that we are interested at this point in the actual amount of equity capital available to the firm for use as the foundation of the total supply of money capital funds. Looking, therefore, at the existing firm, we are interested now in the total available realization value of the existing equity ownership. This, it will be realized from our earlier discussion of the financial procedures of the firm, will be estimated from the following data: (1) the realization value of the assets, plus (2) the total of the accumulated replacement sinking funds, minus (3) the debt liabilities. Given the availability of equity capital, the decision problem is then concerned with calculating the maximum attainable economic value that could be created or generated by alternative *de novo* enterprise plans and comparing this value with what could be expected to be generated if the existing enterprise structure were retained.

This is simply the question, pervasive in investment economics, of comparing a going-concern value with the values attainable by investing realization proceeds in alternative uses. This is of the essence of economic opportunity costs. But between the two extreme behavior reactions of variations in short-run interplanning-date operations on the one hand and the thorough reevaluation at any given planning date on the other, there exist any number of possibilities of reassessment and reorganization. To the extent that it is desired to leave particular asset structures undisturbed in plan assessments, the availability of the corresponding real factor capacities can be taken in as production function constraints in the planning analysis, and the gross book value of the undisturbed assets (assuming that the original sinking fund arrangements designed to provide for the assets' replacement and preserve their original values are proceeding according to plan) can be taken in as available equity in the capital constraint. The remaining equity in the firm assessed for planning purposes may then be based as before on the realization values of the remaining assets and the relevant sinking fund accumulations and debt liabilities. All this is tantamount to saying that at the sequential-planning dates the management of the firm will conceivably be able to consider not simply one investment or reconstruction plan but several such possible schemes of growth or reorganization, and will be able to choose between them in accordance with the economic interests of the owners. This latter will be expressed in terms of the total capitalized value of the ownership investment.

In whatever way the decision problem is resolved, the management action precipitated will be that which is necessary to move the firm from its previously existing size and structure to the new preferred size and structure recommended by the planning analysis. This implies, in the spirit of an earlier argument, the bringing into existence of a new structure of the productive process, an altered optimum factor combination, a differently specified optimum asset investment, and a new optimum combination of money capital sources. It can be visualized also how such variations will be reflected in the firm's periodic income statements and in the assets and liabilities sides of its balance sheet. For the present it will be useful to concentrate on the implications such envisaged changes will have for the third of the points it was desired to examine in this chapter. This has to do with the question of the actual investment expenditures of the firm and with the necessary time lags between plan decisions and plan implementations.

Capital Changes and Investment Expenditures

Clearly, the models presented in this book, emphasizing as they have the logical priority of the comparative static, structural decision problem of the firm, have led precisely to a theory of optimum capital stock or optimum capital usage. It is true, of course, and it will already have been recognized as implicit in the preceding arguments, that a theory of money capital investment is in some sense a logical precipitate of the theory of real capital stock. In a meaningful sense it can be said that our theory of optimum capital stock or usage implies that the investment expenditure necessary at any given date will simply be that required to change the size and asset structure of the firm from its previous position to the size and structure inherent in the new and presumably economically superior plan. Fastening in this way on the notion of the theory of investment as a theory of changes in capital stock, we can confront a question that has troubled the literature for some time: Is a judgment possible as to the relative superiority of different investment theories such as accelerator models, capacity models, or those based on profit rates, liquidity constraints or interest rates or the cost of capital? Our answer has to be that all these factors are shown in the planning model to be mutually relevant.

Insofar as the optimization model traces out the implications of optimum factor usage for the capital stock requirements decision, and thus determines the direction of investment expenditures, our theory of investment is a capacity theory. But it is not a capacity theory shackled to the assumption of a constant capital-output ratio such as might be found in some of the cruder formulations of the accelerator-capacity models. As in the other aspects of the solution values of the optimization model, the capital stock and investment decision will be what it is simply because the input-planning data and the related postulates and parameters are what they are. On the other hand, insofar as the capital stock requirements, and therefore the money capital investments, are shown in the model to depend on maximized profit opportunities consistent with optimized ownership values, our theory of investment is a profitability theory.

Or again, bearing in mind our interpretation of the μ coefficient of the money capital availability constraint as the marginal productivity of money capital, our theory of investment is a marginal efficiency theory. But again, it is not a marginal efficiency theory in the crude sense that looks at investment expenditures on a project-by-project basis and says that investment expenditures should continue until the marginal efficiency of the last investment dollar is equal to the cost, or marginal cost, of capital. We have seen that an optimization proposition akin to this is indeed inherent in the solution conditions of the model. But the determination of the outcome has been seen to be much more complex, and to take account of a larger number of interdependent causal relations, than the kind of propositions we have just encountered. In particular, not only has the availability of money capital in one particular form, debt or equity, been seen to affect the cost at which, and the terms on which, other forms of money capital are available, but the overall conditions on which money capital is available determine also the optimum capital intensity of the productive process.

The economics of the investment problem are not exhausted by looking simply at the cash flow stream that an investment project might generate, and calculating on the basis of it an expected rate of profit on the project. It is continually necessary also to consider whether new supplies of money capital that become available from time to time might not be better invested in changing the structure or capital intensity of existing enterprise processes than in engaging in such new activities as may be presented for consideration. The relevant optimization analysis has been examined at length in earlier chapters and the conclusion noted that the problem of capital deepening in the firm is as intimately bound up with the provision of money capital as the related problem of capital widening. Indeed, these are different aspects of the common issue of capital optimization. But the complexity we found in the resolution of the issue prevents us from espousing any simple characterization of investment theory such as those noted above.

But it is still true to say that our planning model has provided us with a comparative static, optimum capital stock or optimum total investment decision. It still says nothing about the calendar time lags in the implementation of optimum structural plans. This, of course, in raising the problem of the rate of time flow of investment expenditure, is pointing to a full-scale dynamic analysis of enterprise adjustment. Into that province it is not desired or necessary to enter in this book. It is our prior concern to show the genesis and logical nature of the issue. The dynamic analysis of lagged adjustments in the economic system, and in particular their bearing on investment expenditures, has become itself a specialized part of economics and may be consulted in many parts of the literature.[4]

Comparative Static and Dynamic Models

Before we leave this question of the time rates of investment outlays and the methodological issue of the relation between, or the logical priority of, comparative static versus dynamic enterprise models, it will be useful

---

[4] See, for example, Edwin Kuh, *Capital Stock Growth: A Micro-econometric Approach*, North Holland Publishing Company, Amsterdam, 1963, and R. G. D. Allen, *Mathematical Economics*, Macmillan & Co., Ltd., London, 1959. See also the recent and important work of Dale W. Jorgenson, "Capital Theory and Investment Behavior," *American Economic Review*, vol. 53, pp. 247–259, May, 1963 (reprinted in *Readings in Business Cycles*, American Economic Association, Richard D. Irwin, Inc., Homewood, Ill., 1965), and "Anticipations and Investment Behavior," *Brookings Quarterly Econometric Model of the United States*, James S. Duesenberry et al. (eds.), Rand McNally & Company, Chicago, 1965.

to refer at slightly greater length to a problem previously noticed but not discussed. This has to do with the possibility of constructing growth models of the business firm and with the logicoempirical interpretation that is to be attached to them. We have already referred to the growing literature concerned with this question.[5] As for the logical significance of the growth model, the internal validity of the exercise and the coherence of the model turn, as in all such analytical work, on the nature of the assumptions, in this case notably the growth rate assumption, introduced into the argument, and on the nature of the mutually determinate relations deemed to exist between the parts of the model. The empirical significance, on the other hand, would seem to turn on three kinds of questions: first, whether the model actually attempts to account for the principal forces that determine the position and stance of the firm in its economic environment; second, whether actual firms do in fact proceed with their planning by locking themselves into assumed rates of growth over time, and whether they are, from a normative point of view, advised to do so in the interests of the optimization of their owners' economic positions; and third, whether the nature of change in the determinant forces of the economic world, for example production, revenue, cost, factor, and money capital supply functions, really is amenable to analysis by the kind of enterprise growth models that have appeared to date.

Apart from the empirical investigation of capital stock growth at the business firm level such as referred to above, the theoretical development that abuts most directly on the problems we set out to analyze in this book is that which has stemmed from the model of common stock price valuation developed in the early work of Gordon.[6] The most interesting development in this direction from our present point of view occurs in the recent work of Lerner and Carleton.[7] Without attempting to examine their interesting and provocative work in detail, we shall draw attention to the main features that give it significance for the kind of problems we have examined.

First we are interested in the very valuable methodological awareness exhibited by the work. This is the consciousness that the thing needed in the theory of the firm is an integrated model that attempts to combine the various forces determining the economic position of the owners. We noted at due length in Chapter 6 the history of the attempts that economists have made to live comfortably with this realization. For our own

---

[5] See footnote 1, Chap. 10.

[6] Myron J. Gordon, *The Investment, Financing, and Valuation of the Corporation,* Richard D. Irwin, Inc., Homewood, Ill., 1962.

[7] Eugene M. Lerner and Willard T. Carleton, "The Integration of Capital Budgeting and Stock Valuation," *American Economic Review,* vol. 54, pp. 683–702, September, 1964, and *A Theory of Financial Analysis,* Harcourt, Brace & World, Inc., New York, 1966.

part we have tried to come to grips with this logical integration problem by bringing the analytical trilogy of the theories of production, capital, and finance to bear on what we interpreted as the three main divisions of the enterprise optimization problem: the production problem, the investment problem, and the financing problem. Our procedures and results have been illustrated fully in the preceding chapters. But for the question immediately in hand, an interesting methodological development can be noticed in the relevant theoretical literature. The significant work of Smith, for example, in effect addressed itself to the first two legs of our trilogy, his main interest having been that of developing "a unified theory of production and investment."[8] Lerner and Carleton, on the other hand, were interested, in effect, in the last two legs of our trilogy, the investment and financing problems. Their earlier article noted the absence from previous work of a "widely accepted theoretical apparatus linking the market valuation of common stock to a corporation's investment-opportunities schedule, dividend payout function, and capital structure." Their analytical procedure, therefore, was to "depart from the single-equation convention and explicitly introduce two equations: an investment-opportunities (or capital-budgeting) schedule and a stock-valuation equation."[9] In their subsequent book a fuller discussion was given also of the supply and use of debt capital and of the associated question of the risks introduced into the firm by variations in the financing structure.

It is not necessary to repeat at this stage the ways in which Smith's treatment of production and investment differs from our own work, or to examine at length how Lerner and Carleton handle the investment and financing questions. But in the interest of preserving perspective, the following brief substantive comments on the latter work are in order. It is emphasized that our only interest at this point is that of considering whether the Lerner-Carleton attempt to achieve an integrated theory of the valuation of the ownership of the firm is asking the most meaningful questions or moving in the most significant directions. These issues need to be raised, if only because the Lerner-Carleton model is the most ambitious of its kind yet to appear in the literature.

The Lerner-Carleton model, quite apart from the reasonableness of its assumptions or its own internal coherence, with neither of which we are primarily concerned at this point, sets out to optimize certain decision variables, principally equity reinvestment rates or dividend policy on the one hand and the usage of debt capital on the other. The objective is that

---

[8] Vernon L. Smith, *Investment and Production: A Study in the Theory of the Capital-using Enterprise*, Harvard University Press, Cambridge, Mass., 1961, p. vii.

[9] Lerner and Carleton, "The Integration of Capital Budgeting and Stock Valuation," p. 683.

of optimizing the market price per share of common stock ownership, and the optimization task is achieved in the model subject to a set of so-called constraint conditions. First, a financial constraint is introduced, describing the interest costs at which debt capital is available to the firm as a function of the financial leverage ratio. Second, an earnings opportunities constraint is introduced to describe the average rate of return that can be earned on the total assets of the firm, dependent on the total amount of assets employed or, as subsequently argued, on the time rate of increase in the total assets. The interest cost is a monotonically rising function of the financial leverage in the firm, and the rate of return on assets is a monotonically declining function of the total asset investment.[10] The objective function into which these constraint functions are substituted in order to find the optimized solution values of the decision variables is the familiar Gordon-type growth model share price equation. This shows the price of a share of common stock as equal to the dividend expectation capitalized at a capitalization factor equal to $k - g$, where k refers to the investors' required rate of return and g refers to the assumed constant expected rate of growth of dividends.[11]

The interesting feature of the Lerner-Carleton model for our present purposes is the contention that the declining functional relation between the amount of asset investment in the firm and the average rate of return on the assets takes account of "the prevailing conditions in the product market in which the firm sells its output and the factor market in which it purchases its inputs."[12] Of course if it could be shown that these output and input market conditions are really taken into account and are really allowed to determine the solution values of the decision variables, the Lerner-Carleton model might genuinely have made an advance in considering what we have termed in this work the production problem, and, even more significantly, might have achieved some integration of the production problem with the investment problem of the firm. But it is clear, unfortunately, that such high hopes cannot be held. For all that the output and input analysis amounts to is a restatement of a familiar threefold proposition: First, the unit selling price function will be negatively inclined in an imperfectly competitive firm; second, the average cost function will be rising; and third, the average rate of return on assets can therefore be expected to decline as the asset investment increases.

---

[10] Reference should be made to the full discussion in Lerner and Carleton's recent book, *A Theory of Financial Analysis*.

[11] For a guide to the fuller development of the Gordon model and a consideration of the logical paradox inherent in it, see Douglas Vickers, "Profitability and Reinvestment Rates: A note on the Gordon Paradox," *Journal of Business*, vol. 39, July, 1966.

[12] Lerner and Carleton, *A Theory of Financial Analysis* p. 10.

The analysis we have just referred to, and which for complete perspective should be inspected in its original source, is hardly sufficiently robust to support the claim that "we have now fashioned all the tools necessary to specify the determinants of the rate of return on assets and to determine those conditions under which a change in the level of assets will lead to a fall in the rate of return."[13] The thing that is missing, of course, and that puts the analysis on the wrong track so far as an integrated theory of ownership valuation is concerned, can be summed up as follows. First, the Lerner-Carleton scheme does not really address itself to the firm's output or production optimization problem, for it says nothing of the production function characteristics of the firm and offers no analysis of the determination, or the relevance to the optimum structure of the firm, of the optimum combination of factor inputs with which the firm should produce. In the thought forms of the analysis of this book, the Lerner-Carleton scheme, by not confronting what we called the production problem, has not taken full account of what is vital and significant in the neoclassical theory of production.

Second, the contribution we are at present discussing does not therefore take real account of the way in which the firm's investments in assets, and therefore its money capital requirements, are actually embedded in its optimum factor usage. In the thought forms of our earlier analysis again, the Lerner-Carleton scheme does not address itself to what we called the investment problem, and therefore does not take account of the vital elements from which we should build a microtheory of capital. It may seem, therefore, if the foundation concepts of our early chapters are meaningful for the progress of the theory of the firm, that the Lerner-Carleton analysis, in passing over the integrated contribution of production and capital theory, is unlikely to make significant progress in the theory of enterprise optimization. The concepts of capital theory and the vital notion that Lange insisted upon as long ago as 1936, "the distinction between money capital and real capital,"[14] are logically quite foreign to the Lerner-Carleton analysis.

With this in hand it need hardly be said that the Lerner-Carleton financing constraint, which is analogous to the debt capital supply function in our models, is not set in juxtaposition with a money capital requirement function, and again no integration of the firm's financing problem with its investment and production problems is achieved. On the analytical level the theory of finance is not finally integrated with the theory of capital and the theory of production. When, moreover, the Lerner-Carleton

[13] *Ibid.*, p. 80.
[14] Oskar Lange, "The Place of Interest in the Theory of Production," *Review of Economic Studies*, vol. 3, p. 178, June, 1936.

scheme incorporates as a final building block the assumption of a constant periodic growth rate of earnings and assets, the problems of optimum structural planning for the firm, and the sequential decision making and reconstruction for which we have argued at length, are avoided completely. Hopefully, of course, it will be recognized that the foregoing critical arguments have been adduced only because this book shares with Lerner and Carleton a common realization and theoretical awareness. Before the nascent financial theory of the firm can make progress, an integration of its thought forms into the main corpus of economic analysis must somehow be achieved. The work of Lerner and Carleton is the most ambitious attempt at a contribution to this objective from the side of the finance theorists. Though we have elaborated alternative and hopefully more productive approaches, the Lerner-Carleton volume must be read, alongside the contributions from the economic theorists we noted earlier, as a significant milepost on the road to the more general theorems which, as economic scientists, we hope to discover.[15]

[15] The issues we have referred to here might be compared with the exchange of views on the Lerner-Carleton analysis in the *American Economic Review*, vol. 57, pp. 209–222, March, 1967, including comments by Haim Ben-Shahar and Abraham Ascher, and Jean Crockett and Irwin Friend, and a reply by E. M. Lerner and W. T. Carleton. With reference to our own decision to work with a comparative static, sequential structural model, rather than a growth model of the kind we have already referred to, it is of interest to note that in the course of their perceptive remarks Jean Crockett and Irwin Friend also refer to considerations that "seriously prejudice the usefulness of the extremely popular constant growth model. . . ." Though their immediate context refers to a different level of analysis from what we have been concerned with, a significant insight is suggested by their summary argument: "It may be useful to demonstrate more directly that a stock-valuation formula can be combined with an investment opportunities schedule (and if desired with other relevant equations) without affecting the validity of the traditional theory. For this purpose it is desirable to introduce an alternative valuation equation which allows for the interdependence of investment decisions in a more explicit and flexible way than does the constant growth model. . . ." But all such theorizing, including, of course, that which has engaged us in this book, enjoys only varying degrees of internal inconsistency, logical generality, and empirical applicability. The intricacies in subsuming the real world forces that bear on the optimum position of the firm in the mathematical thought forms of the study are probably intractable in an ultimate sense. The concluding methodological observations in the "Reply" by Lerner and Carleton already referred to bear eloquently on this point. But valuable work can be done in uncovering and restructuring with a radical thoroughness the important modes of causation and directions of logical relationships in the optimization nexus of the firm. The manner in which this essential logical task might be faced and the foundations laid for further development of analysis will be clear from our preceding chapters.

12

Final
Considerations

Our analysis to this point has examined fairly completely the logical structure of the optimization model of the firm. The important point at issue has been consistently that of showing the real nature of the causal forces operative in the optimization nexus and the interconnections that exist between them. There remain, however, as is clear from the level of approximation with which we have worked, many problems in building the connections between the logical constructs on the one hand and their application to actual enterprise optimization on the other. Our preceding analysis, it is clear, is embedded in empirical categories, but it has concentrated on providing perspectives and avenues for empirical applications, rather than cultivating directly such new areas as might thereby be opened up. In this chapter, therefore, it will be useful to draw attention to several questions of a more specialized kind, as a means of exhibiting the logical flexibility and the procedural adaptability of the argument.

In the ownership optimization models we have developed, the revenue function, the cost function, and the money capital requirement function have all been described in terms of the firm's usage of factors of production. Equation (9-11), for example, and the solution conditions based upon it may be consulted again in connection with the following discussion. Our problem now is to recognize that the structure of the real world enterprise is such that certain costs may be incurred periodically, quite without any very direct relation to the employment of what might be envisaged as factors of production in the firm's production function. Admittedly, one of the forward steps now required in the theory of the firm is a more thoroughgoing analysis, by a partnership of economists and engineers, of the problem of specifying the firm's production function in a form amenable to both theoretical analysis and empirical manipulation. We have already noted the important work, at the level of the individual firm, that has been done in this connection by Vernon Smith and other economists. But even after a fuller logicoempirical specification of this kind it will still be true that certain indirect overhead costs are incurred by the firm and must therefore be incorporated in the cost and profit functions and integrated with the optimization analysis.

Ad Hoc and Overhead Costs

The incorporation of these items into the optimization model does not give rise to any conceptual difficulty, and need not therefore be discussed at length. Examples of such items would be the firm's administrative and general office salaries and various related expenses. These may be introduced into the firm's profit function as a fixed cost, in which case the optimum factor combination condition will not be affected, or they may be introduced as a definable function of the level of output or the size of operations of the firm. Consider, for example, the following attenuated form of the optimization model based on Equation (9-11) and shown as follows only for illustrative purposes:

$$\varphi = [p(Q)f(X,Y) - \theta(Q) - \gamma_1 X - \gamma_2 Y] + \mu[\overline{M} - \alpha X - \beta Y] \quad (12\text{-}1)$$

In Equation (12-1) the first expression in brackets on the right-hand side is the familiar profit function, into which an administrative cost function, $\theta(Q)$, has been introduced. The final expression in brackets is the general form of the money capital availability constraint in which, for simplicity, the available money capital is assumed to be fixed at an amount equal to $\overline{M}$.

We can again generate solution conditions to Equation (12-1) by taking partial derivatives with respect to the same basic decision variables as previously, namely the factor inputs X and Y.

$$\frac{\partial \varphi}{\partial X} = \left(p + Q\frac{dp}{dQ}\right)f_x - \frac{d\theta}{dQ}f_x - \gamma_1 - \mu\alpha = 0 \quad (12\text{-}2)$$

$$\frac{\partial \varphi}{\partial Y} = \left(p + Q\frac{dp}{dQ}\right)f_y - \frac{d\theta}{dQ}f_y - \gamma_2 - \mu\beta = 0 \quad (12\text{-}3)$$

By rearrangement of Equations (12-2) and (12-3) the solution condition follows:

$$\left(m - \frac{d\theta}{dQ}\right)f_x = \gamma_1 + \mu\alpha \quad (12\text{-}4)$$

$$\left(m - \frac{d\theta}{dQ}\right)f_y = \gamma_2 + \mu\beta \quad (12\text{-}5)$$

where m refers to the marginal revenue of output. If Equation (12-5) is divided into Equation (12-4) it is again seen that solution conditions for optimum factor combinations may be specified, similar to those encountered in earlier models of this kind.

In a similar way, various cost and asset purchase decisions may be confronted by the firm in actual practice, where the linkage to the firm's factor usage, and therefore its operating structure, is of this indirect kind. The money capital constraint function in the basic model may be amended, for example, by including as part of the money capital requirements the amount needed to finance the construction of an administrative office building. Since the investment decision involved at this point is logically distinct from the more general and pervasive investment problems that affect the operating structure of the firm, the office building investment decision will be subject to its own suboptimization engineering and cost criteria. The decision outcome will in turn be reflected in various ways in the firm's planning model and in its regular financial statements: in the money capital requirements function and the balance sheet so far as the investment outlay is concerned and in the profit function and the income statement so far as the annual amortization and maintenance cost is concerned.

Perhaps of more intriguing interest in its implications for the optimization model is the question of the advertising and selling expenses of the firm. In our arguments to this point we have assumed that adequate generality was achieved by imagining a single-product, imperfectly competitive firm, engaging only in price competition, whose average revenue function could be visualized simply as a negatively inclined function of the quantity of output produced and sold. In our preceding arguments, therefore, the total revenue function has been implicitly specified as

$$R = p(Q)Q \qquad (12\text{-}6)$$

and the basic Equation (9-11) may again be taken as illustrating the point. If, however, the firm is engaging in certain forms of nonprice competition, for example sales promotion expenditures, the gross revenue function of the firm will need to be specified in a more general form. In that case we may write

$$R = R(p,Q,\theta) \qquad (12\text{-}7)$$

where the new argument, θ, refers to the amount of sales promotion expenditure.

A useful way of incorporating the sales promotion expense into the optimization model is to argue that the market price at which any given quantity of output can be sold is dependent on the amount of selling expense incurred by the firm. Or alternatively we can summarize by saying that the larger the sales promotion expenses, the larger will be the price at which a given output can be sold, or the larger the output that can be sold at a given price. In any event it will be useful to change the form of the unit selling price function, or the firm's average revenue function, from $p = p(Q)$ to

$$p = p(Q,\theta) \tag{12-8}$$

This price function and the amended cost function may then be incorporated into the profit function in the firm's optimization model.

It may be decided, moreover, that the managers wish to restrict the sales promotion budget to some maximum level in any operating period. If such a maximum budget of $\bar{A}$ is specified, the relevant constraint incorporated into the decision model will be of the form

$$\theta \leq \bar{A} \tag{12-9}$$

An amended optimization model could then be written in attenuated form as follows:

$$\varphi = [p(Q,\theta)f(X,Y) - \gamma_1 X - \gamma_2 Y - \theta] \\ + \lambda[\bar{A} - \theta] + \mu[\bar{M} - \alpha X - \beta Y] \tag{12-10}$$

In this case we now have an optimization model in the three decision variables X, Y, and θ and in the Lagrange multipliers λ and μ. The solution conditions of the model can be specified in the usual manner by taking the partial derivatives of Equation (12-10) with respect to each of these five variables. The exercise is similar to those considered in corresponding contexts previously, and we need consider at this stage only the interpretation of the variable θ and its relevant constraint coefficient λ. We write the partial derivative of Equation (12-10) with respect to θ as follows:

$$\frac{\partial \varphi}{\partial \theta} = Q\frac{\partial p}{\partial \theta} - 1 - \lambda = 0 \tag{12-11}$$

It follows that, at the equilibrium or optimization situation indicated by the solution values of the model,

$$Q\frac{\partial p}{\partial \theta} - 1 = \lambda \tag{12-12}$$

Now it is possible, in the same manner as previously and for the mathematical reasons examined earlier, to interpret the Lagrange variable λ in Equation (12-12) as the marginal productivity of sales promotion expenditures. Moreover the left-hand side of Equation (12-12) can be recognized as the net marginal revenue of sales promotion expenditure. This equation, therefore, is simply interpreting the solution condition that, at the equilibrium situation, the marginal productivity of the sales promotion expenditure can be expressed as its marginal net revenue.

More significant, however, is the interpretation of the policy implications of the conclusion we now have before us. If the marginal revenue of sales promotion expenditure is greater than unity, or if the left-hand side of Equation (12-12) is positive, then the value of λ is positive. This means, therefore, that so long as λ is positive, the profit of the firm can be increased by relaxing the sales promotion budget constraint of $\bar{A}$, as shown in Equations (12-9) and (12-10). In fact, the policy objective of the firm in this connection could be interpreted as that of progressively relaxing this particular constraint until, at the mutually determinate solution values of the system, the value of λ has been driven to zero. At that point no further profit could be derived from further sales promotion expenditures. For the marginal productivity of this activity will then have been driven to zero. It follows, of course, from the underlying mathematical theorems we considered previously, that if the initial budget allocation to sales promotion expenditures is larger than that warranted or required by the optimum output volume otherwise decided upon by the system, the budget will not be fully utilized, the relevant budget constraint in Equation (12-10) will not be operative, and the solution value of λ will be zero.

Further Modifications of the Model

Additional variations of the basic optimization model need not detain us at length. Again taking Equation (9-11) as describing the standard model, it will be realized that one or more of the γ_i may be expressed as functionally dependent on the corresponding factor input acquired. The mathematics for the solution of the system become more complicated in such a case, and the economics of the model require us to speak of conditions of imperfect competition in the factor markets and of marginal factor costs instead of fixed direct unit factor costs. But no change will have occurred in the economic interpretation of the model's solution conditions, and the description of the optimum enterprise structure as determined by the model remains the same.

We have seen also that the money capital requirement coefficients of the factors, α and β in the model, may be functionally related to the amounts of the respective factors acquired. But again this makes no change in the logical nature of the solution conditions of the model, or in the general nature of the optimum structural characteristics of the firm.

If, finally, it were desired, as a matter of ownership or management policy, to set a maximum limit to the debt-equity ratio in the firm's financing structure, this again could be introduced as a further side condition or constraint on the solution values of the model. Though the quantitative description of the structural characteristics of the firm may be changed in such a case, depending on whether the critical debt-equity ratio would be reached in a solution outcome of the model that was not bounded in this respect, the qualitative nature of the result would again remain unaltered.

Leases or Rental of Assets

A final respect in which the basic optimization model might be modified in practice, even in the case of a single-product firm, relates to those instances in which instead of purchasing the assets necessary to provide productive capacity the firm obtains the use of them under lease or rental arrangements. In the case of leasing rather than purchasing, no investment is being made by the firm, and its total money capital requirements are therefore lower. The lower level of asset investments, as described on the assets side of the balance sheet, will be reflected in a lower level of total money capital employed as described on the liabilities side of the balance sheet. But there will at the same time be an annual flow cost of the factor capacities provided by the asset being leased, and this can again be interpreted analogously with the gamma terms in the cost and profit function in the basic model.

The precise nature of the analogy, however, and the implications for enterprise optimization of a choice between leasing and purchasing assets can be explored a little more fully. When assets are purchased, it has been seen, the units of factor capacity thereby provided will be costed to the firm at the margin of employment, or at the optimum factor combination, at what we referred to as the factor's effective marginal cost. This appears again in the right-hand sides of Equations (12-4) and (12-5); it is made up of (1) a direct marginal factor cost, or gamma term, and (2) the marginal imputed money capital cost, which in turn is equal to the marginal money capital requirement of the unit of factor capacity times a cost imputation rate equal to the marginal productivity of money capital. If, now, assets are leased rather than purchased, no money capital is being raised or invested, the fixed asset requirement coefficient of the factor is zero, and the cost of the unit of factor capacity provided by the leased asset will be determined simply by the lease rental charged under the relevant lease agreement. We are confronted then with the need to estimate a periodic flow cost per unit of factor capacity as that would appear if the asset were leased.

The lease rental in the case envisaged would presumably be large enough to afford the lessor, the owner of the asset, an acceptable rate of return on his investment in the asset, and it may be higher or lower depending on whether the agreement provided that maintenance and servicing were to be supplied by the owner or user. The conditions may be expected to vary depending on the kind of asset involved. In any event the lease rental can be regarded as being made up of components akin to those included in the effective marginal factor cost in our basic enterprise model. Given this kinship of cost components, then, the decision makers in the firm can confront the question whether the provision of factor capacities by leasing or purchasing best serves the economic interests of the owners. This latter can be interpreted here, as throughout our work, as the maximization of the economic value of the owners' investment in the firm.

Conceivably, the technological nature of the production possibilities confronting the firm will indicate at what points a meaningful choice exists between leases and purchase of assets. At each such point it would be possible to construct a function defining the unit cost of factor services as they would exist under the lease arrangements, taking account, in addition to the rental payments, of the maintenance and servicing costs that might be incurred during the lease period. This being done, constrained objective functions analogous to those already examined could be constructed under any number of desired assumptions as to asset lease arrangements. There could thus be determined a set of optimum solution outcomes showing, for each different set of assumptions, the optimized enterprise production structure, factor combination, money capital employment, and mix of financing sources. Similarly, the same kind of optimized solution outcomes could be determined on the assumption that no assets would be leased and that all asset requirements would be purchased. From the possible alternatives that could thus be arrayed, the decision makers could determine the optimum plan and structure of the firm, including the optimum extent of leasing, consistent with the technological production possibilities involved.

It is not necessary for our present purposes to consider all the accounting variations related to leasing rather than purchasing assets, including the different impacts on the firm's taxation liability. But some important issues should be noted briefly, consistent with the methodology adopted throughout this work. First, the choice between leasing and purchasing in a generalized optimization nexus of the kind we are considering has traceable effects on all levels of our trilogy of production, investment, and financing problems. Discussion of leasing in the context of partial optimization analysis has generally focused on the balance sheet and financing effects, and has regarded this problem mainly as one of alternative financing methods. It can be seen on reflection, however, that insofar as money capital usage is in this way affected and the amount and optimum mix of the money capital employed are changed as a result, this must ripple through and affect, via the implicit determination of the marginal efficiency of money capital, the rate at which marginal money capital costs are to be imputed to factor capacities employed in the firm, depending on their fixed asset requirement coefficients. This, in turn, must affect the optimized solution outcomes at which the optimum factor combination is decided upon. Previously we saw in considerable depth that the terms on which money capital was available and the form in which it was employed influenced the decision as to the optimum enterprise structure and the factor combination. It is not necessary to rehearse all the details of the argument at this point. But it must be noted that the very same kind of interdependence and mutual determination of solution outcomes is present again in the leasing versus purchase decision.

It can be pointed out finally that if the firm is adopting a fairly general policy of leasing assets, it is introducing a fixed financial charge into the profit function, and this will tend to have the same kind of effects on the expected value and stability of the residual owners' income stream as would be caused by a fixed financial charge in the form of interest on debt. This means that the presence of fixed lease rental obligations may induce a change in the form of the interest cost or debt capital supply function confronting the firm and in the equity owners' capitalization rate function. It is sufficient to remark only that this implicit increase in the riskiness of the firm's income stream must be taken into account by the decision makers when their view is being formed of the terms on which further capital may be obtained from the money capital market. One way of proceeding would be to work not in terms of the actual debt-equity ratio shown on the firm's balance sheet, but in terms of what can be called an effective financial leverage ratio, in which the debt capital figure includes not only the actual debt on the balance sheet, but also the equivalent capitalized value of the annual lease rental obligations.

Multiproduct Firms

Perhaps the most serious restriction we have so far imposed on the optimization process for the firm is involved in the assumption that it is producing only a single product. In actual fact, of course, this is unlikely to be the case, and an acknowledgment must be made of the ways in which the logic of our models might be affected by the economics of multiproduct outputs. Essentially, we shall see, the logical relationships in the model which takes account of multiple product outputs are perfectly analogous with those already examined at length. It was for this reason that the procedure was adopted of clarifying initially the interdependent causal relations between the determinant functions in the single-product model. For the nature of the causation does not change when the single-product assumption is relaxed. This procedure, of course, is consistent with the usual methodology in the neoclassical exposition of the subject and has served the important additional purpose in our preceding work of permitting a new integration of the firm's functional problems of production, investment, and financing.

But even though the logic is unchanged, the actual task of optimum structural planning in the multiproduct firm is rendered acutely complex by the large number of functional relations involved. It will be necessary, for example, to specify an expected revenue function for each product, with or without the added complexity we introduced in connection with sales promotion expenditures and nonprice competition. Similarly, a production function for each product will have to be specified, and an amended interpretation must be given to the factor inputs and their optimum employment. In particular, the inputs of factor services will now need to be classified, not simply in terms of their physical characteristics, but in terms also of their technical or functional uses. Physically homogeneous units of labor, for example, may be considered as different factors of production depending on whether they are allocated to the production of product A or product B. Thus it will be possible to discover the optimum combination of factors with which to produce each product and the optimum combination of products for maximum ownership values.

The solution of the multiple-product case will be indicated in what follows, not by means of a general model that leaves the possible number of products unspecified, but by using a simple two-product model. This will enable us to draw out rigorously the principal relationships inherent in the problem and its solution, analogous with the preceding models of the single-product firm.

Consider, then, a constrained objective function of the following form:

$$\varphi = [p_1(Q_1)f(X_1, Y_1) + p_2(Q_2)g(X_2, Y_2)$$
$$- \gamma_1 X_1 - \gamma_2 Y_1 - \gamma_3 X_2 - \gamma_4 Y_2 - r(D)D]$$
$$+ \mu[\overline{K} + D - \alpha_1 X_1 - \alpha_2 X_2 - \beta_1 Y_1 - \beta_2 Y_2] \quad (12\text{-}13)$$

In this equation, which is similar in form to those adduced in corresponding contexts earlier, the first bracket on the right-hand side contains the expression for the profit function of the multiple-product firm. The first two terms in this expression represent the revenue functions for the respective products. Throughout the model the outputs, selling prices, and factor inputs are subscripted with the numeral 1 or 2 to indicate reference to the first or second product respectively. The factor input flow cost prices are indicated as γ_1 and γ_2 for the factors employed in producing the first product and as γ_3 and γ_4 for the second product. It will be realized, as indicated previously, that X_1 and X_2 may be physically homogeneous units of factor services, but for purposes of solving the problem in hand they are regarded as different factors. In the specification of the money capital requirement function, therefore, the money capital requirements of the factor may be different if it is employed in producing the first rather than the second product. Thus the description of the relevant constraint function in the second bracket on the right-hand side of Equation (12-13) contains both the α_1 and the α_2 terms. Subject to this distinction, these money capital requirement coefficients have the same interpretation as the analogous terms in the earlier models.

While it is hardly necessary at this stage to generate the full solution conditions of the model, it will be useful to notice the factor employment conditions in order to clarify at least the principal features determining the optimum structure of the productive processes of the firm. The nature of the mutual determination of the optimum amount and direction of employment of debt capital will be recognized as similar to that already discussed. We proceed then to take the partial derivatives of Equation (12-13) with respect to the four factor input decision variables X_1, Y_1, X_2, and Y_2.

$$\frac{\partial \varphi}{\partial X_1} = m_1 f_{x_1} - \gamma_1 - \mu\alpha_1 = 0 \qquad (12\text{-}14)$$

$$\frac{\partial \varphi}{\partial Y_1} = m_1 f_{y_1} - \gamma_2 - \mu\beta_1 = 0 \qquad (12\text{-}15)$$

$$\frac{\partial \varphi}{\partial X_2} = m_2 g_{x_2} - \gamma_3 - \mu\alpha_2 = 0 \qquad (12\text{-}16)$$

$$\frac{\partial \varphi}{\partial Y_2} = m_2 g_{y_2} - \gamma_4 - \mu\beta_2 = 0 \qquad (12\text{-}17)$$

In Equations (12-14) through (12-17) the subscripted m variable represents the marginal revenue obtainable from the sale of the respective products. The subscripted f terms represent the marginal physical products of the factors in producing the first product, and the subscripted g terms have an analogous interpretation with reference to the second product.

If now we combine Equations (12-14) and (12-15), the equilibrium condition for factor usage for the first product is obtained:

$$\frac{f_{x_1}}{f_{y_1}} = \frac{\gamma_1 + \mu\alpha_1}{\gamma_2 + \mu\beta_1} \qquad (12\text{-}18)$$

Again, as before, the optimum combination of factors will be such that the ratio of their marginal physical products is equal to the ratio of their effective marginal costs. In the same way, the combination of Equations (12-16) and (12-17) provides the corresponding optimization condition for the employment of factors for the second product.

A more interesting proposition emerges, however, if the case is considered in which X_1 and X_2 are physically homogeneous factor services, even though they are employed in the production of different products. Consider now the relationship between Equations (12-14) and (12-16). Dividing the latter into the former yields the following expression:

$$\frac{m_1 f_{x_1}}{m_2 g_{x_2}} = \frac{\gamma_1 + \mu\alpha_1}{\gamma_3 + \mu\alpha_2} \qquad (12\text{-}19)$$

The expression on the left-hand side of Equation (12-19) is the ratio of the marginal revenue productivities of the factor in its respective possible employments. At the optimization solution values of the model, this ratio must equal the ratio of the effective marginal cost of the factor in its respective uses. It is not necessary, of course, that the effective marginal cost of the factor be the same in both its possible uses, for this marginal cost depends on the differing possible γ terms and α coefficients. These, it was seen at greater length in Chapter 7, may depend in turn on the volume of the relevant factor usages and on the volume of output of the product on which they are employed.

By the very nature of the model, of course, the μ terms in Equation (12-19) will be identical, for the periodic rate at which money capital costs are to be imputed to the factors of production will be the same, irrespective of the direction in which the factors are employed. On the basis, therefore, of a comparison between Equations (12-18) and (12-19), propositions can be adduced regarding (1) the optimum combination of factors with which to produce a given product, and (2) the optimum allocation of a given factor over different product employments.

It is possible also, on the basis of the multiple-product model, to derive an optimization theorem relative to the use of available money capital. From Equations (12-14) and (12-16), for example, it is possible to derive solution values for μ and to establish the following equality:

$$\mu = \frac{m_1 f_{x_1} - \gamma_1}{\alpha_1} = \frac{m_2 g_{x_2} - \gamma_3}{\alpha_2} \qquad (12\text{-}20)$$

The numerator terms in this expression can be referred to as the surplus marginal revenue products of factor X in its different employments. A similar interpretation was employed in an analogous argument in Equations (10-3) and (10-4). It follows from Equation (12-20) that at the optimized solution values of the model, the marginal profit contribution per dollar of money capital employed will be the same for all directions of use in the firm. This can be shown to hold whether the different uses of money capital relate to the employment of different factors in producing a given product or to the employment of the same factor in producing different products. It is not necessary to explore the solution properties of the multiple-product model further to establish its consistency with the basic methodology of the earlier arguments in this book.

It might be noted, however, that in leaving the multiple-product analysis at this point we are leaving unexamined two potentially significant questions. These relate to the joint production of product outputs and to the joint supply of factor inputs. If, in the first case, product outputs are jointly produced, it may be necessary to describe a joint revenue function for the sale of them if they are producible only in fixed proportions.

In such a case, also, the factor employments necessary to produce the outputs can be combined in a single joint production function.

In the second case, it may be possible for factor capacities required for both products to be supplied from a single asset. The provision of warehouse space is a simple example. In this event it is unrealistic to conceive of a separate money capital requirement coefficient assigned to the factor capacity in each of its separate uses. In Equation (12-13), for example, factors Y_1 and Y_2 may be homogeneous warehouse space allocable to products A and B respectively. In such a case, it would be inappropriate to conceive of β_1 and β_2 as logically and empirically separable money capital requirement coefficients. Particularly is this so when it is remembered, as was argued at an earlier point of the analysis, that the magnitude of the money capital requirement coefficient associated with the use of a particular factor may be functionally dependent on the quantity of that factor employed. In the situation now in hand, therefore, the money capital requirement coefficient in the capital availability constraint in Equation (12-13) should read, not $\beta_1Y_1 + \beta_2Y_2$, but $\beta(Y_1 + Y_2)(Y_1 + Y_2)$, where the expression to the close of the first term in parentheses represents the form of the β function and the term in the second parentheses describes the total number of units of the factor capacity required for both products.

A Partial Geometry of Financial Optimization

The complex forms of the mutually determinate functions in the optimization model make it quite impossible to give a geometrical representation of the entire solution process. In Figure 9, however, we have brought together in summary form several of the principal determinants and outcomes of the model. In the first (northeast) quadrant is shown a total productivity of capital function. Continuing to assume consistently the standpoint of the economic interests of the owners of the firm, the function in this quadrant shows the amount of residual profit that can be earned for the owners as increasing amounts of debt capital are added to a given amount of equity capital in the firm. If, for example, debt capital of OL is employed, the residual profit will be OM.

In the fourth quadrant is shown the leverage ray which, for a given equity capital base, establishes the debt-equity ratio implicit in the employment of varying amounts of debt capital. Thus OL debt implies a leverage ratio of ON. Then in the third quadrant the equity capitalization rate function describes the rate of increase in the owners' capitalization rate for variations in the debt-equity ratio. Working through the relationships, therefore, the figure suggests that the debt capital of OL will induce an equity capitalization rate of OP.

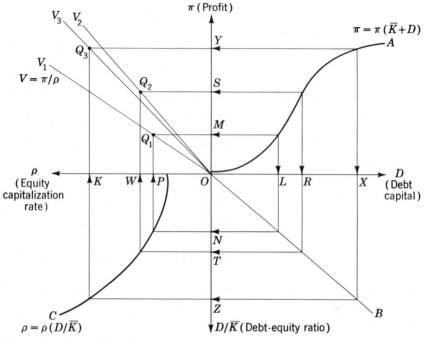

Figure 9. Financial optimization

We are interested principally, however, in the economic values that are being generated for the owners by differing structures of the firm, and we have accordingly drawn in the second quadrant of Figure 9 a family of isovalue vectors. Any given isovalue vector will be the image in the π-ρ plane of the different combinations of profits and capitalization rates that will provide a specified total economic value. Thus if the employment of OL debt capital, together with the given amount of equity capital, produces equity earnings of OM and if these earnings are capitalized at the rate OP, the economic value described by the point Q_1 can be understood to lie on isovalue vector V_1 in the second quadrant of the figure.

It will be clear, of course, that the relationships in Figure 9 have not been drawn to provide arithmetical accuracy, and nothing more than a partial and impressionistic view of the optimization model is intended. Consider, for example, the profit function in the first quadrant. In a fuller geometrical treatment it would be necessary to envisage in this quadrant, not a single profit function, but a family of such functions, each member of which would refer to a given equity capital base. The higher the equity base, the higher the profit function would stand above the debt capital axis. Similarly, we should have in the fourth quadrant a family of leverage rays, each member of which would be associated with a given member of the family of profit functions in the first quadrant. The higher the equity base, the closer the leverage ray would lie to the debt capital axis.

Finally, it will be recalled from earlier discussions that the equity capitalization rate function is only partially described by the function in the third quadrant of Figure 9. The intercept of this function on the capitalization rate axis can be understood, consistent with the argument in Chapter 2, to describe the rate at which the owners' profit would be capitalized if no debt capital were employed. The intercept is therefore the capitalization rate appropriate to a pure equity, or unlevered, capital structure, and its determination was seen in Chapter 4 to depend principally on the degree of risk, measured by the coefficient of variation in the net operating income stream of the firm. Thus in the third quadrant of Figure 9 we might expect to find again a family of capitalization rate functions, each of a different level and shape. The intercept of each such function on the capitalization rate axis would be explained by a different coefficient of variation of the net operating income stream of the firm. The different possible shapes of the functions would depend on the form of the owners' risk aversion characteristics, deriving from their utility functions as postulated at the beginning of our analysis.

Given, however, the partial representation of the optimization model shown in Figure 9, we can summarize the objectives of the planning decision by saying that the aim should be consistently that of achieving and remaining upon the highest attainable isovalue vector in the second quadrant of the figure. If, for example, the debt capital at work in the firm were increased from OL to OR, the residual profit would rise to OS, and when capitalized at the induced higher capitalization rate of OW this would move the ownership onto the higher isovalue vector V_2, passing through the π-ρ coordinates at Q_2. The relationships in the figure suggest, however, that if the debt capital were increased as far as OX, the economic position of the owners would be as described on the lower isovalue vector V_3. In such a case the optimum amount of debt capital would have been exceeded, and the structure of the firm could not therefore be said to be optimum in the sense of our earlier models. It is hardly necessary to emphasize that the partial relationships shown in Figure 9 do not take up the further stage of analysis we elaborated in Chapter 10 under the heading of the *maximum maximorum* position of the owners of the firm. It is for this further analysis that the families of functions we referred to in connection with Figure 9 would be required.

13

Conclusion

The stance we have adopted in this book in relation to the large and growing body of literature on the financing and capital budgeting of the firm will have become clear as the argument developed. Our primary concern was not to continue in the line of development of recent work on business financing nor on what is beginning to be called the financial theory of the firm. We argued at the beginning for the need to refurbish a sound theoretical foundation for work in the financial analysis of the business enterprise, and it is for this reason we have been concerned so largely with new perspectives on the economic theory of the firm. Though our work has been motivated by the recognition of the need for more general theoretical models than have thus far been offered, it is possible at this stage to refer in the most general terms to some of the principal problems the literature has raised. A deeper probe must await further work on some empirical aspects of the approaches we have suggested. The two main areas of controversy in recent work have been concerned with (1) the specification and ordering of the profitabilities in alternative investment opportunities confronting the firm, and the selection of the optimum set of such projects for inclusion in a firm's periodic capital budget, and (2) the specification of the firm's cost of capital, its significance for capital budget decision making, and the relationship, if any, that exists between the firm's average cost of capital and the structure of financing sources employed.

Various works that we have referred to throughout this book present fairly completely the arguments for and against the use of the present value of a project or the internal rate of return in the project as criteria for assessing its economic desirability and for ranking it among other projects in an order of worthwhileness. So far as our own model touches on this kind of question, it is a present-value model. But there is clearly a much deeper point at issue. Our model requires that in the interest of maximum ownership values, we do not concern ourselves solely or even principally with the desirability of a particular project or group of projects. Rather, our concern at the firm's sequential-planning and decision-making dates is consistently with the question: What will be the effect on the structure and value of the firm if one or the other of possibly several alternative plans is adopted? The methodological importance of this is that it does not ask directly for the present value or the expected rate of earnings of a particular project or set of projects. It asks instead for the net change in the value of the business if a certain plan of action is followed, compared with the value of the business if its existing size and structure are undisturbed, or if some alternative plan is followed. And, as our theoretical analysis has alerted us to recognize, the importance of this approach lies in the fact that the adoption of a particular project, or set of projects or plan, may call for induced changes in the structure of the firm or in the way of doing things in more respects than need to be recapitulated at this point.

Most notably, we have seen that a relative shortage of capital, or the fact that we are continually planning subject to a capital constraint, forces us to optimize at a factor combination (that is, operate at a locus on the production possibility contour implicit in the production function) different from what we would adopt for similar optimization purposes if our capital constraint were relaxed. To proceed, therefore, to the calculation of rates of return potentially available in new investment projects without considering how the existing operations and the attempted realization of new objectives should be mutually solved for overall value maximization is to avoid the real task of economic and financial planning and organization. Rather than thinking in terms simply of candidate projects for inclusion in a periodic capital budget, therefore, or even in terms of optimum sets of new projects, we think in terms of alternative enterprise structures. The objects of choice are (1) the various combinations of products, activities, or investment structures that include more or less of what already existed in the firm prior to the sequential-planning date now under contemplation, and (2) various combinations of more or less of certain new alternatives. We have already looked, in the theoretical parts of our work, at what this implies for periodic changes in production functions and valuations of sunk investments. Clearly the task of business economic planning thus envisaged will be, for firms of any significant size, both continuing and complex. Happily, the extensive and burdensome nature of the continuing reappraisals of the structure and expansion of the firm is likely to be alleviated rapidly in the future with the development of programming techniques and related management tools.

The logic of these arguments for a continuing structural analysis of the firm determines also our attitude to much of the recent controversy on the cost of capital. Insofar as we are interested in the question from the point of view of corporate optimization planning, the cost of capital controversy has often been an empty one because the wrong question has been asked. Instead of asking what is the *cost* of raising capital, the real question should be what is the *effect* of raising capital and investing it in income-earning assets. If this latter is the question asked, the answer will emerge from the analysis we have proposed in the form of indications of the structural changes that would be implied in the firm's total production, investment, and financing operations. Without repeating even the leading arguments again at this point, it suffices to say that the same question can be expected to be asked, and the same kind of answers can be expected to be forthcoming, whether new capital funds contemplated are debt or equity. It is economically meaningful to focus, in every instance associated with a proposed structural change in the firm, on the effect on the owners' wealth position, and the criteria for judging such effects have already been elaborated. But the predilection economists have shown for speaking of the "cost" of capital is probably related to the frequent mistake, which we discussed in an earlier chapter, of thinking of money capital as a factor of production, with the attendant need to compute its cost. We have seen that it is not for this reason that capital costs are to be incorporated in the optimization analysis, and the contributions that the constructs of economic analysis can make to business planning are of a different kind.

Finally, we ask: What analytical relevance attaches to the arguments for and against the hypothesis that the average cost of capital for the firm is invariant with respect to the structure of money capital sources it is employing? Our model permits us to make some generalizations on this question. First, the hypothesis may or may not be a reasonable description of an individual firm as it confronts the capital market and considers the form of what we have called its interest cost function and its equity capitalization rate function, as influenced by all the factors that make the firm economically unique. But our arguments related to the probable elasticities of the money capital cost functions — and the possibilities of monopsonistic discrimination in the money capital market — lead us to expect that a minimum average cost of capital is in fact achievable. Second, we conclude that once again a preoccupation with the need for an affirmative or negative answer to this invariance question shunts analysis off in the direction of an empty controversy so far as the decision problems of the individual firm are concerned. The functions that enterprise planners perforce must use as best approximations to describe interest costs and capitalization rates may take on any of many possible forms, having regard again to the possibilities of monopsonistic discrimination in the markets for capital funds. And in any event the invariance question has generally been part of what we have called a partial optimization analysis, a level of argument with which we have not been primarily concerned.

Thus we leave the task of erecting new and more fruitful perspectives on the theory of the firm. No further apology for the venture and no further hopes for its usefulness and success are in order. We have tried to provide a scheme of analysis that makes a step toward what Robbins called, in a different but not totally unrelated context, "a theory of moving equilibrium through time."[1] Whatever now the rate, or even the direction, of hoped-for theoretical advances, it is likely that the clarification of issues and problems we have attempted might assist in clearing the way for the larger tasks of business analysis that lie ahead.

---

[1] Lionel Robbins, *An Essay on the Nature and Significance of Economic Science*, Macmillan & Co., Ltd., London, 1935, p. 71.

Bibliography Of Works Cited

Allen, R. G. D.: *Mathematical Analysis for Economists*, Macmillan & Co., Ltd., London, 1938.

——: *Mathematical Economics*, Macmillan & Co., Ltd., London, 1959.

American Economic Association: *Readings in Price Theory*, G. J. Stigler and K. E. Boulding (eds)., Richard D. Irwin, Inc., Homewood, Ill., 1952.

——: *Readings in the Theory of Income Distribution*, W. Fellner and B. F. Haley (eds.), Richard D. Irwin, Inc., Homewood, Ill., 1951.

Ascher, Abraham: See Ben-Shahar, Haim.

Barges, Alexander: *The Effect of Capital Structure on the Cost of Capital*, Prentice-Hall, Inc., Englewood Cliffs, N.J., 1963.

Baumol, William J.: *Business Behavior, Value and Growth*, The Macmillan Company, New York, 1959.

——: *Economic Theory and Operations Analysis*, 2d ed., Prentice-Hall, Inc., Englewood Cliffs, N.J., 1965.

——: "The Transactions Demand for Cash: An Inventory Theoretic Approach," *Quarterly Journal of Economics*, vol. 66, November, 1952.

——: See Makower, H.

Ben-Shahar, Haim, and Abraham Ascher: "The Integration of Capital Budgeting and Stock Valuation: Comment," *American Economic Review*, vol. 57, March, 1967.

Beranek, William: *Analysis for Financial Decisions*, Richard D. Irwin, Inc., Homewood, Ill., 1963.

——: *The Effect of Leverage on the Market Value of Common Stock*, The University of Wisconsin Press, Madison, Wis., 1964.

——: *Working Capital Management*, Wadsworth Publishing Company, Inc., Belmont, Calif., 1966.

Bierman, Harold, and Seymour Smidt: *The Capital Budgeting Decision, Economic Analysis and Financing of Investment Projects*, 2d ed., The Macmillan Company, New York, 1966.

Boulding, Kenneth E.: *Economic Analysis*, 4th ed., Harper & Row, Publisher, Incorporated, New York, 1966.

——: *A Reconstruction of Economics*, Science Editions, Inc., New York, 1962.

—— and W. Allen Spivey: *Linear Programming and the Theory of the Firm*, The Macmillan Company, New York, 1960.

Brigham, Eugene F.:   See Weston, J. Fred.

Buchanan, N. S.:   *The Economics of Corporate Enterprise*, Holt, Rinehart and Winston, Inc., New York, 1940.

Carleton, Willard T.:   See Lerner, Eugene M.

Carlson, Sune: *A Study on the Pure Theory of Production*, published in Stockholm, 1939, republished by Augustus M. Kelley, *Reprints of Economic Classics*, New York, 1965.

Chamberlin, E. H.:   *The Theory of Monopolistic Competition*, Harvard University Press, Cambridge, Mass., 1933.

Clower, R. W.:   "Business Investment and the Theory of Price," *Proceedings of the 28th Annual Conference of the Western Economic Association*, 1953.

————:   "An Investigation into the Dynamics of Investment," *American Economic Review*, vol. 44, 1954.

Cohen, Jerome B., and Sidney M. Robbins: *The Financial Manager*, Harper & Row, Publishers, Incorporated, New York, 1966.

Cohen, Kalman J., and Richard M. Cyert: *Theory of the Firm: Resource Allocation in a Market Economy*, Prentice-Hall, Inc., Englewood Cliffs, N.J., 1965.

Cournot, Augustin: *Researches into the Mathematical Principles of the Theory of Wealth*, 1838, republished by Augustus M. Kelley, *Reprints of Economic Classics*, New York, 1965.

Crockett, Jean, and Irwin Friend: "The Integration of Capital Budgeting and Stock Valuation: Comment," *American Economic Review*, vol. 57, March, 1967.

Curley, Anthony J.:   *A Stochastic Simulation of the Personal Investment Decision*, unpublished Ph.D. dissertation, University of Pennsylvania, 1967.

Cyert, Richard M.:   See Cohen, Kalman J.

Davidson, Paul: "Keynes's Finance Motive," *Oxford Economic Papers*, vol. 17, March, 1965.

Dewey, Donald: *Modern Capital Theory*, Columbia University Press, New York, 1965.

Dorfman, R.:   "A Graphical Exposition of Bohm-Bawerk's Interest Theory," *Review of Economic Studies*, vol. 26, February, 1959.

————, **Paul A. Samuelson, and Robert M. Solow:**   *Linear Programming and Economic Analysis*, McGraw-Hill Book Company, New York, 1958.

Durand, David: "The Cost of Capital, Corporation Finance and the Theory of Investment: Comment," *American Economic Review*, vol. 49, September, 1959.

Encarnación, José, Jr.:   "Constraints and the Firm's Utility Function," *Review of Economic Studies*, vol. 31, April, 1964.

Farrar, Donald E.: *The Investment Decision under Uncertainty*, Prentice-Hall, Inc., Englewood Cliffs, N.J., 1962.

Ferguson, C. E.: *Microeconomic Theory*, Richard D. Irwin, Inc., Homewood, Ill., 1966.

Frazer, William J.: "Firms' Demands for Money: The Evidence from the Cross-section Data," *Federal Reserve Bulletin*, vol. 53, January, 1967.

Friend, Irwin: See Crockett, Jean.

Furubotn, E. G.: "Engineering Production Functions and Capital-Labor Substitution in Metal Machining: Comment," *American Economic Review*, vol. 56, September, 1966.

Gabor, Andre, and I. F. Pearce: "A New Approach to the Theory of the Firm," *Oxford Economic Papers*, vol. 4, October, 1952.

—— and ——: "The Place of Money Capital in the Theory of Production," *Quarterly Journal of Economics*, vol. 72, November, 1958.

Gordon, Myron J.: *The Investment, Financing, and Valuation of the Corporation*, Richard D. Irwin, Inc., Homewood, Ill., 1962.

Gordon, Myron J., and G. Shillinglaw: *Accounting: A Management Approach*, Richard D. Irwin, Inc., Homewood, Ill., 1964.

Hadley, G.: *Nonlinear and Dynamic Programming*, Addison-Wesley Publishing Company, Inc., Reading, Mass., 1964.

Hart, Albert G.: *Anticipations, Uncertainty, and Dynamic Planning*, The University of Chicago Press, Chicago, 1940.

Henderson, James M., and Richard E. Quandt: *Microeconomic Theory: A Mathematical Approach*, McGraw-Hill Book Company, New York, 1958.

Hertz, David B.: "Risk Analysis in Capital Investment," *Harvard Business Review*, January–February, 1964.

Hicks, J. R.: *Value and Capital*, Clarendon Press, Oxford, 1946.

Hillier, Frederick S.: "The Derivation of Probabilistic Information for the Evaluation of Risky Investment," *Management Science*, April, 1963.

Hirshleifer, J.: Investment Decision under Uncertainty: Applications of the State-preference Approach, *Quarterly Journal of Economics*, vol. 80, May, 1966.

Horwich, G.: "Money, Prices and the Theory of Interest Determination," *Economic Journal*, vol. 67, December, 1957.

Jaedicke, Robert K., and Robert T. Sprouse: *Accounting Flows: Income, Funds and Cash*, Prentice-Hall, Inc., Englewood Cliffs, N.J., 1965.

Jevons, W. S.: *The Theory of Political Economy*, 1871, Reprint Kelley & Millman, Inc., New York, 1957.

Johnson, Robert W.: *Financial Management*, 3d ed., Allyn and Bacon, Inc., Boston, 1966.

Jorgenson, Dale W.: "Anticipations and Investment Behavior," *Brookings Quarterly Econometric Model of the United States,* James S. Duesenberry et al. (eds.), Rand McNally & Company, Chicago, 1965.

——: "Capital Theory and Investment Behavior," *American Economic Review,* vol. 53, May, 1963, reprinted in *Readings in Business Cycles,* American Economic Association, Richard D. Irwin, Inc., Homewood, Ill., 1965.

Kuh, Edwin: *Capital Stock Growth: A Micro-econometric Approach,* North Holland Publishing Company, Amsterdam, 1963.

——: "Capital Theory and Capital Budgeting," *Metroeconomica,* vol. 12, December, 1960.

Kuhn, H. W., and A. W. Tucker: "Nonlinear Programming," *Proceedings of the Second Berkeley Symposium on Mathematical Statistics and Probability,* U. Neyman (ed.), University of California Press, Berkeley, Calif., 1951.

Lachmann, L. M.: *Capital and Its Structure,* London School of Economics, G. Bell & Sons, Ltd., London, 1956.

Lange, Oskar: "The Place of Interest in the Theory of Production," *Review of Economic Studies,* vol. 3, June, 1936.

Lave, L. B.: "Engineering Production Functions and Capital-Labor Substitution in Metal Machining: Comment," *American Economic Review,* vol. 56, September, 1966.

Lerner, Eugene M., and Willard T. Carleton: "The Integration of Capital Budgeting and Stock Valuation," *American Economic Review,* vol. 54, September, 1964.

—— and ——: *A Theory of Financial Analysis,* Harcourt, Brace & World, Inc., New York, 1966.

Lintner, John: "Security Prices, Risk and Maximal Gains from Diversification," *Journal of Finance,* vol. 20, December, 1965.

Lutz, Friedrich, and Vera Lutz: *The Theory of Investment of the Firm,* Princeton University Press, Princeton, N.J., 1951.

Magee, John F.: "Decision Trees for Decision Making," *Harvard Business Review,* July–August, 1964.

——: "How to Use Decision Trees in Capital Investment," *Harvard Business Review,* September–October, 1964.

Makower, H., and William J. Baumol: "The Analogy between Producer and Consumer Equilibrium Analysis," *Economica,* vol. 17, 1950.

Markowitz, Harry M.: *Portfolio Selection,* John Wiley & Sons, Inc., New York, 1959.

Marshall, Alfred: *Principles of Economics,* 9th (variorum) ed., C. W. Guillebaud (ed.), Macmillan & Co., Ltd., London, 1961.

Merrett, A. J., and Allen Sykes: *The Finance and Analysis of Capital Projects,* John Wiley & Sons, Inc., New York, 1963.

Miller, Merton H.: See Modigliani, Franco.

Modigliani, Franco, and Merton H. Miller: "The Cost of Capital, Corporation Finance and the Theory of Investment," *American Economic Review*, vol. 48, June, 1958, reprinted in Ezra Solomon (ed.), *The Management of Corporate Capital*, The Free Press of Glencoe, New York, 1959.

———— and ————: "Some Estimates of the Cost of Capital to the Electric Utility Industry, 1954–57," *American Economic Review*, vol. 56, June, 1966.

Myers, Stewart C.: See Robichek, Alexander A.

Porterfield, James T. S.: *Investment Decisions and Capital Costs*, Prentice-Hall, Inc., Englewood Cliffs, N.J., 1965.

Quandt, Richard E.: See Henderson, James M.

Quirin, G. David: *The Capital Expenditure Decision*, Richard D. Irwin, Inc., Homewood, Ill., 1967.

Robbins, Lionel: *An Essay on the Nature and Significance of Economic Science*, Macmillan & Co., Ltd., London, 1935.

Robbins, Sidney M.: See Cohen, Jerome, B.

Robichek, Alexander A., and Stewart C. Myers: "Conceptual Problems in the Use of Risk-adjusted Discount Rates," *Journal of Finance*, vol. 21, December, 1966.

———— and ————: *Optimal Financing Decisions*, Prentice-Hall, Inc., Englewood Cliffs, N.J., 1965.

———— and ————: "Valuation of the Firm: Effects of Uncertainty in a Market Context," *Journal of Finance*, vol. 21, May, 1966.

Robinson, Joan: *The Economics of Imperfect Competition*, 1st ed., Macmillan & Co., Ltd., London, 1933.

Rose, J. R.: "The Cost of Capital, Corporation Finance and the Theory of Investment: Comment," *American Economic Review*, vol. 49, September, 1959.

Samuelson, Paul A.: *Economics*, 6th ed., McGraw-Hill Book Company, New York, 1964.

————: "General Proof That Diversification Pays," *Journal of Financial and Quantitative Analysis*, vol. 2, no. 1, March, 1967.

————: See Dorfman, Robert.

Schlaifer, Robert: *Introduction to Statistics for Business Decisions*, McGraw-Hill Book Company, New York, 1961.

Schumpeter, Joseph A.: *History of Economic Analysis*, Oxford University Press, Fair Lawn, N.J., 1954.

Schwartz, Eli: "Theory of the Capital Structure of the Firm," *Journal of Finance*, vol. 14, March, 1959.

Scitovsky, Tibor: *Welfare and Competition*, Richard D. Irwin, Inc., Homewood, Ill., 1951.

Sharpe, William F.: "Capital Asset Prices: A Theory of Market Equilibrium under Conditions of Risk," *Journal of Finance*, vol. 19, September, 1964.

————: "Security Prices, Risk, and Maximal Gains from Diversification: Reply," *Journal of Finance*, vol. 21, December, 1966.

Shillinglaw, G.:   See Gordon, Myron J.

Shubik, Martin: "Objective Functions and Models of Corporate Optimization," *Quarterly Journal of Economics*, vol. 75, August, 1961.

Simon, Herbert A.: "New Developments in the Theory of the Firm," *American Economic Review*, vol. 52, May, 1962.

————: "Theories of Decision-making in Economics and Behavioral Science," *American Economic Review*, vol. 49, June, 1959.

Smidt, Seymour: See Bierman, Harold.

Smith, Vernon L.: *Investment and Production: A Study in the Theory of the Capital-using Enterprise*, Harvard University Press, Cambridge, Mass., 1961.

————: "The Theory of Investment and Production," *Quarterly Journal of Economics*, vol. 73, February, 1959.

Smithies, A.: "The Austrian Theory of Capital in Relation to Partial Equilibrium Theory," *Quarterly Journal of Economics*, vol. 50, November, 1935.

Solomon, Ezra: "Leverage and the Cost of Capital," *Journal of Finance*, vol. 18, May, 1963.

————: *The Theory of Financial Management*, Columbia University Press, New York, 1963.

———— **(ed.):** *The Management of Corporate Capital*, The Free Press of Glencoe, New York, 1959.

Solow, Robert M.:   See Dorfman, Robert.

Spivey, W. Allen: See Boulding, Kenneth E.

Sprouse, Robert T.:   See Jaedicke, Robert K.

Sraffa, P.: "The Laws of Return under Competitive Conditions," *Economic Journal*, vol. 36, December, 1926.

Stigler, G. J.: *The Theory of Price*, The Macmillan Company, New York, 1949.

Sykes, Allen: See Merrett, A. J.

Tobin, James: "The Interest Elasticity of Transactions Demand for Cash," *Review of Economics and Statistics*, vol. 38, August, 1956.

Triffin, Robert: *Monopolistic Competition and General Equilibrium Theory*, Harvard University Press, Cambridge, Mass., 1949.

Tucker, A. W.:   See Kuhn, H. W.

Vickers, Douglas: "Elasticity of Capital Supply, Monopsonistic Discrimination and Optimum Capital Structure," *Journal of Finance*, vol. 22, March, 1967.

————: "On the Economics of Break-even," *Accounting Review*, vol. 35, July, 1960, reprinted in Hector R. Anton and Peter A. Firmin (eds.), *Contemporary Issues in Cost Accounting: A Discipline in Transition*, Houghton Mifflin Company, Boston, 1966.

————: "Profitability and Reinvestment Rates: A Note on the Gordon Paradox," *Journal of Business*, vol. 39, July, 1966.

Vickrey, William S.: *Metastatics and Macroeconomics*, Harcourt, Brace & World, Inc., New York, 1964.

Walter, James E.: *The Investment Process*, Harvard University Press, Cambridge, Mass., 1962.

Walters, A. A.: "Production and Cost Functions: An Econometric Survey," *Econometrica*, vol. 31, January–April, 1963.

Weintraub, Sidney: *Intermediate Price Theory*, Chilton Company, Philadelphia, 1964.

————: *Price Theory*, Pitman Publishing Corporation, New York, 1956.

Weston, J. Fred: "A Test of Cost of Capital Propositions," *Southern Economic Journal*, vol. 30, October, 1963.

———— **and Eugene F. Brigham:** *Managerial Finance*, 2d ed., Holt, Rinehart and Winston, Inc., New York, 1966.

Wicksell, Knut: *Lectures on Political Economy*, Lionel Robbins (ed.), Routledge & Kegan Paul, Ltd., London, 1934.

Wippern, Ronald F.: "Financial Structure and the Value of the Firm," *Journal of Finance*, vol. 21, December, 1966.

Yamane, Taro: *Mathematics for Economists*, Prentice-Hall, Inc., Englewood Cliffs, N.J., 1962.

Index

Index

668